WHERE IN THE WORLD IS THE BERLIN WALL?

Edited by Anna Kaminsky
on behalf of
The Federal Foundation for the Reappraisal of the SED Dictatorship

Project management: Ruth Gleinig

Compiled by Ronny Heidenreich and Tina Schaller

WHERE IN THE WORLD IS THE BERLIN WALL?

BUNDESSTIFTUNG
AUFARBEITUNG

Where in the World is the Berlin Wall?
Published on behalf of
The Federal Foundation for the Reappraisal of the SED Dictatorship
Kronenstraße 5
10117 Berlin
www.bundesstiftung-aufarbeitung.de
buero@bundesstiftung-aufarbeitung.de

1st edition – Berlin: Berlin Story Verlag 2014
ISBN 978-3-95723-017-1

Editorial deadline: 30th March 2014
© Bundesstiftung zur Aufarbeitung der SED-Diktatur, 2014
Berlin Story Verlag GmbH
Unter den Linden 40, 10117 Berlin
Tel.: (030) 20 91 17 80
Fax: (030) 69 20 40 059
www.BerlinStory-Verlag.de, E-Mail: Service@BerlinStory-Verlag.de
Translation: Simon Hodgson
Cover and Typesetting: Norman Bösch
Cover pictures:
Simi Valley, California, Ronald Reagan Presidential Library and Museum (s. p. 132),
Sosnówka, Poland (s. p. 96), Yokohama, Japan, TÜV Rheinland Yokohama (s. p. 229)

WWW.BERLINSTORY-VERLAG.DE

TABLE OF CONTENT

PREFACE 8
Anna Kaminsky

FROM THE BUILDING OF THE BERLIN WALL TO THE FALL OF THE BERLIN WALL 10
A SHORT HISTORY OF THE DIVISION
Maria Nooke

"THERE ARE PLENTY OF GOOD REASONS TO ALSO NOT LOSE SIGHT OF THE 13TH AUGUST." 27
REMEMBERING THE WALL SINCE 1990
Anna Kaminsky

WHERE IN THE WORLD IS THE BERLIN WALL. 35
Europe 35
North America................................ 113
Central America 197
South America 205
Africa 213
Asia 215
Australia and Oceania 241
Mars 244

BETWEEN DISAPPEARANCE AND REMEMBRANCE 246
REMEMBERING THE BERLIN WALL TODAY
Rainer E. Klemke

THE MESSAGES OF THE WALL SEGMENTS 260
Leo Schmidt

FROM CONCRETE TO CASH. 268
TURNING THE BERLIN WALL INTO A BUSINESS
Ronny Heidenreich

LIST OF AUTHORS 282

ACKNOWLEDGMENT 283

Geographic Register................................ 285

From the 13th August 1961, the Wall – built by the communist rulers in East Berlin – not only divided the German capital into East and West. The Wall was also a symbol of the inhuman regime behind the 'Iron Curtain' and of the divided world – the Soviet ruled communist dictatorship in the East block and the democratic states in the western hemisphere.

In the summer of 1989, the communist states were already in a state of ferment and their people had already begun to voice their protests with ever growing courage. Neither those in the East, nor those in the West could have imagined that the Wall would fall anytime soon, nor could they have imagined that the communist dictatorship would be vanquished and the Cold War would come to an end.

Whilst the GDR government continued to talk at great length about the permanency of the Berlin Wall, trade union federation 'Solidarity' was celebrating the first legislative elections in Poland. The GDR government continued to open fire on citizens who wanted to choose their own path in life and fled to the West. At the same time, Hungary began to open the 'Iron Curtain'.

As late as 5th February 1989, East German border troops shot 20 year old Chris Gueffroy as he attempted to get over the Wall and into the West. Hundreds of people were shot at the Berlin Wall and inner-German border as they tried to flee East Germany. The inhuman border regime and the Wall ruined the lives of countless people who lost their friends, family or homes.

The Peaceful Revolutions in almost all countries in the former East Block and the Fall of the Berlin Wall make up some of the most significant events in history. With these revolutions, the people of the GDR and Central and Eastern Europe vanquished the communist dictatorships and brought about the beginning of the end of German and European division.

As a result of the revolutions in Central and Eastern Europe, the Soviet Empire collapsed within a few months. As hundreds of thousands of people danced and celebrated on top of the Berlin Wall, the Wall also became a symbol for free will and the triumphant struggle against oppression and dictatorship.

Almost all traces the Wall left on the cityscape had disappeared within a few years. After experiencing freedom, democracy and unity, it seemed there was a strong desire to remove any traces left by this awful past. It was not until 15 years after the Fall of the Wall, when there was almost nothing left to see of the monument that once divided the city, that the Berlin Senate began to work on a memorial concept to remember the Berlin Wall and the division of the city. What was left of the Wall should be preserved and the relationship between the remains told as part of the memorial concept.

Whilst people in Berlin began to dispose of the Wall as quickly as possible, interest in the Wall from around the world was massive. Countless sections of the Wall, which had once surrounded and walled in West Berlin (each weighing tonnes), found new homes all around the world. Today, they can be found on every continent, where they stand as historical memorials, victory trophies, as symbols of freedom or as works of art and commemorate overcoming German division and the struggle for freedom and democracy. 146 sites all over the world, each home to a piece of the Berlin Wall, have been chosen for this book. 241 complete segments of the Berlin Wall and a further 45 smaller pieces, from both the exterior Wall and the so called 'hinterlandmauer' – which marked the border in West or East Berlin – are presented in this book. The

owners of the pieces of Wall have been asked to tell the story behind 'their' pieces of Wall. Some of the stories that have been uncovered are exciting and peculiar, some are tragic. They reflect the multifaceted and complex ways in which the Berlin Wall is remembered. The stories are by artists who wanted to create memorials to freedom, by politicians whose political careers were influenced and shaped by the Berlin Wall. The stories are also by private individuals whose fates were in some way linked with divided Germany. Art museums and collectors display the sections of Wall at their exhibitions due to their bright graffiti. They are often put on display in historical museums and stand as representatives of the confrontation between East and West and the victory for freedom and democracy against oppression and dictatorship. One section of the Wall was blessed by the Pope in the Portuguese city of Fátima and today, pilgrims from all over the world flock to it. There is also a section of the Wall in the gardens in Vatican City and thanks to NASA, the Wall has even left its mark on Mars. The Wall has been the starting point for many moving, artistic and sometimes funny and peculiar stories and works of art.

The remains of the Berlin Wall have been scattered across the globe and serve as witnesses to the Cold War and the confrontation between democratic states and dictatorships. Unattached from the concrete interpretations from where the segments of Wall once stood, they make one thing very clear: people allover the world remember the division of Germany and the joy felt when the Wall fell. The Wall is still seen today as a symbol of the collapse of the totalitarian communist systems.

We would like to sincerely thank all those who have shown support or contributed to this book, be it by supplying photos, researching or anything else. Without your willingness to share your stories and experiences, photos and memories as well as going to the most remote places in search of traces, we would not have been able to show and tell many of the stories included in this book. Many thanks!

Berlin, March 2014
Anna Kaminsky

**FROM THE
BUILDING OF
THE BERLIN
WALL TO THE
FALL OF THE
BERLIN WALL**
A SHORT
HISTORY OF
THE DIVISION

Maria Nooke

O n 31st August 1969 at 1:00am, the lights went out at the Brandenburg Gate and police and members of the East German army moved towards the sector border. Ten minutes later, the GDR announced that measures were being taken which would help to "guard and control".[1]

Within a few hours, the GDR government had closed the border to West Berlin with barbed wire. An impermeable border fortification was built over the next days and weeks – the Berlin Wall. Pictures of this formidable border installation were sent around the world. Confused faces and a wall of armed soldiers at the Brandenburg Gate have become engraved on collective memory.

28 years later, on 9th November 1989, the Brandenburg Gate was again the focus of worldwide attention. The Wall had fallen. There were images of people dancing with joy on the concrete Wall in front of the Brandenburg Gate.

The euphoria felt when the division came to an end was not only felt by Berliners, not only by Germans in the East and the West, but by people all over the world.

The Wall had divided Berlin for over 28 years. The beginning and end of the Berlin Wall marked significant landmarks in world history, which history books would later refer to as the 'Cold War'. The Berlin Wall was a physical construction which showed the inhumanity of the GDR government. A government that became known for shooting its own citizens if they tried to escape. When the Wall fell on 9th November 1989, it became a symbol for the peaceful victory over German division. The fate of the GDR had been sealed with the Fall of the Wall and German reunification was made possible.

The Brandenburg Gate after the Fall of the Wall

GERMANY UNDER OCCUPATION AFTER THE SECOND WORLD WAR

The reasons leading to the building of the Berlin Wall go back to the Second World War, which had been instigated and lost by Germany. When it became clear that Hitler was going to lose the War, the Allies began to negotiate plans to split Germany into new territories once Hitler had been defeated. Germany was to be divided into three, later four, zones of occupation and a special status was arranged for Berlin, the capital city. The city was also to be divided into four sectors with an Allied Kommandatura. Former county borders were used to help decide where the sector borders should lie. Hitler's system of power was to be destroyed once and for all by dividing the country. At the Yalta conference in February 1945, it was decided that an *Allied Control Council* would be established and should govern Germany. The Allies assumed that there would be no division of power amongst the individual zones, but that they would be governed together.

---

1   Hertle, Hans-Hermann: Chronik des Mauerfalls. Die dramatischen Ereignisse um den 9. November 1989, Berlin, 8. Ed. 1999.

On 2nd August 1945, the *Potsdam Agreement* by the Allies aimed to reconstruct Germany, both socially and politically. This meant democratisation of the political system, demilitarisation and denazification, radical changes to the economy and decentralisation in politics, administration and the economy. However, it became clear during the talks at the *Potsdam Conference* that the powers, once united, would find it difficult to agree how to govern Germany and that such an agreement was no longer possible.

The effects of conflicting interests became clear in the subsequent period, especially when looking at the varying political and economical systems put in place.

In the Soviet occupation zone (SBZ), social economical conditions changed and became the basis for a people's democracy according to the Soviet model.

A communist one-party dictatorship was quickly put in place and the economy became a planned economy through communisation of property.

In the western occupation zones, in contrast, economical and political structures were put in place which reflected traditional western democracy and a private system of ownership took shape. The relationship between the Allies deteriorated due to these conflicting positions. In March 1948 the Soviets left the Allied Control Council and plans for the Four Powers to govern Germany together failed. The two sides of Germany developed into increasingly independent states.

After the War, the German people reacted to the situation in occupied Germany in their own way, and millions of people flocked over the demarcation line. They were in search of home, family members or simply looking for ways and means to survive. Migration from the Soviet occupied zone to the western zones was, from the beginning, greater than that from the western zones to the East. The majority of the refugees were displaced people from the former eastern territories of Germany which once belonged to Poland. The continued economical and political sovietisation in the East was also a reason for the increasing numbers of people fleeing west. The final break between the Allies was caused by introducing a new currency in the western zones. Aimed at putting a stop to the flourishing black market and to create a stable economy – thereby strengthening economical development in the West – the West Mark was officially introduced on 20th June 1948 in the western zones. A reaction from the Soviet zone was inevitable – otherwise the SBZ economy would have crashed – the old currency flowed where it was still worth something, in particular to East Berlin.

The Soviet military administration in Germany (SMAD) retaliated by introducing the East Mark within its zone on 24th June. The SMAD requested the Mayor of Berlin to make this currency compulsory for the western sectors in Berlin – this was deemed to be inoperative and the D-Mark became the official currency for West Berlin. In Berlin, there were now two currencies in circulation.

At the same time the monetary reform was introduced, the Soviets began the Berlin Blockade. All access points to West Berlin were blocked. The existence of the western side of the city was under threat. Essential supply channels were cut off from one day to the next. There were no means of delivering coal, electricity or food. By depriving West Berlin of such essentials, the Soviets hoped to put the people under pressure and remove Berlin from the power of the western Allies. However, the western Allies did not give up and instead they organised an airlift to provide West Berlin with essential supplies. Planes from the American and English airforces took off and landed every minute, loaded with goods to prevent West Berlin from starvation. This resulted in a change in the relationship between the citizens of West Berlin and the western Allies: they could trust the Allies and the occupiers became friends. The airlift had a lasting effect which was seen again immediately after the Fall of the Wall when the city was once again found itself in an extreme situation.

RESTRICTIONS BETWEEN ZONES AND SECURING DEMOCRACY

The foundation of the two German states in 1949 and the escalation of the Cold War had a grave influence on the safeguarding of a demarcation line between the occupation zones in Berlin.[2]

At first, the borders between the occupation zones and the sectors within Berlin only served as governing borders. However, in the course of the political developments, they became much more influential and eventually real customs and economical borders.

Crossing the inner-German border was initially possible without significant problems – but officially illegal. By 1946, the Soviets had founded the border police. At the same time, the border between the Soviet and western Zones was closed for three months to curb the huge numbers of people and goods leaving the East. From 1948, so called *border violators* were increasingly searched for by the Soviet side. They were trying to curb smuggling and the black market, but also to chase down saboteurs and spies.

From 1950, the border police were given the task of surveying the crossing points. In order to better govern the flow of people moving between the borders, the Soviets introduced border passes in 1946. They were valid for 30 days and were issued for urgent family or business trips. During the Berlin Blockade, the Soviets made it compulsory to be issued also with a temporary residence permit alongside the border pass. By doing this, the aim was to reduce the flow of people travelling between the Zones. Crossing the borders illegally was, however, still possible. Many still chose the less dangerous route through Berlin as Berlin was still quite accessible due to its special status.

On 1st April 1948, on orders from the Soviet zone, a police reform was put in place: a 'ring around Berlin' was created along a path of 300 km surrounding the entire city (including West Berlin) and controls were carried out. This made it possible to survey the open border as well as was possible at a time when the migration of people from the Soviet zone of occupation was becoming an ever increasing problem.

When the GDR was formed in October 1949, 1.9 million people had already left for the West.

Conflicting interests from the Soviets on one side, and those from the USA, Great Britain and France on the other prevented a peace treaty from being signed. In 1952, the Soviet Union made a step towards solving the problems caused by conflicting political interests and agendas, and the first Stalin Note was sent. Stalin offered the reunification in a neutral unified Germany – free elections should take place under Allied control. By doing this he, wanted to prevent Germany from becoming part of the *Western Defence Alliance*. The western Allies rejected his offer as they feared it to be a bluff and saw it instead as an attempt to spread the Soviet influence over Germany.

This rejection of terms, alleged activities of sabotage and the constant migration of people prompted the GDR officials, under Soviet influence, to close the border between the GDR and West Germany in May 1952 and gain control of movement between borders.

The border was now a real inner-German border. A five kilometre exclusion zone was set up on the GDR side of the border to secure the 1,378 km long border – an order from the Soviet occupiers. This area could only be entered or traversed with permission. Meetings and events were prohibited from 10:00pm.

A ten-metre-wide control strip was dug up along the border. Deforestation was carried out in green areas along the border. Ramparts, ditches and alarmed trip wires were installed behind the border. Crossing the ten metre long control strip was an arrestable offence. Border police were ordered to shoot those

---

2   For information on the development of the inner-German border see Ritter, Jürgen/Lapp, Peter Joachim: Die Grenze. Ein deutsches Bauwerk, 5. Ed., Berlin 2006. See also Lapp, Peter Joachim: Grenzregime der DDR, Aachen 2013, p. 22-33.

who did not follow their orders. A 500 metre-wide protection strip was closed around the ten-metre stripe in which approximately 110 villages lay. Inhabitants of these villages were subjected to particularly harsh regulations: being outdoors in the 500m area was only permitted during the hours of sunlight and all traffic was forbidden after dark and alterations to land was forbidden without permission. Numerous restaurants and hotels were forced to close down after the protection strip had been constructed. Routes along the Brocken Railway, which linked the Harz mountain range in North Germany, had to be closed as the trains were no longer allowed to travel through western territory.

People living in the restricted area were no longer issued with passes to travel between zones, and people from West Germany were also no longer allowed to travel over the 5km long strip. To put an end to the cries of outrage from the people, a special scheme was put into place which saw the forced resettlement of so called enemies, criminals and 'suspicious' people from the protection strip.

'Operation Vermin' was the name given to the actions that saw 11,000 residents forcibly moved out of the border area in a matter of days. Violence was used in part to move these people from their homes.[3]

Not only did these people lose their communities, but also a great deal of their personal possessions. Around 3,000 people avoided forced resettlement by fleeing to the West.

Closing the border also meant closing many transport links. 32 railway lines, three motorways, 31 A-roads, 140 country roads and thousands of other roads were blocked.[4]

A consequence of this was a zone surrounding the West which had negative implications on the economical situation in areas close to the border and on the quality of life for the people living nearby.

The West German government created incentive programmes which aimed to help minimise the effect the precarious situation having on the people. People on the GDR side of the border were kept quiet with special discounts and benefits. They were treated to pay rises, tax deductions and improved pensions. They were also supplied with better consumer goods.

In Berlin, too, there were similar incisions when the border was closed in 1952: 200 streets were closed. Almost 75% of transport links between West Berlin and the surrounding areas were no longer in use. Control strips were dug up on numerous sites around Potsdam and West Berlin. Vast areas of private land (often belonging to the West) fell victim to securing the border.

Compensatory damages to land owners were few and far between and many land owners received absolutely nothing. As well as the measures being taken along the border, telephone lines and electricity supplies between East and West Berlin were cut off. The GDR wanted an independent infrastructure for East Berlin.

However, the number of people leaving East Berlin did not decrease. Most of the escapees continued to try their luck over the border in Berlin, which remained open. Controversial domestic political situations, like those during collective farming and the forced development of Socialism ahead of the people's uprising on 17th June 1953, were reasons for many GDR citizens to leave East Germany.

In 1953, the West German government set up a refugee centre in Marienfelde in West Berlin to help manage the number of people entering. At this refugee centre and other similar centres, refugees had to go through an official procedure. Successful refugees could obtain residency permits and be integrated into West German society.[5]

---

3   Bennewitz, Inge/Potratz, Rainer: Zwangsaussiedlungen an der innerdeutschen Grenze, Berlin 1994
4   For these and the following figures see Ritter/Lapp, 2006, p. 24.
5   Effner, Bettina/Heidemeyer, Helge (Ed.): Flucht im geteilten Deutschland, Berlin-Brandenburg 2005.

The western powers chose to suspend compulsory inter-zone passes in November 1953 and stopped issuing temporary permits of residence. Therefore, there were no longer restrictions on travel in the West. In contrast, a law passed by the GDR in 1954 which made fleeing the GDR illegal.[6]

Fleeing the GDR was now punishable with up to three years imprisonment. The laws were tightened further in 1957 when preparations to flee and attempted escapes were also made punishable.[7] Restrictions by the GDR officials on approved travel to the West also followed. Permission to travel to the West depended on one's age and job. Students, for example, were not permitted to travel to West Germany or any western countries.

THE BERLIN ULTIMATUM AND CRISIS

In autumn 1958, Soviet party leader, Nikita Khrushchev, gave the western Allies an ultimatum and caused the second crisis for Berlin. He ordered the "transformation of Berlin into an autonomous political entity – a free city", that should be demilitarised and "free from interference from any state including the two German states".[8]

If the Allies did not comply with these orders within six months, he would carry out his planned measures within the GDR and grant it its own statehood. Khrushchev wanted to use Berlin's weak position as a lever for his political aims and cement the recognition of Europe's situation, achieved during the Second World War. Furthermore, he wanted to prevent nuclear disarmament and reduce the West German military.

His suggestion to make Berlin a "free city", aimed to get rid of the four-power-status and left the West fearing that the Soviets did actually intend to integrate West Berlin into their zone.

With this solution intending to weaken the West[9], Khrushchev also wanted to close the loophole around Berlin and gain control of the refugee problem. The Soviets were no longer striving for reunification. However, the western Allies were not prepared to give up their rights and rejected his suggestions. This advance from the Soviets caused more unrest amongst the people and, in turn, led to a renewed wave of refugees. Many GDR citizens feared that the escape route over Berlin would be lost forever.

On 3rd-4th June 1961, a meeting was held in Wien between the newly elected US President, John F. Kennedy and Soviet leader, Nikita Khrushchev, against this tense backdrop.

Khrushchev pushed for the signing of a peace treaty and threatened once again to enforce this on the GDR if America was not prepared to agree to his suggestions. A separate peace treaty would also be offered to West Germany. Such a treaty would mean the end of the war and nobody would be forced to surrender. This would concern the entire law of occupation as well as access to Berlin including the airlift. Khrushchev threatened that any violation of GDR ruling would be classified as a declaration of war.

On the other hand, Kennedy emphasised that part of the responsibilities resulting from the war would mean that by leaving Berlin, the US would lose credibility in the eyes of the Allies. Therefore, due to his political responsibility, he could not approve this. It was not about Berlin, it was about the whole of western Europe as well as US state security, to which Berlin was of crucial strategical importance. Kennedy wanted to maintain the balance of power in the post-war order as he thought any shift would be detrimental. Both representa-

---

6 Passport law by the GDR on 15th September 1954, GDR law journal 1954 p. 786.
7 Eisenfeld, Bernd/Engelmann, Roger: 13. August 1961: Mauerbau, Bremen 2001, P. 25-28.
8 Steininger, Rolf: Der Mauerbau. Die Westmächte und Adenauer in der Berlinkrise 1958-1963, München 2001, p. 41. For information on the Berlin crisis cf. also Wilke, Manfred: Der Weg zur Mauer, Berlin 2001, p. 196-251 and Lemke, Michael: Die Berlin-Krise 1958-1963, in: Henke, Klaus-Dietmar: Die Mauer. Errichtung, Überwindung, Erinnerung, München, 2011, p. 32-48.
9 Cf. analysis by Gerhard Wettig in Wilke, 2011, P. 211-212.

tives of the major powers left Vienna without reaching agreement. At a speech on 25th June 1961, Kennedy once again named the 'Three Essentials' directing the US course of action in West Berlin: 1) the right of western Allies to be present in Berlin, 2) the right to free access to the city, 3) securing the livelihood of West Berlin and its citizens. The 'Three Essentials' were proclaimed worldwide in a large-scale campaign. Kennedy formulated them specifically for West Berlin and not the whole of the city, as the special status would have implied. This position signalled to the Soviet Union the need to accept the originally reserved rights for their sector and to agree to the closure of the border in the interest of avoiding military confrontation.[10]

THE GDR BEFORE THE BUILDING OF THE WALL

At the start of the summer holidays in 1961, the amount of people fleeing the GDR soared. Many people disguised their escape as a holiday. This was a reaction to the foreign policy as well as the dramatic economic climate and the drastic supply problems that continually escalated.[11]

As part of a propaganda offensive, the GDR government depicted the refugee movement as a specific method of alienation from the West. In order to prevent further escapes, the GDR set up 'human trafficking committees'. Alleged 'human traffickers' were sentenced to harsh sentences in staged trials. By doing this, the government wanted to distract attention from the truth that people were leaving the GDR of their own free will. So called border workers were also targeted. These were people who lived in East Berlin but travelled to work in West Berlin. They were inspected more frequently at the border and some had their passports and ID taken from them so that they were no longer able to go to work in the West. Due to the economic divide between West and East Berlin, the number of border workers rose to 56,000 before the Wall was built.[12]

Border workers were paid partly in West German currency and the GDR government used this as propaganda to cause jealousy and resentment amongst the people towards the border workers and also as a means to justify the harsh state treatment towards them. Any wages paid in West German currency were subject to a compulsory exchange. Many services could be exchanged in the GDR for West German cash. In early August, the border workers were forced to give up their jobs in the West and register as job-seekers in the GDR.

GDR propaganda aimed to denounce West Berlin as a dangerous trouble spot in the East-West conflict. The GDR's campaign accused the FRG government of intensive war preparations, aiming to conquer the GDR and parts of Poland.

The increasing measures taken against refugees and border workers, as well as the fierce propaganda campaigns in the GDR, made suspicions in the West all the more great that it would not just be individuals who were victimised by the GDR government. A televised speech by Khrushchev on 7th August 1961 caused many of those watching to fear that a Wall may be built along the Berlin border. People assumed, however, that the measures would be enforced along the 'ring around Berlin'. Nobody thought that the city would be cordoned off. That was a massive error of judgement, as would soon be proved.

---

10 Cf. Wilke, 2011, p. 308-311.
11 For the development of escape attempts and reasons behind escapes see Effner, Bettina/Heidemeyer, Helge: Flucht im geteilten Deutschland, Berlin 2005. Documents relating to the building of the Wall and background in: Camphausen, Gabriele/Nooke, Maria: Die Berliner Mauer. Ausstellungskatalog, Dokumentationszentrum Berliner Mauer, Dresden 2002.
12 SBZ-Archiv year. 12 (1961) pp. 234.

DECISION TO BUILD THE WALL AND PREPARATIONS TO CLOSE THE BORDER

According to claims by the Czech Minister of Defence, which were televised in the West in 1968, Ulbricht had already put forward a suggestion to lay a barbed wire fence through Berlin during a Warsaw Pact meeting in March 1961.[13] In light of this, Ulbricht's words at a press conference in June 1961 make more sense, "nobody has the intention to build a wall" – words which would later be revealed to be lies. The fact that large amounts of building materials including fence posts and barbed wire were being stored in Berlin, further suggested that plans had long been underway to build a wall. However, the decision to build a wall was first finalised in July and the start of August 1961.[14]

After the Vienna summit and the dramatic supply crisis in the GDR, which in turn lead to increasing levels of people fleeing the GDR, Ulbricht decided upon a propaganda offensive. He made propaganda relating to the Berlin question and the peace treaty. At the same time, Ulbricht urged the Soviets to close the borders immediately. Khrushchev called for his decision (which should be made by 20th July), and insights into the intelligence agencies regarding the military strength of the western powers, American politics and planned defensive measures.[15] The Warsaw Pact states would also be involved in the decision. From 3rd-5th August 1961, a conference for party leaders was held in Moscow. The problems surrounding a peace treaty and West Berlin were discussed. Walter Ulbricht was criticised by his counterparts for slow economic growth and high consumer spending in the GDR. Ulbricht underlined his own position that the border to West Berlin was to be held responsible and demanded it to be closed with immediate effect. However, the states of the Warsaw Pact feared economic sanctions of unpredictable proportions in the event of closing the border. Sanctions which would not only have an impact on the GDR.

There were only two possible solutions to the problem: complete control over all access points to the West, including air corridors, or to build a wall. Since complete control of the air corridors was impossible to implement, Ulbricht's calls for the border to be closed – meanwhile supported by Khrushchev – led to the planned measures being supported.[16]

A central argument for the decision was the volatile economical situation in the GDR and the increasing numbers of people leaving for the West. When Ulbricht returned from Moscow, the SED politburo began putting the plans, which had been discussed in Moscow, into action. (Which, in agreement with the Soviet side, were technically already being prepared.)

On 10th and 11th of August, the People's Parliament, the cabinet and the East Berlin Magistrate passed a decree in typical SED wording explicating the closure of the border. Only comrades in the highest political ranks were let in on the plans in order to keep them secret for as long as possible. At the same time logistical preparations were being made and all the stops were pulled out on the propaganda front to prepare citizens for the radical measures.

It was via this propaganda offensive that Ulbricht invoked fears of military action from the West from which the GDR needed to protect itself. But for the GDR government, this was not actually about protecting GDR citizens, it was about preventing them to free access West Berlin. The aim was to stabilise the GDR.

The action was led by Secretary of the SED, Erich Honecker. He coordinated the complex task of closing the border. An operational group was formed at the Department for National Security to carry out

---

13 Eisenfeld/Engelmann: 13. August 1961: Mauerbau, Bremen 2001, p. 41.
14 Cf. Wilke, 2011, p. 296-311.
15 Ibid., p. 301-304.
16 Wilke, 2011, p. 322-327.

the planned action. Whilst Soviet troops in the GDR and adjacent Eastern Bloc countries had only been reinforced between May and July 1961 with several hundred thousands[17], cordoning off the border was to be conducted by the GDR border police, riot police and the company brigades. Entities of the National People's Army had to be on emergency standby to stop potential attacks from the West. A third squadron was formed by Soviet troops at the Ring of Berlin.

The GDR Ministry of State Security was in charge of securing the building of the Wall domestically. The mission operated under the names "Mission Rose" and "Mission Ring" and took place right across GDR territory. The records of intensive supervision of the people of the GDR were to be passed on to the Ministry hourly for the first two days. All mail in corss-border traffic was subjected to controls and telephone lines to western Germany were cut off completely. A state of all-encompassing supervision was to be established.

CLOSING THE BORDER AND THE CONSEQUENCES OF BUILDING THE WALL[18]

The systematic closing of the 160 km border around West Berlin began on Sunday 13th August at 1:00am. Members of the People's and Border Police, as well as members of the Combat Groups of the Working Class were deployed along the border. They had 30 minutes to seal off 81 streets. At 1:30am, the forces also entered numerous train stations and rail traffic between the two halves of the city was permanently blocked. The station at Friedrichstraße was the only exception and remained in service as an interchange station for inter-sector traffic. Passenger trains from the West also stopped at this station.

The streets were sealed off in the following three hours. Pavements were pulled up, railway connections split, barriers erected and barbed wire laid. When the city began to wake up at 6:00am, everything had been closed off. Only 12 road links remained open where people could pass between East and West and they were strictly regulated. The Brandenburg Gate was cordoned off in the following days as well as further streets. Only eight crossings remained and strict controls were carried out at such crossings.

On 15th August, two days since the border had been closed, East Germany's National Defence Council decided that the border should continue to be fortified by the military. In the hours of darkness between 17th and 18th August, work began

Special edition of 'BZ' about the construction of the Wall
© Archiv Bundesstiftung Aufarbeitung

---

17 Ibid. p. 329
18 For the building of the Wall and the consequences see Hertle, Hans-Hermann: Die Berliner Mauer – Monument des Kalten Krieges. The Berlin Wall – Monument of the Cold War, Berlin, 2008. detailed information and documents on www.chronik-der-mauer.de

to replace the barbed wire with concrete blocks. The people of Berlin were deployed to seal up their own border – despite Ulbricht's claim just two months earlier that "No one has any intention of building a wall". The Wall became more and more insurmountable with each day that passed.

Citizens in both the East and the West looked on, bewildered. They faced the Wall, furious and powerless.

Members of the People's Police kept citizens at bay with machine guns under their arms. Those who protested were arrested. People had also begun to gather on the west side of the border. West Berlin police had also been deployed along the border to push people away from the Wall and help prevent the situation from escalating. Everyday life in the city had been turned on its head from one day to the next. Tens of thousands of families were torn apart by the Wall, couples split in two, parents kept from their children, friendships destroyed and neighbourhoods ruined. Countless people lost their jobs, their way of life and their prospects. Indescribable human tragedy went on as the world watched. Some people still managed to escape the East where it was possible. Many broke through the barbed wire or jumped from windows onto safety nets held out by the West Berlin fire brigade. In September and October, more then 2000 people were evicted from their homes along or near the border. People at the inner-German border were also forced to resettle as a result of "Operation Consolidation".

POLITICAL REACTION

The world held its breath. Was the West going to let this happen on the most tense section of the Iron Curtain? Indeed, Willy Brandt was publicly criticising the closing of the border and referred to it on 13th August as "outrageous injustice", but could do little more than to call the protecting powers.[19]

The break with the Four-Power-Agreement by the Soviet Union was also a blow to Konrad Adenauer, Chancellor of the FRG and he made sure not lose sight of the goal for reunification.[20]

However, Adenauer came under fire due to his reservations, especially assuring the Soviet Union that he would take no actions that would harm the relationship between the Federal Republic of Germany and the USSR and which could harm international relations even further. The situation was tense and fears grew that the outbreak of war was imminent. 300,000 citizens of Berlin gathered in front of Rathaus Schöneberg (in the West) on 16th August 1961. They called for serious action to be taken by the western powers and safe guards for West Berlin. The allies had hardly reacted and anything they had done in reaction was only by means of verbal protest. The discontent felt by the people is clear to see in their banners: "70 hours and no action – doesn't the West know what to do?" or "Paper protests do not stop tanks".[21] These banners illustrated the fear that the West had given up on Berlin.Willy Brandt wrote a letter to the American President in which he wrote "Berlin expects more than words, Berlin expects political action". He made a speech directed at those in the East, "to all functionaries of the zone regime, all officers and units", he appealed to them and told them, "don't be made fools of! Display human behaviour wherever possible and above all do not shoot at your own people!"

On 19th August 1961, in an attempt to try and calm the people of West Berlin and in order to demonstrate that the island city could rely on him, John F. Kennedy sent Vice President, Lyndon B. Johnson, to Berlin. Accompanying him was General Lucius D. Clay, who had masterminded the Berlin Air Lift. One day later, US troops arrive in Berlin to strengthen the troops already stationed there. 1,500 men arrived.

---

19 www.chronik-der-mauer.de, Chronik, 13. August 1961, In: Erklärung des Regierenden Bürgermeisters von Berlin, Willy Brandt, auf einer Sondersitzung des Abgeordnetenhauses, 13. August 1961.

20 See explanation by Federal Chancellor Adenauer about the building of the Wall on 13. August 1961 on: www.bpb.de/themen, Geschichte der Mauer, Adenauer zum Mauerbau. Zur Kritik an Adenauer siehe Steininger 2001, p. 277-279.

21 For the course of the rally and the extracts quoted from the speech see www.chronik-der-mauer.der, Chronik, 16. August 1961.

In his letter of reply, Kennedy wrote to Willy Brandt: "As this brutal closure of the border is a clear admission of failure and political weakness, it obviously means a fundamental Soviet decision that could only be undone by war."[22]

The western powers did not wish to risk a war and were forced to respect the Soviet Union's sphere of influence. Germany appeared to be forever divided. The crisis in Berlin, however, was not ended with the building of the Berlin Wall.

When American officials were prevented from crossing the border at Checkpoint Charlie, tanks were put in place at the border crossing. It was not long before Soviet tanks were brought in and the two sides found themselves in a face-off.

The stand-off lasted 16 hours, finally – as agreed upon in secret negotiations – the Russian tanks moved back first, followed by the American tanks.

It became clear to the world that America had a right to be in Berlin, but could not do anything about the division of the city. America's promise for a safe and free Berlin was strengthened on 26th June 1963 when President Kennedy visited West Berlin. Berliners cheered as he made his famous "Ich bin ein Berliner" speech.[23]

ESCAPCE AND ESCAPE AID AFTER THE BUILDING OF THE WALL

On 15th August 1961, 19 year old East German soldier, Conrad Schumann, jumped over the barbed wire into the West. Schumann, from Zschochau, Saxony, had been sent with his police unit to Berlin and was supposed to guard the border. Doubts about the sense of what he was doing at the border made him leap into freedom. Schumann was the first of over 2,500 border soldiers who evaded service on the border and having to shoot their own compatriots by fleeing to the West.[24]

The first deadly shots to be fired at the border fell 10 days after the Wall was built. On 24th August 1961, Günter Litfin attempted to escape via a small canal.[25] Litfin lived and worked in West Berlin and had been visiting his family in the East. He was shocked to find his way back to the West suddenly blocked. He began to look for a way to get back to his home and job. When he was spotted by border troops, he jumped into the water at Humbolthafen, a small harbour in the River Spree, and began swimming towards the West Berlin banks. The border troops tried to prevent his escape attempt with curtain fire and then aimed for his head. He was hit and disappeared under the water. A little while later, he was pulled from the water – dead. Günter Litfin was the first victim to be shot at the border. He was, however, not the last. Despite the deadly threat, many continued with escape attempts until the Wall fell.[26]

Citizens from West Berlin were still permitted to enter East Berlin in the days immediately after the Wall was built. Many took this opportunity to smuggle friends and relatives back over the border using West Berlin papers and passports. Passes for West Berliners visiting the East were made obligatory on 23rd August.

This rule was made obsolete on 25th August after the Allies and West Berlin Senate refused to set up GDR permit offices. There was no further direct contact between citizens in the East and the West until

22 Ibid., Chronik, 18. August 1961, In: Brief des amerikanischen Präsidenten John F. Kennedy an den Regierenden Bürgermeister von West-Berlin, Willy Brandt, 18. August 1961.
23 Cf Wentker, Hermann: Der Westen und die Mauer, in: Henke, Klaus-Dieter (Hg), München 2011, p. 196-210, here p.200.
24 See Nooke, Maria: Geglückte und gescheiterte Fluchten nah dem Mauerbau, in ibid., S. 163-180, here p. 171f.
25 See Brecht, Christine: Günter Litfin, in: Hertle, Hans-Hermann/Nooke, Maria et al.: Die Todesopfer an der Berliner Mauer 1961-1989. Ein biographisches Handbuch, Ed. Zentrum für Zeithistorische Forschung Potsdam und der Stiftung Berliner Mauer, 2. Ed., Berlin, 2009, p. 37-39.
26 See biographic portraits of victims in ibid.

Memorial stone for
Günter Litfin in Berlin Mitte
© Archiv Bundesstiftung Aufarbeitung

the first border-pass agreement was made in December 1963. Only those in possession of a West German passport and foreigners could cross the border – or refugees who used forged papers to get over the border. Others escaped to West Berlin via sewage systems – until the sewers were also blocked up with metal bars. Coming up with new and innovative means to escape knew no boundaries.[27]

Holes and weak points were constantly searched for. Many disguised themselves as foreigners and escaped to Scandinavia on the interzonal train. Cars were converted, people concealed in cases, diplomats won over to help with escape attempts, paths made over East Europe and hot air balloons built.

The digging of escape tunnels under the border installations was particularly spectacular.[28] Underground burrowing led to 70 tunnels being dug out, however, only a quarter of these were used in successful escape attempts.Many of those trying to escape were arrested or shot. For each escape route discovered, measures were taken to increase security and perfect the border installations.

---

27 Detjen, Marion: Ein Loch in der Mauer. Die Geschichte der Fluchthilfe im geteilten Deutschland 1961-1989; Nooke, Maria/Dollmann, Lydia: Fluchtziel Freiheit. Berichte von DDR-Flüchtlingen über die Situation nach dem Mauerbau – Aktionen der Girrmanngruppe, Berlin, 2011.
28 Keussler, Klaus-M. v./Schulenburg, Peter: Fluchthelfer. Die Gruppe um Wolfgang Fuchs, 2. Auflage, Berlin 2011; Arnold, Dietmar/Kellerhoff, Sven Felix: Die Fluchttunnel von Berlin, Berlin 2008; Nooke, Maria: Der verratene Tunnel. Geschichte einer verhinderten Flucht im geteilten Berlin, Bremen 2002.

UPGRADING AND PERFECTING THE BORDER INSTALLATIONS[29]

Until the mid-nineteen sixties, the inner-city Wall was built using concrete blocks and barbed wire. In the areas between West Berlin and the surrounding land, metal fencing was put up in place of the Wall.

As time went on, a border strip was gradually introduced – it was introduced according to locality and the extent to which the GDR could monitor the area. The border strip was complemented by two, sometimes three, rows of barbed wire fencing, antitank barriers, trip wires, dogs on cable-runs and watch towers. In June 1963, a border area (at some points stretching over hundreds of metres) was set up. Residents and visitors to this area were only allowed to pass with special permits.

Work began on the so called "hnterlandmauer" (hinterland wall), which bordered the death strip on the East and made up the actual border line for citizens of the GDR.

Upgrading the Wall followed in the mid-nineteen sixties and was carried out according to detailed plans by the military. After the first and second generations of Wall, followed the third generation. The third generation Wall was made up of slabs of concrete and was 3,4 metres high. "Grenzmauer 75" (border wall 75) followed in the mid-nineteen seventies. It was an L-shaped wall made from steel reinforced concrete and was 3,6 metres high. This type of wall had been tested for its stability and insurmountability and served as the primary border installation facing the West.

The death strip was 15-150 metres wide and was made up of varying security systems to prevent escape. It was built up from East to West until the end of the 80s as follows: not far from the East facing hinterland wall was a signal fence made up of many electrical wires. If it was touched, an alarm went off. At some points, the fence went half a metre into the ground to prevent people from crawling underneath it. After the fence came watch border troop watch posts and towers – they were built within visibility range to each other and were occupied by two soldiers. A so called "Kolonnenweg" then followed, this was a path along which border troop's vehicles constantly patrolled. It was lined with floodlights which lit up the death strip and a sand path that went right to the Wall itself. This way, visibility was always good and the field of fire always visible. Right in front of the Wall was a ditch, it was slanted and strengthened with concrete making it almost impossible to overcome in a vehicle. Along the top of the Wall itself was a round pipe which prevented people getting any kind of grip with their hands if they attempted to climb over. At certain weaker points along the border, guard dogs were also put on patrol. The dogs were tied to a wire which ran parallel to the signal fence and could move up and down the length of the wire. In 1989, the border around West Berlin was a total of 156,4 km long, 43,7 km of which ran between the two halves of the city and 112 km between West Berlin and Potsdam.

According to a lineup of the border troops, the strip consisted of 63km of developed land, 32km of wood land and 22,65km of open terrain as well as 37km of "water border". Along the border there were 41,91km of Grenzmauer 75 (Border Wall 75), another 58,95km consisted of the 3rd generation Wall made up of concrete slabs and 68,42km were cordoned off by an expanded metal fence. The light strip was 161km in length and the signal fence comprised of 113,85km. On the death strip, there were 186 watch towers and 31 leading posts for the border troops. Access to West Berlin was possible via 13 street border crossings, 4 rail way crossings and 8 waterway crossings, which were all safeguarded.[30]

---

29 Cf. Hertle, Hans-Hermann: Die Berliner Mauer – Monument des Kalten Krieges. The Berlin Wall – Monument of the Cold War, Berlin, 2007, p. 90-101
30 Cf. www.chronik-der-mauer.de/Material/Statistiken, in: Grenzsicherung in Berlin 1989, Auskunftsbericht zum Grenzkommando Mitte (GK Mitte) und der Staatsgrenze der DDR zu Westberlin, März 1989.

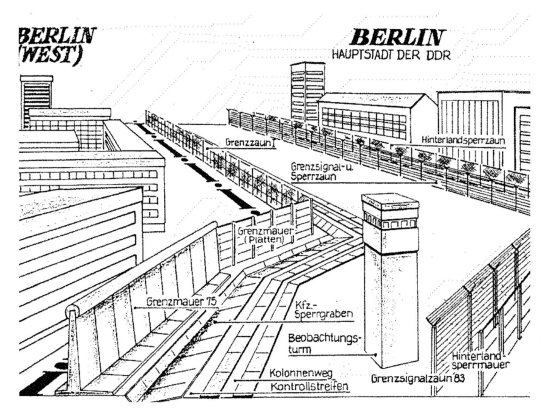

BERLIN (WEST)

BERLIN
HAUPTSTADT DER DDR

Grenzzaun I

Grenzsignal-u.
Sperrzaun

Hinterlandsperrzaun

Grenzmauer
(Platten)

Grenzmauer 75

Kfz.-
Sperrgraben

Beobachtungs-
turm

Kolonnenweg
Kontrollstreifen

Grenzsignalzaun 83

Hinterland-
sperrmauer

Diagram showing the
border fortifications

© Bundesarchiv-Militärarchiv,
GTÜ AZN 17130 Bl. 205

SHOOT-TO-KILL ORDER AND FATALITIES

The real danger was not the almost insurmountable barrier, nor was it the People's Police who worked alongside and supported the border troops. It was not the unofficial staff or volunteers who helped the border police. The deadly threat to those trying to flee the GDR was the fact that they were shot. Even if leaders of the GDR government and military continued to deny that there was an official order to kill (even during court proceedings in the 1990s), killing people at the Wall was common practice.[31]

From a legalistic point of view, the laws, service regulations and the use of fire arms only implied that it was "allowed legally" to kill, but there was no compulsory order to shoot-to-kill. However, the explicit order for border troops to prevent any escape attempts and destroy anyone violating the border led to 136 deaths at the Berlin Wall alone – most of them killed by gunfire. Amongst the victims were 98 would-be escapees, 30 people from the East and the West who had no intention to flee but were nevertheless wounded or killed after being shot and 8 soldiers serving at the border. The majority of the victims were young men aged between 17 and 29. Furthermore, more than 250, mostly elderly people, died whilst crossing official border control points between East and West Berlin.[32]

31 Hertle, Hans-Hermann/Nooke, Maria: Todesopfer an der Berliner Mauer. Kooperationsprojekt des Vereins Berliner Mauer und des ZZF, in: Potsdamer Bulletin für Zeithistorische Studien, no. 34-35 (2005); Hertle, Hans-Hermann/Sälter, Gerhard: Die Todesopfer an Mauer und Grenze. Probleme einer Bilanz des DDR-Grenzregimes, in: DeutschlandArchiv 39 (2008) ed. 4.
32 Results of the research project about victims in: Hertle, Hans-Hermann/Nooke, Maria u.a., 2009

View of the death strip between

East and West Berlin 1981

© Archiv Bundesstiftung Aufarbeitung /
Coll. Michael von Aichberger
No. 698

The last person shot trying to escape over the Wall was 21 year old Chris Gueffroy who was shot on 5th February 1989 whilst trying to escape along the Britz district canal.[33] He had heard from a friend that the order to shoot had been lifted and by escaping to the West, he hoped to avoid his compulsory service in the National People's Army. Whilst the four soldiers who broke off the escape attempt were given a cash reward of 150 Marks and military awards for their actions by the border police, Gueffroy's friend, who also tried to escape and suffered substantial injuries, was sentenced to three years imprisonment. Significant international pressure led Honecker to lift the order to kill on 3rd April 1989. For Chris Gueffroy this order came too late.

HUMANITARIAN INTERVENTIONS AS A SIGN OF THE DÉTENTE POLICY

Despite the deadly threat and many failed escape attempts, 40,101 people managed to flee from the GDR to the West in the 28 years that Germany was divided. 5,075 escaped over the border fortifications in Berlin.[34] In order to alleviate the inhumane situation that had come about as result of German division, the government began looking for humanitarian solutions for those who had been affected. The West Berlin Senate negotiated with GDR officials to introduce a travel permit scheme (Passierscheinabkommen) that made it possible for West Germans to visit relatives in the East for the first time since the Wall had been built. 730,000 citizens made use of this between 19th December and 5th January. In total, 1,2 million visits were registered.

33 Baron, Udo/Hertle, Hans-Hermann: Chris Gueffroy, in: Herlte, Hans-Hermann, Nooke, Maria et al., Berlin, 2009
34 For these and following information see Hertle 2008, p. 57 and p. 84.

ing on Bornholmer Bridge were faced with thousands of people wanting to cross. They saw no alternative than to open the border immediately. This was the night the Wall fell under pressure from the masses, the word "Wahnsinn" (madness) became the word of 1989.

DEMOLISHING THE WALL

The fate of the barrier was sealed with the Fall of the Berlin Wall. In the city centre, between Bernauer and Eberswalder Straße, sections of the Wall had already been removed to make way for a border crossing point. The Wall was open at many points within a very short period of time.

People danced joyously on the Wall, delighted that the hated construction had finally been made redundant. Berliners and visitors all came to the border, equipped with tools and began making holes and securing themselves a piece of the historic Wall. Around the same time plans to dismantle the rest of the border installations were being made. As early as December 1989, the decision to tear down the Wall had been made by the provisional GDR government and the East Berlin authorities. Any traces of the brutal border should be vanquished from the city landscape. The demolition process did not only mean tearing down the Wall, but all of the security systems in place along the border which had prevented escape.

On the 1st July 1990, controls at the remaining border crossings ceased and the official economic and monetary union came into effect. By now, more than 100 streets that had crossed the border had been reopened and were now back in use. The last sections of the inner-city Wall were removed in November 1990. The swift dismantling of the Wall was a reflection of the social consensus: "The Wall has to go". The people of Berlin did not want to be faced with the Wall any longer, the city should become one again. Whilst institutions and individuals from all over the world secured themselves sections of the Wall to put up as memorials to the Cold War and overcoming German division, all traces of the Wall should be eradicated from Berlin. Very few voted to maintain parts of the Wall in Berlin for future generations to see. This was to happen on Bernauer Straße which, due to the many events that took place there during the time the Wall stood, has become part of collective memory. A 212 metre long section of Wall stands there today and has been preserved as a memorial to the history of the divided city and the victims of the communist dictatorship. Part of the Berlin Wall Memorial on Bernauer Straße runs across the former death strip. There is a wealth of information about the former border regime, as well as information about how life was for people living alongside the Wall in the divided city. It is also explained how the Fall of the Wall was forced upon the GDR government and how the peaceful revolutions which led to the Fall of the Wall came about.

"THERE ARE PLENTY OF GOOD REASONS TO ALSO NOT LOSE SIGHT OF THE 13TH AUGUST"[1]
REMEMBERING THE WALL SINCE 1990

Anna Kaminsky

"Some of you will have asked yourselves: Why has the Enquête Commission of the German Bundestag been campaigning so hard to remember the building of the Berlin Wall 35 years ago today? Is it not enough that the first Enquête Commission tried to analyse the event in several expert groups and hearings? Is the 17th June not an appropriate day to remember everything carried out by the SED dictatorship until its downfall in autumn 1989? I think there are plenty of good reasons also not to lose sight of the 13th August."[2]

FROM 9TH-13TH AUGUST

In 1996, in his welcome speech at a commemoration service in the Bundestag, Rainer Eppelmann used these words to justify the committee's decision to use the 35th anniversary of the building of the Wall as an opportunity to both remember and to dedicate a number of events to it. 18 years later, remembering the building of the Wall and life in a divided city and a divided world has not only been brought back to the forefront of the city's memory, the Wall and its construction now have a firm place in public discussion and collective memory. Moreover, in the 50th year after the Wall was built, remembering the building and the weeks leading up to it received greater attention by June 2011 in research and from the media than the uprisings of 17th June 1953.

The actual division of the city had been relegated to second place on the city's self-image agenda years ago, but the situation seemed to have changed by the 50th anniversary of the Building of the Wall. One sign of this was that the anniversary had pushed other events into the background of public discourse during the time leading up to it. Moreover, it became clear that the policy of eradicating the Wall in the first years after its fall had led to calls for a reconstruction of the Wall in order to "bring history to life"[3], as former governing mayor of Berlin, Eberhard Diepgen, requested.

Despite various ideas of how to keep the memory of the Wall and the division alive, it seems as though the city has found its way back to its traumatic history after 20 years. Forgotten are the first 15 years after the Fall of the Wall which were characterised by the attempts to completely eradicate all traces of the construction and the division of the city which lasted 28 years. Before this, commemorating the Wall had only been a topic for victim's associations, private societies and a few concerned citizens. Whilst public events mainly celebrated the Fall of the Wall, public attention only turned to the 13th of August by way of detour on the 9th of November. The happiness and euphoria brought on by the Fall of the Wall, coupled with the nostalgia of the 90s, seemed to change the general consensus about what exactly had fallen in 89: it was a dictatorship that had denied its citizens basic human rights and shot or imposed long prison sentences on all those who had tried to escape its sealed borders.

SO WHERE WAS THE WALL?

The images from the night of 9th-10th November are equally as iconic in world history as those from 12th-13th August 1961.

The crowds of people who stormed the opened border and the people sitting and dancing on the Wall are no less a part of cultural memory than the people standing in disbelief in front of the rolls of barbed

---

1   Revised edition of the speech from 18th June 2001 at the Berlin Wall Memorial (www.berliner-mauer-gedenkstaette.de/de/der-mauerbau- 1961-970. html)

2   Rainer Eppelmann: Begrüßung zur Gedenkstunde zum 35. Jahrestag des Baus der Berliner Mauer. Öffentliche Sitzung der Enquete-Kommission „Überwindung der Folgen der SED-Diktatur im Prozeß der deutschen Einheit" des Deutschen Bundestages am 13. August 1996 in Berlin. Special edition ed. by Deutschen Bundestag. Bonn 1996, p. 7.

3   Werner von Beber: Diepgen will Teile der Mauer neu aufstellen lassen. Der Tagesspiegel on 19.6.2011, p. 10.

wire, or those jumping from windows on Bernauer Straße who considered these dangerous jumps the only possibility to make it to the West and, ultimately to freedom.

Although it was by no means a forgone conclusion to SED rulers in the GDR that the Wall and the border were to remain open, deliberations were already being made on 10th November as to what should happen to this 'historical monstrosity'. Whilst Willy Brandt – then the reigning mayor of West Berlin – called for sections of the Wall to be preserved as a memorial in his speech in front of the Schöneberg City Hall, others were already thinking of turning the Wall into a business. And so, on 10th November 1989, the first enquiries were sent from Bayern to the GDR government offering cash in return for "unwanted pieces of your border fortifications no longer needed".[4] On 14th November 1989, a business consultant got in touch with the GDR's Permanent Representation in Bonn and – since trade with the Wall could no longer be hindered – recommended that the GDR should think about any "conflicting nature", the consultant went on to say that "trade will be made with sections of the Wall, no matter where they come from. I consider it therefore all the more reasonable to make money from it."[5]

Almost overnight, the Wall became a highly sought-after object, a trophy of the Cold War, an export hit and a symbol. If, during its 29 years in existence, the Wall had simply been a symbol of the Socialist system's inhumanity and oppression, overnight, it had become a symbol of civil courage and the will for freedom. No other construction in Germany, and perhaps Europe, had had such grave consequences on so many people in the second half of the 20th century. No other construction from this period became a symbol of oppression and dictatorship, contempt for basic human rights and, finally, for taking hostage of millions of people by a regime formed on injustice. After the Fall of the Wall, no other construction went from being a symbol of oppression and contempt for mankind to a symbol of the will for freedom and civil courage.

In the weeks and months after the Wall fell, requests from all over the world for pieces of the Wall increased and on 7th December / 4th January 1990, the GDR government, under Hans Modrow, decided to sell it. It was hoped that selling the Wall would help save the GDR economy which was heading towards bankruptcy. With offers of up to 500,000 DM per section[6], these hopes were warranted.

Since the political development by the end of 1989 had already shown that the SED regime could no longer be saved, and, furthermore, that not only the Berlin Wall, but the entire inner-German border had been opened, dismantling what was once the most heavily guarded border was at the top of the agenda.

It was immediately suggested that at least part of the costs of dismantling the fortifications should be financed by selling the Wall.

 The GDR government launched an information campaign around Christmas 1989 to outline the reasons for the sale of the Berlin Wall to the angry and rattled people in the GDR. The campaign aimed to pick up the points made in the letters of complaint received by the government and justify the sale of the Wall to which the government saw no alternative.

Anger at the sale of the Wall was directed at the government who had locked in its citizens for decades, ruthlessly shot at escapees and who now wanted to sell this 'Wall of shame' – at which people had been murdered – in order to make money. The government used three arguments to justify selling the Wall to the western World:

---

4   Letter to the Minister of Foreign Trade on 10.11.1989, quoted by Ronny Heidenreich: From Concrete to Cash. Turning the Wall into a Business. p. 268
5   Telefax from a Ministry of Foreign Trade business consultant to the GDR's Permanent Representative in Bonn, 14.11.1989. BArchB DE 10/21, quoted by Ronny Heidenreich: From Concrete to Cash. Turning the Wall into a Business. p. 271
6   For the sale of the Wall see the Text by Ronny Heidenreich: From Concrete to Cash. Turning the Wall into a Business. p. 268

1) The GDR's need foreign exchange,

2) the Wall is public property and, therefore

3) any profit made by the sale would go to the entire GDR population, and social projects, for example, would therefore benefit from such a sale. Irrespective of any further reservations about the sale of the Wall, the border troops in Mitte – whose job had been to protect the Wall and prevent anyone penetrating the border until December 1989[7] – began work on dismantling the Wall in January 1990. Work began on sections of the Wall which had been painted by Wall artists, and, therefore, were particularly lucrative. The majority of the concrete sections were crushed and used, amongst other things, for road and motorway construction.

In less than a year, that which had once separated the people along a 156 km long border and was made up of 54,000 concrete segments – each 2.6 tonnes in weight and 3.2 metres in height – had all but disappeared from the city landscape. Other objects from the border to disappear included hundreds of kilometres of barbed wire and strips of lighting, equipment used to harness guard dogs and 186 watch towers from which guards had shot live-ammunition.

The desire for the city to return to some sort of normality after the long years of division was quite understandable. In 1990, very few could have imagined that there would one day be calls for the city and its people to make their wound visible once more. Removing the Wall from the city completely seemed a suitable way to overcome the division and its consequences as quickly as possible.

It was not only visitors to Berlin, whose interest in the Wall was warranted, who were increasingly baffled and asking: "So, where was the Wall?" At the same time, people had to accept that the notion of what the Wall had meant for the city and its people had waned considerably.

THE CONFLICT SURROUNDING COMMEMORATING THE WALL

From very early on, some had voiced their opinion that the Wall should be preserved, at least in some areas of the city, as a memorial.

Willy Brandt was the Mayor of Berlin at the time and, on 10th November 1989, during a speech in front of the Schöneberg City Hall, he had already called for "a piece of the construction (…) to be be preserved as a memorial to a historic monstrosity."[8] After almost all sections of Wall in the inner-city had been removed by the Mitte border troops, the East Berlin Magistrate decided to put the existing "ensemble" on Bernauer Straße under monument protection. Despite this decision, the sale and building, also on Bernauer Straße, proceeded. Almost 15 years would pass before a plan for the Berlin Wall would be developed and the majority of the former border fortifications would disappear without trace from the city landscape.[9]

Whilst the Wall itself was removed from the city with German efficiency, sections of it were becoming hugely popular all around the world. In the first years after the Fall of the Wall, memorials were created from its concrete sections in more than 40 countries worldwide. Meanwhile, 600 sections of the Wall make up 140 memorials worldwide.

In 1991, there were few reminders of the Wall left in Berlin, except a few building sites along the former death strip. In the same year, Berlin remembered 30 years since the Wall was built. The memorial service

---

7   The firing order was not revoked until 22nd December 1989.

8   Quoted in "Streit um das Symbol des Schreckens", in Süddeutsche Zeitung on 13.8.21991, p. 3.

9   Leo Schmidt and Axel Klausmeier made an inventory of all the remains of the former border fortifications in Berlin. The book contains a lot of information that only informed observers can detect: concrete elements etc. Mauerreste – Mauerspuren, Westkreuz-Verlag Berlin 2004

was attended by the Federal Minister of the Interior and the Mayor of Berlin. Until the Berlin Wall Memorial on Bernauer Straße was opened in 2001, the ceremony had taken place at the Peter Fechter memorial on Zimmerstraße.

On one hand, media coverage caused a stir about the missing millions made from the sale of the Wall. There were, however, on the other hand, concerned reports and urgent warnings which pointed out that not all sections of the Wall and border installations should be disposed of without a concept for commemorating the Wall in the future.

Whilst the cultural administration pleaded for a memorial to be constructed on Bernauer Straße and for the fortifications to be reconstructed, the road traffic authorities followed with plans to build a multi-lane by-pass. The distorted image of a memorial as a "Wall-Disney-Land"[10] at this site made the idea seem unappealing.

Christoph Stölzl, director of the German Historical Museum warned that "It may appear as irony of history to future generations if the German capital does not display pieces of this chapter in German history."[11]

Within the same context, discussions about the "Wall in people's minds" attracted great attention since this imaginary wall had long replaced the real-life Wall.

By this time, there were only four noteworthy sections of the Wall left in Berlin – on Niederkirchner-straße, the 'hinterlandmauer' at Invalidenfriedhof and the section on Bernauer Straße. The fourth, a section of hinterlandmauer along the banks of the Spree, north of the Oberbaum bridge, had been decorated with paintings and was already famous all around the world as the East Side Gallery post-1989. Former minister for urban development, Volker Hassemer, wanted to preserve it, but was met with opposition from the city district of Friedrichshain. The district officials wanted the land between the Spree and the Wall closed to the public and used instead for commercial benefit. The individual districts within the city were free to decide what was to happen to the sections of Wall within their districts. This "regionalism" within Berlin hindered the founding of a Wall memorial and the development of a general concept for years.

In the following years, there was a threat that the discussion about a general memorial concept could be ground down by the conflict of interest from the preservationists on one side, and the those with economical interests on the other. Questions of remembrance, memorial and the importance of retelling history had no place in this disagreement.

On 13th August 1991, the Berlin Senate adopted a resolution to build a "central memorial" on Bernauer Straße. For this purpose, a section of Wall, 70 metres long with signal fence, hinterlandmauer and watch tower[12] should be reconstructed alongside the remains that still stood. It would still take three years before a competition to design the memorial would be announced in 1994 and which 'Kolhoff und Kolhoff' would win. The memorial, which was finally realised by 1998, consisted of a section of the Wall which could only be looked over from a viewing platform – offering a vague perception of the scale of the Wall and border strip. (ill.1)

One of the most frequently made points of criticism to the complete demolition of the Wall and border fortifications was that – even where sections of the Wall had indeed been preserved – the actual structure around the border could no longer be seen. For this reason, it was almost impossible to comprehend exactly how the city had been divided – not just by a Wall, but by a deep city wound.[13]

---

10 The Minister of Transport had presented his plans for a four-lane street on 15th July
11 Was von der Mauer bleibt. in. Berliner Morgenpost on 13.08.1991.
12 See also the entires from monument protection website ("Was weg ist, ist weg" – und darf nicht mehr rekonstruiert werden)
13 Lore Ditzen: "Die ausrasierte Stadtwunde". In: die tageszeitung on 13.08.2001, p. 19.

III. 1

© Bundesstiftung Aufarbeitung

Furthermore, the Wall continued to sell well and development on the area that was once the border went on full steam ahead. The memorial on Bernauer Straße was officially opened in 1998 and received criticism due to its abstract design which gave no real idea of what the Wall had actually been or meant.

FORGOTTEN VICTIMS

At the same time, the representatives for the victims continued to complain about the general indifference towards 13th August. This was a complaint which had already been formulated as early as the 35th anniversary by Klaus-Peter Eich who was a representative for the victims.

The facility, opened in 1998 on Bernauer Straße, was also unable to change anything fundamentally. For one thing the memorial site was, as before, run by volunteers workers and the church. The financial and personnel situation had become more than precarious over a number of years. The fact that the site at "Bernauer Straße" could develop itself into a Berlin Wall memorial, was above all down to the enthusiasm of those there. It seemed, from a political perspective, that the memorial had faded into obscurity – with the exception of memorial days like 13th August and 9th November.

The 40th anniversary of the building of the Wall on 13th August 2001 made it obvious that there were various expectations for a dignified and earnest memorial to the Berlin Wall and the division and, through that, also a way of remembering the SED dictatorship.

At the height of a wave of nostalgia for the East (Ostalgie), speculation around a Social Democrat and Socialist coalition in Berlin characterised the 40th anniversary of the building of the Wall. The PDS (Party of Democratic Socialism), who had received a steady 20% of votes during the GDR, prepared themselves to become a political party in the German capital. To generate votes in the western side of the city, a new explanation for building the Wall was deliberated. Apologising to the victims was not on the agenda: "We regret the injustice caused by the SED"[14], read their dry statement.

In the media, comments on the political exploitation of the anniversary stood in the foreground, which, amongst other things, was described as "disgraceful"[15] in a comment by Rolf R. Lautenschläger in the 'Tageszeitung' (German newspaper) on 13th August 2001. For the victims of the SED regime, on the other hand, it was unthinkable that an SPD and PDS coalition could govern the fate of the capital at this point in time, with the latter being the successor of the party – the SED – that stood for injustice, the Building of the Wall, arbitrariness, repression, hundreds of thousands of unjust political verdicts and hundreds of deaths at the border and the Wall. Much attention was also given to the fact that the PDS had still not apologised for the border regime, constructing the Wall or the deaths caused by the regime. Governing mayor, Klaus Wowereit, also requested that the PDS "apologise to the many victims of the SED dictatorship".[16] And CDU member, Frank Steffel, explained that "yesterday's party of riflemen from the Wall should not supply the senators of tomorrow".[17] PDS leading candidate, Gregor Gysi, declined the request for an apology, but

14 Süddeutsche Zeitung on 11.8.2001, p.6.
15 Die tageszeitung on 14.8.2001, p. 19.
16 Quoted from die tageszeitung on 14.08.2001, p.19.
17 Ibid

pointed out that the "inhumane border regiment" could not be justified in any way.[18] For the victims of the SED, the games being played out by the coalition were unbearable. They renewed their calls for a dignified memorial in central Berlin and threatened to boycott the upcoming memorial event. When PDS representatives appeared on Bernauer Straße with a wreath during the memorial event, political prisoner of the GDR, Alexander Bauersfeld, removed it and stamped on it amidst loud protest in front of the memorial Wall. He was arrested by the police for his actions.

"GUERILLA REMEMBRANCE" AND VISIBLE COMMEMORATION

Anyone who had hoped that the Berlin Senate would work on making a memorial in the city (more) visible after the 40th anniversary of the building of the Wall was to be disappointed. The memorial centre on Bernauer Straße continued to be run on a voluntary basis and only received limited project financing. Whilst this did not derogate the decisions of the members in the organisation, it meant that a long-term project in a safe institution could not be granted.

Any change in the poor treatment towards the official memorial site to the Berlin Wall and division was not on the horizon.

An initiative by the director of the Wall Museum at Checkpoint Charlie filled this gap in 2004 on the day of the 15th anniversary of the Fall of the Wall. Her temporary memorial to be put up on a abandoned area at Checkpoint Charlie did not only cause a stir on the Berlin politics scene. The memorial was made up of a replica of the Wall and over 1,000 wooden crosses – most of which were given a name. For many victims and their families, as well as many visitors to Berlin, the memorial satisfied their need for an authentic place of memorial for the Wall (ill.2). The memorial and the public reception to it made it undeniably clear that the public need for a demonstrative area which remembered the Wall and the division had not been satisfied. References to the memorial on Bernauer Straße came to nothing – it was considered too objective and its location outside the centre of the city made it remote. For the first time, may victims felt they had been taken seriously by Alexandra Hildebrandt's emotional memorial and its use of forms (ill.3).

Whilst victims and tourists to the city welcomed the memorial as a powerful symbol, criticism was aimed at the instillation's style. It was argued that the number of crosses could be seen as a reference to the number of victims, which was not possible to prove. The use of forms was also criticised for mirroring the Memorial to the Murdered Jews of Europe, which had also only just been opened. Critics claimed that the analogy – 6,000 concrete blocks at the Jewish memorial and over 1,000 crosses at this memorial – would cause an equalisation between National Socialism and the SED dictatorship.

III. 2
© Bundesstiftung Aufarbeitung

Undeterred by the critical voices against the memorial, Alexandra Hildebrandt fought back, as she had done on other occasions, against the dismantling of the memorial, which she had initially claimed would be a temporary one.

She organised demonstrations and victims of the communist dictatorship chained themselves to the crosses to protest against

18 Ibid

the crosses being taken down. They argued that this was the only site in Berlin where the victims of the SED dictatorship were suitably brought into public consciousness. These "guerilla memorials" brought about an end to the inaction in Berlin's politics. In November 2004, the Abgeordnetenhaus (Berlin House of Representatives) submitted two proposals by the CDU and B90/Die Grünen (the Green Party), in which the Berlin Senate was called upon to submit a concept for the preservation of the remaining Wall segments and the remembrance of the SED dictatorship. Both proposals called for the Berlin Senate to be more proactive in their efforts to remember the second dictatorship and its victims in Berlin.

They claimed there were not only "shortcomings in the visible memorials to the Wall as a symbol of the history of the city, Germany and the world, but also in the comprehensive representation of the SED dictatorship in the areas of control, daily life and resistance."[19]

In spring 2005, the Berlin House of Representatives organised a hearing to discuss "public engagement with the history of the capital city, Berlin – Wall memorials and the SED past".

III. 3
© Bundesstiftung Aufarbeitung

In light of the memorial site on Checkpoint Charlie (initiated by Alexandra Hildebrandt) and the public reaction to it, Berlin's Minister of Culture, Thomas Flierl (PDS/Die Linke), had already begun to develop a concept for the design of a Wall memorial in summer 2004. On the one hand, the concept intended to secure and preserve any remains of the Wall still in the city as well as to protect any sites where it was still possible to imagine the extent of the Wall and the death strip from further development. On the other hand, any existing memorials should be made more visible and also refer to each other. There were already around 60 memorials which remembered escapees, or memorials made out of remains from the Wall, like on Potsdamer Platz. Amongst these memorials was the double row of cobbled stones which had marked the path of the Wall since the start of the 1990s. However, recognising the stones was increasingly difficult as they were not used exclusively for marking the path of the Wall, but also for repairing the damaged streets. There were no funds available to introduce a metal strip with the dates of the building and collapse of the Wall, which had made mapping the path of the Wall possible.

The concept by the Berlin Senator for Culture was completed in 2006. It was intended as a comprehensive basis and starting point for finding a way to commemorate the division of the city and the victims of the dictatorship by the 50th anniversary of the building of the Wall in 2011. The area around Bernauer Straße was to be maintained for the memorial; existing sites including the basements of the houses demolished to provide a free field of fire were to be opened in order to create connections between them and people's stories and fates. Until then, the site had drawn its effectiveness mainly from the events and campaigns organised by the

---

19 Statement by A. Kaminsky in light of the hearing on 25.4.2005, p. 1.

a association. A historical park was now to be designed and the plans envisaged a concept which covered the entire area up to 'Mauerpark'. The concept finally achieved what had been called for again and again since 1990.[20]

On 13th August 2011, the newly designed memorial site for the Wall was inaugurated during a moving opening ceremony which was attended by the Federal President and the Chancellor. Thousands of Berliners as well as tourists turned out on this day together with their families to commemorate the building of the Wall and the division of the city. Today, the memorial has seen a record-breaking number of visitors pass through its doors. As perceptions of the 17th June 1953 uprisings in June 2011 demonstrated, the remembrance of the Wall was starting to push other traumatic memories of the second dictatorship into the background. Only the future will show whether or not the memory of the building of the Wall and its dramatic consequences for the people caged in the GDR dictatorship will become the defining memory of this second dictatorship. The potential for it certainly lies in the fact that the historical event is interwoven with emotional images as well as specific buildings in the cityscape and moving fates and stories of courage, despair, sadness and treason. It is warranted that we are curious to see whether the memory of the building of the Wall and the deadly border regime will dominate the remembrance of the communist dictatorship of the GDR.

---

20 Unfortunately, support for a Wall Panometer at Nordbahnhof by Yadegar Asis was not given by the Mitte district authority, The plans were supported by the Federal Foundation for the Reappraisal of the SED Dictatorship, the Berlin Wall Foundation and the Berlin Senator for Culture – the plans were not realised due to a lack of interest from the district.

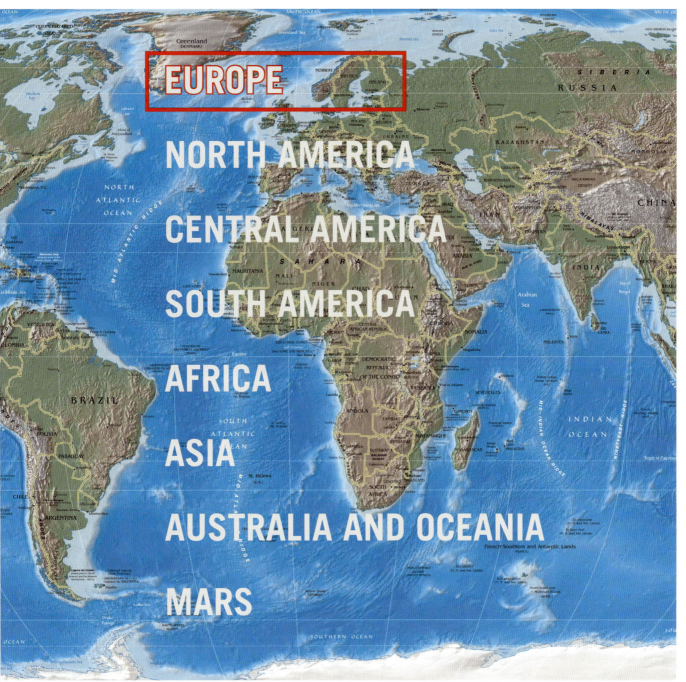

EUROPE

NORTH AMERICA

CENTRAL AMERICA

SOUTH AMERICA

AFRICA

ASIA

AUSTRALIA AND OCEANIA

MARS

Berliner Mauer
Originalteil vom Potsdamer Platz
Von 1961 bis 1989 Symbol der Teilung Berlins, Deutschlands und Europas. Mit ihrem Fall am 9.11.1989 wurde die Vereinigung Ost- und Westeuropas in der Europäischen Union am 1. Mai 2004 möglich.

Mur de Berlin
Pièce originale de la Potsdamer Platz
De 1961 á 1989, symbole de la division de Berlin, de l'Allemagne et de l'Europe. La chute du mur, le 9.11.1989, a rendu possible l'unification de l'Europe orientale et occidentale au sein de l'Union Européenne le 1er mai 2004

De Berlijnse Muur
Origineel deel van de Potsdamer Platz
Van 1961 tor 1989 was de muur het symbool van de scheiding van Berlin, Duitsland en Europa. Met de val van de muur op 9.11.1989 werd de hereniging van Oost- en West-Europa in de schoot van de Europese Unie op 1 mei 2004 mogelijk.

Information board on the Wall behind the European Parliament, Brussels
© Jens Schöne, Berlin

"The Berlin Wall
Original segment from Potsdamer Platz
From 1961-1989 symbol of the division of Berlin, Germany and Europe. With its fall on 9.11.1989, the unification East and West Europe in the European Union on 1st May 2004 was made possible."

BRUSSELS
BELGIUM

Location:
Mini Europe,
Bruparck

Miniature of the Wall in
Bruparck, Brussels
© Jens Schöne, Berlin

The Brandenburg Gate can also be found in Brussels between the Holsten Gate and the Speyer Cathedral. The Berlin Wall runs in front of the gate – people walk alongside it and even sit on it – without hinderance from border soldiers. Low-loading trailers and demolition equipment can be seen on the other side. The dismantling and transportation of the former border fortifications is underway. The famous Wall graffiti, depicting Breschnew and Honecker and the famous Brotherhood Kiss (which was actually painted on a segment at the East Side Gallery), can also be seen.

These miniature replicas can all be seen in the Mini Europe Park at the foot of the world famous Atomium. The miniatures, which were financed by the European Union and the city of Brussels, have all been painstakingly made to a scale of 1:25 and include famous structures from all over Europe.

The park, which was opened in 1989 by Belgian Prince Phillip, is one of Brussels's biggest tourist attractions. 'The Spirit of Europe' – an interactive exhibition, initiated by the European Parliament, awaits guests after they have been on a tour of the park. The exhibition concentrates on the memorable events that took place in Berlin on 9th November 1989.

Location:
Nato Headquarters
SHAPE

The Supreme Headquarters Allied Powers in Europe (SHAPE) is situated in Casteau, north of the small Belgian city of Bons. A building, which was once of special significance during the Cold War, stands on this expansive military site. A special unit made up of western Allies was housed in the so-called 'Live Oak building'. It would have been the unit's job to to defend and support the western sectors if the Soviets cordoned off the West again – as they had done during the Berlin Blockade from 1948-1949.

The Wall in
NATO headquarters, Casteau
© Photo courtesy of NATO

The unit was established in 1959 by France, Great Britain and the USA. Under the codename 'Live Oak', it surveyed access to and from West Berlin.

Originally located near Paris, the unit was transferred to Belgium when France withdrew from NATO in 1967. After the building of the Wall in 1961, a delegate from the Federal Republic was also stationed at the unit and it was this person's job to make contact with the federal government in the event of a crisis.

Information board on the
Wall in NATO Headquarters,
Casteau
© Photo courtesy of NATO

Exactly what went on in the 'Live Oak Building' was kept top secret during the Cold War. It was not until 1993 that information was made public. Just three years earlier, on the evening from 2nd-3rd October, the unit had denied its activities and purpose.

After the Fall of the Wall and the end of the Cold War, the ICC (Implementation Forces Coordination Cell) moved into the building. Amongst other duties, the ICC oversaw the placing of troops and the implication of peace plans in Bosnia. By this time, the Russian military was also part of the ICC. A conference centre was later constructed for consultations by the states involved in the 'Partnership for Peace'.

In the centre of four flag poles, an original piece of the Berlin Wall stands outside the entrance of the 'Live Oak Building'. General Johan Galvin Saceur, the last 'Live Oak' commander accepted the gift from Germany on 27th November 1990. It is flanked by two ever green live oaks – a reference to the building's name. The following text is inscribed on a plaque at the foot of the segment:

"This section of the Berlin Wall symbolizes the division of Germany that existed after WWII until German Unification on 3. October 1990. The Live Oak Organization was dedicated to freedom of access to Berlin from 1959 to 1990.
France, United Kingdom, Federal Republic of Germany, United States of America"

The Gravensteen, the Count of Flanders' castle, stands defiant in the centre of the Belgian city of Ghent. For centuries, counts have summoned people to Flanders' court within its mighty walls. Flemish landgraves were feared for their cruel administration of justice. Countless prisoners were held in the dungeons between 1407 and 1708 – many of them suffered agonising torture. Today, the torture and prison cells make up part of a torture museum and can be visited in the castle.

Mistreatment of prisoners is by no means a problem of the past. Even today, political prisoners are detained worldwide, robbed of their human rights and even killed. The human rights organisation 'Amnesty International' works to protect the rights of such prisoners. In 1998, Amnesty International and the 'Honest Arts Movement' (a Belgian artists' association) initiated the construction of a memorial to commemorate all the 'missing people' worldwide, who have been abducted, imprisoned or murdered due to their beliefs, religion, race or other reasons.

Due to its historical significance, the Gravensteen in Ghent was chosen as the location for the memorial. Belgian artist Freddy de Vos from Drongen took on the task of designing it.

He placed an aluminium sculpture on a cascading base, in the middle of which the silhouette of a person has been cut out. He left the sculpture empty on the inside. To celebrate the official opening on 3rd May 1996, local school children placed letters inside which were addressed to political prisoners. The project, 'Schrijfzevrijdag' (directly translated: 'write them free'), was brought to life by Amnesty International Belgium. The artist himself left a small bronze sculpture as well as three small chunks of the Berlin Wall which had been given to him by a German colleague for the project. Two further small chunks were integrated and are visible from the outside. Alongside this are small stones from South Africa, where human rights activist and later President Nelson Mandela was imprisoned by the Apartheid-regime.

GHENT
BELGIUM

Location:
next to the
Gravensteen castle

GHENT
BELGIUM

Location:
In front of the main building at Flanders Expo, Maaltekouter 1

The Wall at Flanders Expo, Ghent

© Lode Anseel

A segment of the Berlin Wall has been on display in front of the main building at the 'Flanders Expo' multi-purpose indoor arena since 1998. Lode Anseel, former chief accountant for the company and Berlin enthusiast, had the 2.6 tonne section of Wall brought to Belgium. He purchased it alongside a second piece in the mid-90s in Berlin, where he remembered it had once separated Potsdamer Platz into East and West. Anseel succeeded in convincing the former Flanders Expo management to buy one piece and install it is an attraction in the company grounds. During a small public celebration, the segment was finally installed to the sounds of 'The Wall' by British rock band Pink Floyd. The piece, branded on both sides with bright graffiti, is passed by tens of thousands of visitors on their way to the building every year.

The Berlin Wall has become a passion for Belgian photographer, Lode Anseel. The fate of the divided city and its world famous concrete wall have not left him since his first school visit in 1977. Anseel wanted to get back to Berlin immediately on 9th November 1989 when he saw reports about the Fall of the Wall allover the press. However, it was not until 1900 that he actually made the journey. He was in Berlin when the famous border control point 'Checkpoint Charlie' was closed on 22nd June 1990. Anseel took countless photographs as well as a few small chunks of the Wall. He sold the chunks of wall to a street-seller for four GDR Marks. In 1995, he opened his first larger photo exhibition about Berlin in Belgian Menen. Four years later, his pictures were presented to the public in Wingene – ten years after the Fall of the Wall.

By now Anseel's passion for the Berlin Wall had grown even more. He began to collect everything he could find that had anything to do with the former border and the GDR. He was particularly taken by the East German Trabant. Anseel bought four Trabants in the nineties, amongst them a version which was used by the National People's Army. He also owns a first generation Trabant P 50, which he managed to have signed by Soviet Head of State, Michail Gorbachev, Socialist Unity Party of Germany (SED) politician, Günter Schabowski, and GDR figure skater, Katrina Witt. He is particularly proud of one Trabant, which he has covered with banknotes and coins from 75 countries.

It was this passion for Trabants that led him be in possession of two Wall segments. He came across an article in 'Supertrabi' (a magazine for Trabant enthusiasts) by a Berlin-based Trabant fan, who then put him in touch with someone selling parts of the Wall. Anseel also convinced his then employer, the Flanders Expo in Ghent, to buy a piece and organise the transportation. One piece remained at Flanders Expo and Anseel put the second in his garden. It still stands there today, complete with a small white plaque with the words: "ORIGINAL BERLIN WALL / POTSDAMERPLATZ / HOPE, FREEDOM AND PEACE / ALL OVER THE WORLD"

Location:
Ricksteenweg 6

The Wall in Lode Anseel's garden, Zwevedele Wingene
© Lode Anseel

SOFIA
BULGARIA

Location:
Boulevard Bulgaria, next to the National Palace of Culture

The Wall in Sofia
© Fanny Heidenreich

In spring 2006, the Berlin Senate gave a segment of the Berlin Wall to Sofia, the Bulgarian capital, as a 'token gift of appreciation'. The initiative behind this gesture came from the Bulgarian foundation 'Nasledstwo' (heritage). The foundation is dedicated to the preservation of Bulgaria's heritage. The Balkan State branch of 'Funke Mediengruppe' sponsors the project. The city government requested a piece of the Wall in March 2006. On 13th April 2006, after receiving consent from Germany, the decision was made by the city council to place the section of Wall in the park next to the National Palace of Culture. This location was chosen due to its position directly in the vicinity of the nearby monument for the victims of of the communist regime in Bulgaria, which was erected in 1999.

The city council assigned the construction of the Wall memorial to the 'Nasledstwo' foundation. A design by architect, Bojko Kadinow was used, and the concrete segment was erected on an area laid with black flagstones. A tilted wave-like-wall stands behind it. Two texts, in German and Bulgarian, complete the memorial.

Information board in Sofia
© Fanny Heidenreich

"На 13. август 1961 г. една стена раздели Берлин, Германия, а с тях Европа и света на две части. България беше затворена от източната страна на Стената - до 9. ноември 1989 г., когато народът я разруши.
Този отломък от Берлинската стена е дар от гражданите на Берлин на гражданите на София, като знак за възстановеното единство на Европа и доказателство, че българите са вече свободни хора. Берлин май 2006г."
("On 13th August 1961 a wall cut Berlin, Germany and with it Europe and the world in two. Bulgaria remained enclosed on the eastern side – until the Wall was torn down by the people on 9th November 1989. This fragment of the Berlin Wall is a present from the people of Berlin to the people of Sofia – as a symbol of reunified Europe and as proof that the Bulgarian people are now free. Berlin, May 2006")

Work to prepare the site had to be carried out quickly so that the official unveiling of the memorial could coincide with an upcoming visit from Berlin Mayor, Klaus Wowereit, on 16th May 2006. Workers from the company 'Nidel' worked tirelessly to get the memorial site ready whilst the segment was transported from Berlin to Sofia by transportation company 'Militzer und Münch'. Wowereit's visit was eventually rescheduled and the handing over of the Wall to Sofia's mayor, Bojko Borissow, actually took place on 20th June 2006.

Revolutionary events and upheaval also took place in Bulgaria in the autumn of 1989. On 10th November 1989, one day after the Fall of the Wall, the then First Secretary of the Bulgarian Communist Party, Todor Zhivkov, was forced to withdraw from office. Round table discussions were held in autumn between the Communist Party and the opposition alliance, 'The Union of Democratic Forces'. The first free general elections were held in June 1990 and the opposition candidate, Zhelyu Zhelev, was elected president two months later.

ZAGREB
CROATIA

Location:
In front of the Croatian German embassy and Goethe Institute, Ulica grade Vukovara

The Berlin Wall in front of the German Embassy in Zagreb
© German Embassy Zagreb

The 9th November 2009 marked 20 years since the Fall of the Wall. The Fall of the Wall and the events that took place as a result led to the Iron Curtain being opened once and for all and the political, economical and military divisions between East and West being overcome and were also great cause for celebration – Croatia, too, took part in the celebrations. An original section of the Berlin Wall was unveiled in Zagreb by former Croatian President, Stjepan Mesic and former Berlin Mayor, Eberhard Diepgen in front of a

Information plaque at the foot of the Wall segment
© German Embassy Zagreb

crowd of 250 Croatian and German guests.

Stjepan Mesić spoke of the significance of the section of the Berlin Wall:

"The Fall of the Wall was both a beginning and an end. The beginning of profound changes which would be felt throughout Germany, East Europe and the Soviet Union. We felt as though the model we had at this point in time would not survive."

The political and social revolutions that took place in East Europe in 1989 also affected the multinational state of Yugoslavia. At this time, the states were made up of Slovenia, Croatia, Serbia, Montenegro, Macedonia, Bosnia-Herzegovina, and also Kosovo and Vojvodina – two regions in Serbia. New conflicts arose in Yugoslavia at the end of the Cold War, which, in the crumbling multinational state, led to war between the autonomous republics and cost tens of thousands of lives.

Unveiling the Wall segment
© German Embassy Zagreb

German businessman, Axel Brauer, donated the 3.6 metre high and 1.2 metre wide section of Wall to the German embassy in Zagreb. Croatian graffiti artists, Krešimir Golubic and Gordan Orešić, had already repainted the section of Wall. The following quote can be seen in German and Croatian:

"In 1961, Berlin and Germany were forcefully split in East and West by the GDR government. This original section from the Berlin Wall commemorates the peaceful revolution led by the people of East Germany as well as the overcoming of the German division – the symbol of which was the Fall of the Wall on 9th November 1989. Germany was reunified on 3rd October 1990."

coming out of the Baltic Sea with nuclear missiles onboard. Marine commandos sent this information to NATO and the USA. Just a few weeks earlier, American spy planes had observed nuclear launch platforms which had been erected in Cuba. Together with the pictures from Laneland, it became clear that the Soviets intended to set up nuclear missiles in Cuba. When the Cold War came to an end, there was no longer any need for a fort, and in 1993, it was decided that a 'Cold War Museum' should be built. The museum opened on 16th June 1997. It aims to prevent the Cold War from being forgotten.

The piece of Wall in the Cold War Museum in Langelandsfort

© Cold War Museum, Langelandsfort

NYKØBING
DENMARK

Location:

Holtets plads,
Nykøbing, Sjælland

Wall memorial commemorating
the Fall of the Wall 1989
"Muren 89", Nykøbing
© Odsherred Turistbureau

A memorial was erected on the centrally located Holtets-Sqaure in Nykøbing to celebrate the 15th anniversary of the Fall of the Wall. The memorial is simply called 'Muren 89' (Wall 89). A statue of King Frederick VII of Denmark rises out of the ground beside the memorial. Exactly one hundred and fifty years previously, on 9th November 1849, King Frederick had signed the first Danish basic law. The plans for the Wall memorial were made by the mayor when he visited Danish stonemason, Hother Nielsen. The model Nielsen had already completed in 1991 was finally in place in 2004 with support from the local council.

The memorial is made up of a hexagonal fountain with a red granite slab on one side, in which the silhouette of a dove has been cut out. The dove is a symbol of peace and flies through the Wall to freedom. At the same time, the water strengthens and completes the motif of freedom as it flows and makes its own way, unstoppable on its journey – this is the official interpretation given by town officials.

Location:
Sculpture Garden
Odense, Galerie Jens
Galschiøt, Banevänget 22

Model of the Wall memorial
by Jens Galschiøt
© Jens Galschiøt

Two pieces of Wall, each approximately two metres tall, complete with protruding rusty steel cables, can be found in Danish architect Jens Galschiøt's garden. The plan was originally to consolidate the pieces into a memorial, but this never actually happened. The internationally renowned sculptor was so awestruck by the images of the Fall of the Wall on 9th November 1989 that he was keen to create a sculpture that commemorated these historical events. Berlin was the focal-point of the world and he considered it important to capture the euphoric mood in a memorial.

Galschiøt contacted both mayors of the divided city and requested they send him a few pieces of the Wall. The two mayors considered his request with open minds. However, the GDR government had decided in December that the remains of the former border should be sold at as high a price as possible, and Galschiøt was referred to the West Berlin company, 'LeLé Berlin', who had been given the job of marketing the remains of the Wall. The cost for the pieces he requested was between 40,000 and 90,000 D-Mark – a price he could not afford. He contacted the two mayors again and finally reached an agreement to be given two pieces of the so called 'Hinterlandmauer' (interior wall), free of charge.

The pieces of Wall were handed over in Berlin on 18th June 1990. Galschiøt used this opportunity to publicly present the plans for his memorial: on an area of 25 x 8 metres, people, with only half a body, move towards the Wall and only after passing through the wall do they become full-bodied and disperse in all directions. He returned to his studio in Denmark to begin work on this symbolic idea.

By now, the initial euphoria evoked by the Fall of the Wall was seeping away. It was proving increasingly difficult to find sponsors for his ambitious vision, and the plans had to be reduced by more than half. But nobody wanted to erect even the smaller version in Berlin. Galschiøt then got in touch with Willy Brandt in

Artist Jens Galschiøt with his
pieces of Wall, Odense
© Jens Galschiøt

October 1990, hoping to inject new life into the project. The former Mayor of Berlin and former Chancellor supported the project, but were unable to provide materials or funding.

In the meantime, the authorities of the reunited city were busy wiping the wall from the face of the city landscape. By the end of 1990, the Wall had been dismantled. There were debates about what to do with the few remaining leftover parts and where a memorial should be built.

Galschiøt's plans were met with less and less interest. The major corporations who had secured land on the former deathstrip at Potsdamer Platz, did not want to erect the memorial either. In 1992, in a final attempt to gain political support, the artist finally sent miniature models of his memorial plans to all fractions of the Berlin state parliament. Only the museum 'Haus am Checkpoint Charlie' replied, claiming it would be prepared to at least display the model in its exhibition. Two years later, when plans to erect his work at one of the last remaining watch towers at Schlesischer Busch on the border between Treptow and Kreuzberg also failed, Galschiøt eventually gave up on his pursuit.

Alongside the wall segments, that are slowly being weathered in the open-air, a few sculptures remain in the artist's nearby studio, waiting for the possibility that the memorial may still actually be built.

In 1990, road and paving contractor, Klaus Grunske, crushed hundreds of tonnes of the Berlin Wall in Germendorf, just north of Berlin. His company had been given the contract to dismantle the barrier-installation at the border to Brandenburg at Glienicke and Hohen Neuendorf. However, Grunske did not grind all of the segments for building materials, but preserved some for future use. One of the segments found its new home in the southern Finnish city of Tampere. In September 2007, Timo Nieminen, mayor and president of the Finnish Association of Municipal Councils, paid a visit to his colleague, Karl-Heinz Schröder, county commissioner for Oberhavel and vice president of the districts of Germany. Between carrying out inspections for nature conservation and infrastructure project planning, Nieminen learned of the leftover Wall pieces in Germendorf. Klaus Grunske gave a piece of the Wall to his Finnish visitor, and he plans to put it on display at the Museum Centre Vapriikki in Tampere.

Schröder took the piece of Wall with him as a gift on his visit to Tampere on 22nd May 2008. At the official handing over ceremony, Schröder pointed out that Finland was a good location for the Cold War relic due to Finland's intermediary role between East and West and above all due to the Helsinki Declaration of 1975, which had been of great significance to many GDR citizens. The latter especially, since despite the internally agreed freedom of movement, which had the backing of the GDR government, the Wall divided the two German states, Europe and the world for another 14 years. Many citizens of the present-day district of Oberhavel have had their own encounters with the Wall – the southern border to West Berlin ran through the region and was a heavily guarded prohibited zone for decades.

It was not possible to find out exactly where the section of Wall was then permanently put up in Museum Center Vapriikki – an expansive former machine factory on the outskirts of Tampere.

Unveiling the Wall
in Tampere
© Landkreis Oberhavel /
Annemarie Reichenberger

BRINGOLO
FRANCE

Location:
Bringolo, Brittany

Jean Broaweys migrated from Algeria to West Berlin in May 1961, three months before the Wall was built. He worked here for many years in the editorial office for the multimedia company 'Axel Springer'. When the Wall fell in 1989, Broaweys bought two pieces of the Wall in spring 1990 that had previously stood on Potsdamer Platz. He paid for the pieces, weighing tonnes, to be transported to his Breton holiday home. He assembled them in a meadow along with a sky-blue Trabant and a length of barbed wire fence (used before the building of the concrete wall) in Bringolo, a small village with 300 inhabitants.

However, 'Axel Springer Park' received little attention from locals. Divided Berlin is worlds away from Brittany, and the significance of the pair of concrete blocks meant little to the inhabitants, recalls Broaweys with resignation. Nevertheless, the pieces woke the interest of many tourists. Broaweys has welcomed more then 7000 visitors to his park. Now 75 years old, he felt forced to sell his land in 2005. A farmer from Bringolo took over the land together with the pieces of Wall, Trabant and barbed wire fence. The new owner has since tried, in vain, to find an interested party for the ensemble. And so, the pieces of Wall still stand today awaiting an uncertain future in Bringolo.

The words 'Hase bleibt Hase' (rabbit stays rabbit), and countless black and white rabbits adorn the two segments of Wall that stand at Mémorial de Caen. They stand on raised platforms in the permanent anti-war exhibition, and illustrate the section 'The End of the Cold War'. French artist, Daniel Boulogne, donated both segments to the museum in 1999. Whilst many of the pieces of Berlin Wall scattered all over the world are

Location:
Mémorial de Caen,
Esplanade Général
Eisenhower B.P. 55026,
Caen Cedex

The Wall in

Mémorial de Caen

© Benoît Grimbert /
Le Mémorial de Caen

painted mainly on the side facing the West, these two are different. The paintings by Berlin painter, Manfred Butzman, are on side of the Wall that faced the East. This side of the Wall was not accessible until after the Fall of the Wall. The wide deathstrip between the border to West Berlin and the interior East Berlin Wall prevented anyone getting close to the Wall on the GDR side.

Immediately after the border was opened on 9th November 1989, artists from both the East and the West came up with the idea to paint on the eastern side of the Wall as well.

Despite many openings in the Wall, and the fact that traffic was now able to flow between East and West, the deathstrip remained blocked and was still guarded by GDR border guards. In mid-November 1989, Daniel Boulogne was delighted to hear the DDR 'Künstlerbund' (Association of East German Artists) announce its wish to cover the eastern side of the Wall with paint. The French artist loaded a truck with paints and brushes and made his way to Berlin to support the painters in the GDR. After arriving in Berlin it was in the East Berlin 'Palast Hotel' where he met Jean Pichard, an employee from the GDR's French Institute of Culture. He had also recently been appointed the position of manager at the Association of East German Artists. Wolf was excited by the unexpected help and the pair arranged to meet at 'Checkpoint Charlie' on 17th November 1989. From here, they planned to bring the paint supplies brought to Germany in Boulogne's truck. Despite the Fall of the Wall, the border at Checkpoint Charlie, which had been intended for diplomats and foreigners, was still heavily guarded.

Letting through a truck, loaded with two tonnes of undeclared paint supplies, was to prove problematic. At first, the GDR officials denied entry to Boulogne and his driver:

"I went back to the hotel with Jean Pichard. You could still feel the same electrical atmosphere in the lobby. We took two CNN cameramen with us. We really wanted to get at the border guards. Leo Wolf told us which crossings we could pass on foot without any trouble, and so, we took a detour to the east of Checkpoint Charlie. The tricky part was getting the truck over. The CNN cameramen were really hyped-up. They put the cameras right behind the heads of the border guards and began to film. I tried to go in the direction of the wagon, but was approached immediately by one of the guards. It didn't look good, but it turned out

luck was on our side. Whilst I was talking to the guard, a 38 tonne truck drove up in front of Joël's truck which was parked on no-man's land. The guards ran over to the larger truck to check it out. I wasted no time in getting to Joël, he put the truck in gear and his foot on the gas pedal. The cameras were focused on the truck, which was slowly beginning to move. A guard came towards us. He pointed his rifle at me. I pointed towards the cameras that were still filming us. He shouted something at me in German. I tried to answer him in French. The expressions on our faces did the talking for us. I saw the fear in his face when he saw the cameras. He had understood – if the cameras caught him shooting the rifle, they would not be filming a soldier carrying out orders, but a murder, an execution, a crime. He took a step back and lowered his weapon. We had won."

Leo Wolf and his comrades were already waiting on the other side of Checkpoint Charlie. By this time, it had turned to evening and we would have to put our plans on ice until the next day. Work could finally begin on 19th November 1989. With official permission, and under the suspicious gaze of the troops at the border, 30 artists began to paint the four hundred metre long stretch of Wall between Potsdamer Platz and Leipziger Straße in the East. Each artist was designated a section of the Wall to paint however they wanted. The painting carried on until the afternoon, when one of the border police gave the order for us to stop. Surprised, the artists had to cut short their work after his change of mind. But most of the paintings had already been finished. The border guards then began to cover up the graffiti with paint that night. To this day, it is still not known who gave the order. However, the paint they used to cover up our paintings was of such bad quality that our paintings could still be seen through it. Amongst the artists who took part in this first art session in the East on that day was Manfred Butzmann.

The story behind the rabbits, that today stand at Mémorial de Caen, goes back to a child's play area, built in 1972 on Parkstraße, Berlin Pankow. After GDR officials repeatedly refused to build a play area, the people took things into their own hands and remodelled a car park. At the opening, Manfred Butzmann hoisted a rabbit flag – the symbol of overcoming fear and powerlessness. He used this motif again after the Fall of the Wall. The Wall was now gone and the people (the 'fearful, powerless rabbits') had finally overcome the GDR regime.

A few weeks after the Wall painting campaign, the Wall was slowly taken down. Boulogne sent one of his colleagues to East Berlin. It was his job to save as many pieces of the painted Wall as possible from being crushed. It was pure chance that he discovered the pieces with the rabbits and was able to save them from being destroyed. Boulogne had them brought to Paris and gave them to the museum in Caen.

The quotes above were taken from a report by Daniel Boulogne: http://www.memorial-caen.fr/mur_de_berlin/

Location:
Blangy le Chateau,
Normandy

The Wall in Hans-Olaf Henkel's
garden, Deauville
© Hans-Olaf Henkel

S ince 1993, an original section of the Berlin Wall has been on display in the gardens of a property owned by Hans-Olaf Henkel (businessman and former President of the Federation of German Industry). The section was once covered in graffiti, but, over the years, it has been washed away by the rain, leaving almost nothing but grey behind. The life and work of Hans-Olaf Henkel are associated with the divided city and the Wall. Hans-Olaf Henkel was at 'Checkpoint Charlie' in autumn 1961, shortly after the Wall was built, and when Soviet and American tanks were head to head.

He lived for a few months in the, by then, divided city and began his career at the Federation of German Industry in the then West Berlin area of Lankwitz. It was only logical for him to then obtain of a piece of this concrete construction, steeped in history.

"I bought a segment of the Wall in 1991 for around 3,000 Marks and had it brought to Normandy in a lorry. I have a 16th century manor in the area, a place called Blangy le Chateau, there are a few smaller

The Wall in Hans-Olaf Henkel's garden, Deauville
© Hans-Olaf Henkel

buildings there, a cider press and a small distillery where Calvados was once produced. Back then, I was advisor to the then minister-president and was involved, both privately and via the Federation of German Industry, in the reunification and rebuilding of the East. It seemed logical to me to put up a testimony to this at my second home. Transporting the segment (weighing tonnes), was not so easy. The lorry carrying the segment broke down at Reims and the haulage company had to have extensive work carried out on the lorry to get it going again. Erecting the segment in damp Normandy ground was also not easy. Eventually, we got it done with the aid of a pulley. Afterwards, the lorry had difficulties leaving the site. Relentless rain had softened the ground so much that the lorry had sunk right down to the axle. When the piece of Wall was finally up, it got a lot of attention from the people in the village. Entire families came to look at the symbol of the communist dictatorship. There are a few funny stories to tell about it. One neighbour suggested that I should enclose the property with pieces of the Wall. The mayor replied, "What about a watch tower? Then you could guard the property with German shepherd dogs!" As a matter of fact, the houses in the area had been broken into a number of times, making this suggestion not all that absurd to one or two people. With a landmass of 34 hectares, I would have probably had to import the entire Wall though.

Report to The Federal Foundation for the Reappraisal of the SED Dictatorship by Hans-Olaf Henkel

Location:
Place de Coupole,
La Défense

"König Buffo" in Paris
© Deutschland-Zentrum Paris

A piece painted by Kiddy Citny in Kreuzberg in 1984 and entitled 'König Buffo', has a less majestic residence. It can be found at La Défense, a massive commercial complex in the Parisian area of Courbevois. The three sections stand somewhat secluded and unnoticed at the foot of a high-rise building.

Jean-Yves Haby, a young delegate from the Parisian district of Courbevoi, had already asked the East Berlin Mayor for segments of the Berlin Wall in December 1989, which would then be put on display in the French capital. The town administrators paid 'Limex' 300,000 Marks for three pieces of the Wall. 'Limex' had begun marketing the Wall in 1989. The East Berlin government was not prepared to strike up a German-French friendship and simply donate the segments to the French capital. In early 1990, the deal was finally closed and the segments were brought along the Spree to the Rhein, making a stop at the former Bundestag in Bonn. They then moved on to the European Parliament in Strasbourg, where they were a topic of discussion amongst the young. The highlight and end of the European tour was in the business district of La Défense, Paris – built in North-West Paris as a powerful centre for business during the term of former president, François Mitterrand.

Many significant names from the worlds of politics, economy and culture took part in the opening ceremony. The Wall ensemble created big interest amongst the Parisians. A nationwide competition was to take place to design the base for the segments. Until then, the segments had been stored in a cellar, and were fading from the forefront of people's minds. The initial excitement surrounding the project faded and a dispute began between the government and the administrators from the business district as to where the segments should end up. It was not until 1995 that an agreement was made. Just in time for the 6th

"König Buffo" in Kreuzberg, Berlin

anniversary of the Fall of the Wall, 'König Buffo' was put back on public display. However, it was placed on Place de Coupole between a motorway and a footbridge where very few people passed by.

"König Buffo" in Paris

Location:
Esplanade du
9 novembre 1989,
15. Arrondissement

"9th November Square –
Fall of the Berlin Wall " in Paris
© Deutschland-Zentrum Paris

In the same year the Berlin Wall fell, Jean Goujon was elected as the 15th mayor of Paris. He had headed the district for almost twenty years. One of the last projects he was involved with was installing a piece of the Wall at the entrance to the Paris Exhibition Centre. As a member of the UMP, he had accordingly made an application to the senate in Paris by 2003 which also requested the renaming of a site. The government agreed to his request in December 2006 and the area around Port de Versailles was renamed 'Esplanade du 9. novembre 1989 – chute du mur de Berlin' (9th November Square – Fall of the Berlin Wall). In 2006, the senate of the German capital expressed its wish to donate a piece of the Wall to Paris in conjunction with the town-twinning. The same was the case at the end of 2008 when the senate of Berlin Marzahn loaded its last remaining pieces of Wall on to a truck heading for France. The opening ceremony took place on 9th November 2009 alongside the festivities celebrating 20 years since the Fall of the Wall.

PARIS
FRANCE

Location:

Maison de la Radio 116,
Avenue du Prèsident
Kennedy

Transportation and installation
of the Wall section in front of
Maison de la Radio

© Radio France/ Christophe
Abramowitz

On 26th October 2009, a ceremonial press conference was held in the Berlin Cathedral to mark 20 years since the Peaceful Revolution and the Fall of the Wall. Willi Steul, director at Deutschlandradio had a surprise for his French counterpart, Jean-Luc Hees from *Radio France*: an original section of the Berlin Wall. The 2.6 tonne section of Wall, which had originally made up part of the border in Spandau (and had since been stored in Teltow) finally made its way to Paris in November 2009.

The unveiling ceremony took place in November 2009 as part of celebration to mark the opening of another exhibition. The exhibition was made up of photographs by Christophe Abramowitz, who had documented "Germany day" from a French perspective. Reporters, editors and technicians from Paris had all gathered along the Spree in 2009 to make a 24 hour live broadcast of the German celebrations marking 20 years since the Fall of the Wall.

Installing a section of the Wall in front of the *Maison de la Radio* also sealed cooperation between Deutschlandradio and Radio France. The section of Wall is painted with the French national colours and at night, red, black and gold is projected onto the other side. Jean-Luc Hees, director at Radio France talked about the significance of this section of Wall in his speech at the opening ceremony:

"This section of the Berlin Wall, so prominently displayed at the entrance of Maison de Radio France, not only stands as a symbol of the GDR dictatorship's contempt for mankind, but also of the strength and power of the people."

There are more than 800 tanks on display at 'Musée des Blindés' (tank museum) in the western French town of Saumur. The largest collection of military tanks spans from the First World War right through to the end of the Cold War. An entire hall is dedicated solely to Warsaw Pact army tanks. An original piece of the Wall can also be found here. According to the museum management, it was presented to the 11th Air Assault Infantry Regiment when the troops left Berlin in 1994. Berlin presented it as a symbol of their thanks for forty years of French military presence in Berlin. A small red sign commemorates the event:

> „Authentique élément du 'Mur de Berlin'
> Offert par la ville de Berlin en remerciements de la présence française"
> "Original piece of the Berlin Wall Presented by the city of Berlin in gratitude for the French military presence."

When the French army units left Germany in 1999, all items of significant memorabilia were collected in the tank museum in Saumur. It is thought this is how the piece of the Wall came to be part of the exhibition.

SAUMUR
FRANCE

Location:
Musée des Blindés, 1043, route de Fontevraud

The Wall in the Tank Museum, Saumur

© Association des Amis du museé des Blindés

Plaque on the Wall in the Tank Museum, Saumur

© Association des Amis du museé des Blindés

STRASBOURG
FRANCE

Location:
In front of the European
Court for Human Rights,
Avenue de l'Europe

The Wall in front of the
European Court of Justice,
Strasbourg
© Jochen Guckes

After the Fall of the Wall and the storming of the SED regime in 1989, the GDR had to reposition itself internationally. The GDR, up until now, had been tightly embedded in Soviet dominated Warsaw Treaty politics – in early 1990 the methods of reunifying the two German states and the reform of the GDR and its neutral foreign policy was being fiercely discussed. However, those on the international stage were clearly looking towards reunification. NATO and the Warsaw Pact countries met at an 'Open Skies' conference in Ottawa, Canada in February 1990, and agreed to work towards the possibility of a consolidation of states. The GDR carried on trying to build up contacts to European institutions.

In February 1990 (during a meeting between acting foreign secretary, Werner Fleck, and secretary general of the Council of Europe, Catherine Lalumiére), a request for a segment of Wall was made to the GDR government for the proposed 'Palace of Human Rights' in Strasbourg.

At the beginning of March, the then incumbent GDR foreign minister, Oskar Fischer, made the following suggestion to the GDR government, "the request of the secretary general of the Council of Europe (…) should be granted in the interest of a rapid development in the relationship between the GDR and the council."[1] Two days before the first (and only) East German democratic free elections on 18th March 1990, the request was granted by the council of ministers.

---

1 Resolution by the GDR cabinett 18/I.31/90 on 16.03.1990. Bundesarchiv Berlin DC/I/3/2938

From the viewing platform in
West Berlin to the European
Court of Justice – the Wall in
Strasbourg

© Archiv Bundesstiftung Aufarbeitung,
Bestand Rosmarie Gentges, Nr. 122

Interest in the former border fortification in Strasbourg was great. In addition to the one piece of Wall donated, three further segments of Wall were bought from the company 'Limex'. They were offered for public sale during the first large Wall auction in Monaco in June 1990. However, nobody wanted to buy them, and they were sold back to Strasbourg. The freight, weighing tonnes, was brought back to France in 1990 and stored until the completion of the museum in 1995. But even then, a site for the segments could not be found. It was not until 1997 that a site was found in front of the building housing the European Court of Human Rights. They still stand here today, just as they stood in Kreuzberg in 1990 before they were torn down. Four heads, painted by the famous Wall artist, Thierry Noir, and the somewhat cryptic message 'le duo d'enfer a encore frappé' (loosely translated as 'the duo from hell have managed it again') can still be seen on the segments.

VERSAILLES
FRANCE

Location:

Sylvstre Verger Art,
Organisation,
18, rue d'Anjou

Thierry Noir:
„Don't touch this Wall,
it's a crocodile"
© sVo Art 2009

The fact that world history can also be a source of artistic inspiration is highlighted in the unique collection of Wall art by French gallery owner, Sylvestre Verger. A Swiss company invited artists from all over the world to paint 30 blank concrete sections, measuring 1x1.2 metres, however they wished. Internationally known artists including Richard Long, Richard Longo, Dennis Oppenheim, Sol Lewitt and Eduardo Chilida used the pieces as canvases or turned them into sculptures. American, Adam Steiner, turned the concrete segments into a 'Pandora's Box'. Soviet trained artist, Boris Zaborov, painted an image of two children's heads, separated by barbed wire. A piece by Rolf Knie depicts a section of the Wall on an electric chair. The piece bears the name 'The Wall Condemned to Death'. He added the date of 'execution, 9.11.1989' for good measure.

When money from the Swiss initiators ran out, French real estate agent, Pascal Jeandet, took over the collection. He brought in Sylvestre Verger as curator, who was able to present the collection to the public in Madrid in 1991. A further exhibition followed in London before Jeandet also went broke and the pieces of Wall were bought by creditors in Great Britain. In 1993, after court proceedings, Verger managed to save the collection from being split up.

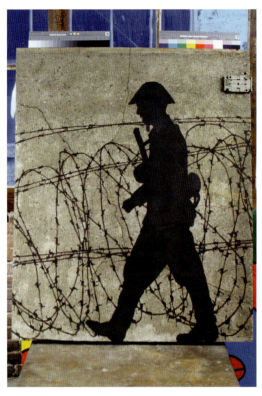

Arman (left):
„Self-destruction-
November 9, 1989"

Gérard Fromanger (right):
„A concrete memory"
© sVo Art 2009

Twelve new pieces were added to the collection including works by Thierry Noir, who had already seen the Wall's potential for art when it split Berlin in two. The famous heads, which had adorned the West Berlin side of the Wall in Kreuzberg in the 1980s, have been in Verger's collection ever since.

The pieces were also shown when the world powers met in French Lyon for the G 7 Summit. Prominent guests included the former Soviet statesman and Communist Party leader, Mikhail Sergeyevich Gorbachev and his wife, Raisa. Gorbachev wrote in the guest book that the exhibition was a 'history lesson'. It was of equal significance when the pieces of the Wall were shown two years later in the Cypriot capital, Nicosia. A national competition was announced in which applicants could win the chance to paint another piece of Wall. Greek-Cypriot artist Theodoulus won with his piece 'The Green Line' and it has since become a permanent part of the collection.

In 2005, Sylvestre Verger showed the artwork in Seoul, the South Korean capital, as well as on the island of Jeju. New pieces were also created by Korean artists. These pieces remained in Korea and are on show today in front of the Jeju-Peace Centre.

THE BERLIN WALL IN GERMANY
OR WHAT IS LEFT OF IT

Tina Schaller

Berlin History Workshop founding document for its initiative "The Wall has to stay"
© Archiv der Versöhnungsgemeinde

"THE WALL HAS TO STAY"

At the end of October 1989, when it was not clear to the world when and under what circumstances the border between the GDR and the Federal Republic would be opened, the "Berliner Geschichtswerkstatt e.V" (Berlin History Workshop) surprised everyone with their initiative "The Wall must stay". The idea behind the initiative was to preserve a piece of the Wall so that future generations would be able to comprehend its injustice. The initiative said this about the Wall:

"The Berlin Wall has been a symbol of oppression over basic human rights for 28 years. Time will pass it by, we are sure of that. If the borders are opened one day, we warn now of cultural barbarity: do not tear the Wall down!!"

At that point in time, nobody was likely to have been aware that the border between East and West Germany would be opened just 10 days later on 9th November 1989. Only a few days later, a piece of the Wall was torn down on Potsdamer Platz, a section of the road tarmacked and a provisional border crossing point made on Potsdamer Platz in the early hours on 12th November 1989. Eight sections of the Wall were lifted out by crane. In the subsequent period, more and more crossings emerged between the two halves of the city, one of these was at the Brandenburg Gate on 22nd December 1989. For the first time, it was possible for citizens on both sides of the Wall to see just how the 'Wall' had been built and that it was by no means just a wall, but a complex system made up of numerous fences, walls, watch towers and the death strip.

The lucrative Wall business began as soon as work to tear down the Wall had commenced. 'Limex' and 'LeLé Berlin', the companies that had been contracted to market and sell the Wall by the GDR government, started selling segments and smaller pieces of the Wall.[1] Parts of the Wall are still sold today and not only by the world's largest online auction site, eBay inc. These pieces of Wall range in size from that of a postage stamp to entire original sections that weigh up to three tonnes – it is even possible to buy a watch tower.

The systematic dismantling of the Wall began in June 1990 and was carried out by members of the National People's Army and the West Berlin police. By November in the same year, the work had almost been completed. Fragments of the Wall which were crushed and used as building material were used to build car parks or, for road construction.[2] However, hundreds of segments were sold and put up as memorials in numerous countries. Many of these Wall memorials can also be found in Germany.

The Berlin Wall has all but disappeared from today's city landscape. The demolition of the inner-city Wall was carried out swiftly and left little time for discussion or contemplation about a suitable way to preserve part of it as a memorial.

---

1   Cf. Article: From Concrete to Cash. Turning the Berlin Wall into a business by Ronny Heidenreich in this volume.
2   Cf. Gerhard Sälter: Mauerreste in Berlin, 2nd Edition, Berlin 2007, p. 18.

The main focus was on bringing the city back to some kind of normality and to heal the wounds that the Wall and the border fortifications had inflicted on the city landscape.

The progressive demolition of the Wall destroyed the border fortifications beyond recognition and today, it is difficult to actually imagine the exact course of the Wall. Only three sections of the so called 'vorderland-mauer' (exterior Wall) still stand at their original locations: Niederkirchnestraße, Liesenstraße and Bernauer Straße.

The longest section of the exterior Wall still intact is located on Bernauer Straße. A section spanning 212 metres still stands there today – albeit with a gap created in 1997 when some segments were taken out.[3]

The side of this stretch of Wall facing the East has been integrated with the Gedenkstätte Berliner Mauer (Berlin Wall Memorial). The idea, its origins and a 2006 Senate resolution to develop the memorial by 2012 "into the central site of commemoration for the Berlin Wall and its victims" originate from political endeavours, but also from both individual and wide-spread civic engagement.

Laying the foundation stone on 13th August 1990 signalised, for the first time, the will on behalf of the city's officials to create a memorial on Bernauer Straße. The decision by the East Berlin magistrate to preserve the area of border which ran across Sophienfriedhof (a Protestant cemetery) as a site of historic interest meant that a milestone had been reached in preserving this stretch of Wall on Bernauer Straße – special thanks for this has to be given to Manfred Fischer, pastor of the Reconciliation Parish.

With the establishment of the foundation in 2009, the Berlin Wall Memorial on Bernauer Straße and the Marienfelde Refugee Centre Museum came together to form the Berlin Wall Foundation.

EAST SIDE GALLERY

Furthermore, the majority of the Wall sections still standing in Berlin are remains of the so called hinterland-mauer, which marked the border on the eastern side (the GDR side).

The largest preserved section of the hinterlandmauer was designed by international artists in 1990 and is now known as the East Side Gallery. It stretches from Ostbahnhof to the Oberbaum Bridge and was listed as a protected historical monument in 1991.

Extensive restoration work was carried out in 2008/2009 and was, in part, financed by the Berlin Senate. 86 artists repainted their work on the Wall which had been especially refurbished. After months of work, pieces of Wall art, including the 'Brotherhood Kiss' and a Trabant breaking through the Wall, were back on public display in 2010.

In the following years, the strip of land behind this section of Wall was developed. Cafés along the river bank then appeared. In 2012, the districts of Friedrichshain and Kreuzberg released parts of the land for development. Permission was given to a developer to build a 63 metre-high residential tower and a hotel directly on the bank between the East Side Gallery and the River Spree.

When the building work commenced in 2013, numerous segments of the Wall were removed to create an entrance to the large building site. In 2006, 34 segments of the Wall were removed as part of the construction work for the O2 World – the gap left behind was 40 metres in length. The East Side Gallery e.V and its chairperson, Kani Alavi, reacted with public protests against any further demolition of the Wall and its pictures and they were met with national and international support. The Berlin Senate announced that a compromise must be reached by the investors of the residential tower (which is currently a shell of a build-

---

3   After disputes with the Sophien congregation, several segments of the Berlin Wall were removed here by its priest as there were World War II graves on this site.

ing), the investors of the proposed hotel as well as the district of Friedrichshain. No compromise has yet been made and it is likely that it will take a while before this happens. For this reason, there is no solution on the horizon to prevent any further destruction of this stretch of Wall, nor is there a possibility that the hole made for the building site will be sealed back up with sections of the Berlin Wall.

DIVIDED CITY MEMORIALS IN THE UNIFIED CITY

Berlin, once a divided city, has the most Wall memorials. Alongside the larger memorials, many sections of the Wall can be found in places which are often overlooked. These sections include those di-

Moving the Wall to the Kollhoff-Tower
© Bundesstiftung Aufarbeitung

Joachim Gauck in front of the Wall section on Kollhoff-Tower
© Bundesstiftung Aufarbeitung

rectly outside the S-Bahn station at Potsdamer Platz, in Ministergärten, in Galerie Lafayette (department store), outside the Märkisches Museum and in residential areas. Fragments can also be found outside many hotels including Hotel Intercontinental, Hotel Westin Grand, Hotel Estrel and Hotel Kolumbus. A further section of the Berlin Wall was installed at the top of the Kollhoff-tower on 15th July 2010. This building on Potsdamer Platz was named after its architect, Hans Kollhoff, and, rising to 103 metres, it is one of the highest in Berlin.[4]

Another impressive Wall memorial by Ben Wagin can be found in Berlin in Marie-Elisabeth-Lüders-Haus (belonging to the Bundestag), and can be viewed by the public.

The Library of the German Bundestag is located on the west side of the multi-purpose building. It has a circular ground plan and consists of four floors. Original segments of the Berlin Wall can be found in the library's basement and commemorate the division of Berlin and the former course of the border which cut through the area where the parliament stands today.

After securing the segments, Ben Wain had one segment of Wall for every year between 1961 and 1989 inscribed with the number of people who died in that year whilst attempting to cross the border. The memorial is complimented with a book edited by Maria Nooke, in which short biographies of those who died at the Wall are recorded. This helps gives faces to the numbers.

Marie-Elisabeth-Lüders-Haus' architect, Stephan Braunfels0, incorporated Ben Wasin's memorial into the building and put up the segments along the original course of the Wall.

Marie-Elisabeth-Lüders-Haus – named after former Reichstag deputy, Marie-Elisabeth Lüders, – has served as the parliament's service and infrastructure centre since its completion in December 2003. After Washington and Tokyo, it is the third largest research library of its kind in the world.

---

4   Further memorial spaces can be traced via documentaries on the SED dictatorship by The Federal Foundation for the Reappraisal of the SED Dictatorship: Erinnerungsorte an die Berliner Mauer und innerdeutsche Grenze, compiled by Ruth Gleinig and Enrico Heitzer, Berlin 2011.

A PIECE OF LIVING HISTORY

Above all, thanks must be given to the individuals who prevented the Berlin Wall from ending up as nothing more than personal trophies in private display cabinets, and who helped to create many memorial sites allover Germany. Such intervention is most likely the reason behind the first section of the Wall finding its way to Silberhausen, a village in Thuringia. It was put up on the village green on 29th April 1990 and unveiled by Rainer Hildebrandt in the presence of former President of the Bundestag, Rita Süssmuth. A lime tree was planted on each side of the 2.7 tonne heavy and 3.6 metre-wide section of concrete to symbolise life.

Michael Spitzenberg was one of the Wall Peckers who made his way to Berlin in 1989. He was so shocked by the actual height of the Wall that he decided to buy a section and take it back to his hometown. Answering the question 'why', he replied he wanted it to serve as "a piece of living history for future generations..."[5]

Michael Spitzenberg and the segment of Wall had already arrived back in Silberhausen on 6th February 1990. On the eastern side of the Wall, Michael Spitzenberg has incorporated a sundial which includes what he considers to be the significant moments in the GDR's history as well as the dates the GDR troops were deployed and surrounded West Berlin.

Original graffiti can still be seen on the side that once faced the West. It is not clear if these sections of Wall are in fact the first sections in Germany to be put up outside Berlin. At the start of the 1990s, Dr. Joachim Zeitz, an ophthalmologist from Düsseldorf, bought three sections of the Berlin Wall which had originally made up part of the border at Potsdamer Platz. Joachim Zeitz had read about the sale of the Wall in a newspaper. He was so attracted to the paintings on these sections (by famous Wall artist Thierry Noir) that he bought all three. One of the sections can be found today in his garden and he donated the other two sections to the town. Two local schools (Büdericher Mataré- Gymnasium and Meerbusch-Gymnasiums) expressed their interest in claiming a section of Wall and suggested displaying a section in their playgrounds. In the end, two sections were given to the Meerbusch-Gymnasium in Strümp and were to be put up on the edge of its playground due to the fact that the area was accessible to the general public. The official unveiling took place on 23rd May 2011 to coincide with the 62nd anniversary of the promulgation of German Basic Law.

TELTOW GALLERY

It is a little-known fact that there is also a Brandenburg version of the East Side Gallery. The idea to construct the Teltow Gallery – a counterpart to the East Side Gallery in Brandenburg – was born in 2009, 20 years after the Fall of the Wall.

At the start of the 1990s, the VEB (publicly owned) concrete plant bought sections of the Wall from the bankruptcy assets of the National People's Army. The sections had originally made up part of the border in Spandau, Berlin. The concrete plant intended to use the segments to store mounds of stone. Around 200 segments of the Berlin Wall finally ended up in storage in the former concrete plant's depot. Steffen Heller, one of the city's councillors and mayor, Thomas Schmidt, went about starting a campaign to create a Teltow gallery.[6]

---

5   2,7 Tonnen Berliner Mauer zur Erinnerung – Silberhausen. Ein kleiner Anger mit einem großen Stück Geschichte, in: Thüringer Allgemeine. 9. April 2011.
6   Cf. Solveig Schuster: Die Mauer muss weg! Es lebe die Mauer!, in: Teltower Stadt-Blatt on November 2013, p. 1–2.

The local council agreed to the project and artists including Thierry Noir arrived in Teltow to brighten up the dull concrete segments. However, a lack of public interest in the project meant that it had to be abandoned. In 2001, Elmar Prost, director of building material company 'Klösters', bought the remaining 164 segments and had them put up in his company grounds in Teltow.[7]

After the failure of the Teltow gallery, he offered professional and non-professional artists the chance to paint the sections of Wall. Each artist who wished to take part had to go through a formal application process and sign a license agreement and code of conduct. The artists were then assigned a numbered piece of the Wall. He now has the time to redesign the segments of the Wall as often as he wants for six months. It is possible to buy one of the unique pieces of art for €500. There are only 40 of the original 164 segments left. Alongside non professional artists, others including Thierry Noir and Victor Landeta have left their mark on these segments. Spanish artist, Victor Landeta, swapped his canvas for sections of the Wall and created larger than life-sized images of Nelson Mandela, Willy Brandt and Albert Einstein. However, building plans in 2014 for Teltow mean that the future of the project is uncertain.

AXEL SPRINGER AG WALL PROJECT

2009 marked 20 years since the Fall of the Wall. To celebrate the anniversary year, the Axel-Springer AG worked with Kai Deikmann, chief editor of 'Bild' on plans to present a section of the Berlin Wall to every federal state. The catalyst for the project was an advert in a Berlin newspaper reporting that the plot of land upon which many segments of the Berlin Wall were being stored was to be put up for forced sale. When Saarbrücken was presented with a piece of the Wall on 17th June 2009 (former Day of German unity), the Saarland became the first federal state to benefit from the project. Baden-Württemberg followed on 9th November 2009 when its segment of the Wall was officially unveiled next to the Landtag in Stuttgart (legislative assembly of a German state). Kai Diekmann presented the segment of the Wall to Wolfgang Schuster, the Lord Mayor of Stuttgart. Other guests in attendance included Minister President of the state of Baden-Württemberg, Günther Oettinger, and Anna Kaminsky, director of the Federal Foundation for the Reappraisal of the SED Dictatorship. In her speech, Anna Kaminsky pointed out that the Berlin Wall has become "...a symbol of overcoming dictatorships and a symbol of the desire for freedom, of overcoming fear, of bravery and civil courage..."[8]

A celebration ceremony was held in the Haus Der Geschichte (House of History) after the official unveiling.

Further places to receive a piece of the Wall as part of the project, initiated by the Axel Springer AG, included Magdeburg (28th September 2010), Bremen (3rd October 2010), Rostock (4th November 2009), Kiel (10th November 2009) and Düsseldorf (12th November 2009).

The piece of Wall between the State Chancellery and the Düsseldorf Landtag can be found in a public park. In his thank you speech, Minister President of North Rhine-Westphalia Jürgen Rüttgers referred to the present from 'Bild' as "a memorial, now accessible to all citizens".[9] This is how each federal state was presented with original pieces of the Berlin Wall, which were mostly put on display in their respective state capitals.

Portraits by Willy Brandt and Nelson Mandela, artist: Victor Landeta, © Victor Landeta

7   Cf. Andreas Conrad: Baustofffirma macht Geschäft mit einstigem Grenzwall, in: Tagesspiegel on 9. November 2013, p. 1–3.
8   The original piece of the Berlin Wall is located between the Berlin House of Representatives and Haus der Geschichte., in: http://www.hdgbw.de/aktuelles/originalstueck-der-berliner-mauer/mehr/
9   Zwei Mahnmale der Freiheit. Bild schenkt Düsseldorf und Braunschweig ein Mauerstück, in: http://www.bild.de/politik/2009/duesseldorf/mahnmale-der-freiheit-bild-schenkt-duesseldorf-und-braunschweig-stueck-der-mauer-10319938.bild.html

THE WALL IN THE FORMER CHANCELLOR'S GARDEN

As part of this project, the Axel Springer AG presented a section of the Wall to former German Chancellor Helmut Kohl in recognition of his services and work towards reunification. The official celebratory unveiling took place in Helmut Kohl's private garden on 9th August 2011 – 50 years since the Wall was built. As well as his wife, Maike Kohl-Richter, and Lord Mayor, Eva Lohse, a group of 100 pupils from Kohl's former primary and high school were also in attendance at the unveiling.

In his thank you speech, Helmut Kohl referred to the symbolic power of the history of the Berlin Wall and the interwoven fate that befell the people – which began with its construction on 13th August 1961 and finally ended with the peaceful reunification of Germany.[10]

Serving for 16 years, Helumt Kohl was the longest serving chancellor of Germany and also became the first chancellor of reunified Germany. The section of Wall was moved to its current location following the unveiling. It stands in Helmut Kohl's garden and can best be seen from his living and dining room or garden terrace.

The Wall in Helmut Kohl's
private garden in Ludwigshafen
© Daniel Biskup/Bild

10 Stephanie Jungholt: 50 Jahre nach Mauerbau. Bild sagt Danke für die Einheit, in: Bild on 10. August 2011, p. 12.

COSFORD
GREAT BRITAIN

Location:
Royal Air Force Museum
Cosford

The Wall in the
Royal Air Force Museum,
Cosford
© Royal Air Force Museum Cosford

Two women and a man stand on a ladder in front of the Berlin Wall and wave to relatives on the other side. Such sights were commonplace in divided Berlin after the Wall was built. Families, friends and neighbours were suddenly torn apart by the Wall.

This scene has been replicated in the Royal Air Force Museum in the English town of Cosford. Embedded in the sculpture is an original piece of the Berlin Wall, alongside it there is a map of the divided city. However, the organisers of the exhibition did make a small mistake: the piece of Wall shown in this scene did not exist as depicted. In 1961, the barrier was of a more provisional nature and was not replaced with the familiar concrete segments until the mid-nineteen-seventies.

The segment found its final home in an Cold War exhibition opened in 2007. The segment of Wall had been given to the British protecting powers at their military airbase in Berlin Gatow in 1994 – shortly before they left Berlin after 49 years. It was then donated to the Royal Air Force Museum, where it was then stored and put on temporary display in 2000.

Location:
Royal Engineers
Museum,
Prince Arthur Road,
Gillingham, Kent

The Wall in the
Royal Engineers Museum

© Royal Engineers Museum,
Library and Archive

The British armed forces also had new tasks to overcome when the Wall fell in November 1989. Royal army units helped with the dismantling of the Wall when the official work began on 13th June 1990. Also helping with the operation was The Royal Engineers 38 Squadron, who helped remove the Wall in

the East Berlin district of Staaken. At the request of Spandau borough mayor, Werner Salomon, the British military was moved to a former border control point between Heerstraße and Brunsbüttler Damm to help with the removal of the Wall there. Working with German federal demolition squads, they dismantled the section of Wall (600 metres) in just a few weeks. To commemorate the presence of the Royal Army in Berlin, three section of the Wall were sent to Gillingham at the start of the 1990s.

They stand today in front of the Royal Engineers Museum in the former Brompton barracks. A giant cobra with its mouth wide open has been painted along the three segments (presumably by family members of the squadron). Above it, the initials RE – for Royal Engineers can be seen.

In 2011, the sections were moved inside the museum in order to better preserve them.

LONDON
GREAT BRITAIN

Location:
Imperial War Museum,
Lambeth Road

Imperial War Museum,
the Wall on the left
© Fanny Heidenreich

Visitors to the Imperial War Museum in London are greeted by a giant mouth yelling, "change your life". The graffiti by Wall artist, Indiano (alias Jürgen Grösse), can be seen on a segment of the Wall that has stood outside the museum in Geraldine Mary Harmsworth since the start of the nineties. Just as the museum claims, the piece of the Wall originated from the Brandenburg Gate and was given to the museum by a donor who wishes to remain anonymous. It is most likely to have come from British patron of the arts, Lord Peter Palumbo, who, in 1994, purchased further pieces of the Wall in London.

There is a further piece of Wall to be found inside the museum in its section on 'Post War Conflict since 1945'. The division of Berlin is depicted here alongside the 1956 Suez Crisis, the war in China, Korea and Vietnam, the decolonising of Africa and the Gulf War.

The small chunk of Berlin Wall, which still has black paint on one side, has an interesting story to tell. It was 'secured' by an officer from the British military police on Invalidstraße. On 20th November 1989, the British military government drew up a certificate of authentication. Shortly after, it left Berlin and was placed in the foreign office in London. Former Foreign Secretary, Douglas Hurd, donated the piece of the Wall along with the certificate to the Imperial War Museum on 5th December 1989. The British military police, who later helped to dismantle the Wall, gave another significant piece of Wall memorabilia to the Museum. The scenes at the border to the British sector had been filmed by a camera team. The images of the events filmed around the Brandenburg Gate are particularly impressive.

The Wall in front of the Imperial
War Museum, London
© Fanny Heidenreich

Location:
National Army Museum,
Royal Hospital Road,
Chelsea

The Wall in front of the
National Army Museum,
London
© Fanny Heidenreich

The segments of the Wall have been on display outside the National Army Museum in London since 1994. They were a gift from the Royal Logistic Corps stationed in Berlin. The grey pieces, without paint, came from the suburbs of Berlin. According to the museum, the graffiti now seen on them was added later by an officer of the Royal Army to make them more attractive. A small bronze plaque commemorates the German division and the families of the British garrison in the city.

„Presented to the National Army Museum by 2. Transport and Movements Squadron. The Royal Logistic Corps (Berlin). 1945-1994."

WAKEFIELD, BRETTON HALL
GREAT BRITAIN

Location:
Yorkshire Sculpture
Park, West Bretton

The Berlin Wall in temporary
storage at Yorkshire
Sculpture Park, Wakefield

© Courtesy of Yorkshire Scupture
Park, photo: Nigel Roddis

Yorkshire Sculpture Park is situated in the grounds of the grand Bretton Hall. The grounds are also famous for being home to the college of the same name until 2004. A landscape garden, complete with ponds and rivers, has been on the site since the 1800s. One of the largest open-air sculpture galleries can also be found on the site today. Works by famous artists including Henry Moore, Andy Goldsworthy, Eduardo Paolozzi and Sophie Ryder can all be found in the park. At the end of the 1990s, British patron of the arts, Lord Palumbo, donated one of the pieces he had bought in 1994 to the sculpture park, where it has stood since then in the open. The graffiti by Jürgen Große (alias 'Indiano') that once decorated the segment has almost been entirely washed away by the rain. The words "Fight your inner" can only just be seen. He painted 'Global Messages' on pieces of the Wall on Niederkirchnerstraße in 1990. The piece of Wall is currently being stored in a depot at the Yorkshire Sculpture Park awaiting restoration work.

Hungary had already opened the Iron Curtain on 27th June 1989, before the Wall fell on 9th November 1989. The gradual dismantling of the Wall had already begun in May on orders from the Hungarian government. The Austrian-Hungarian border had become an 'escape route' for thousands of GDR citizens who had decided to flee East-Germany in summer 1989. Hungary had already decided on a change of policy on the domestic front in 1977/88. The former party leader, János Kádár was ousted and a reform-friendly wing from inside the Hungarian Socialist Workers' Party came to power. The opposition movement became stronger at the same time and founding new parties was permitted.

As well as the Hungarian Democratic Forum (MDF), The Alliance of Free Democrats (SZDSZ) formed their party in 1988 and went on in 1990 to stand for election in the first free elections since 1947.

Going to the polls in 1990, the Democrats could reckon with good public approval and even had the chance to become the strongest party in the new government. With things looking so good, the SZDSZ announced a public festival to be held on Heldenplatz on 31st March 1990.

A piece of the Berlin Wall was also to be erected as a symbol of freedom's victory over oppression. The party leaders got in touch with 'Limex', the company responsible for marketing and selling the Wall. When they found out that the asking price for such a piece was many thousands of Marks, the SZDSZ got in contact with the former GDR Culture Minister, asking him to donate twelve segments of the Wall for free. Two weeks before the election, the request was sent to GDR premier, Hans Modrow – who himself had only been in office for a few days after the free parliamentarian elections on 18th March 1990.

The GDR's foreign ministry obtained an expert opinion about how they should move forward with the request. The appropriate department in the ministry did not appear to be thrilled at the prospect of giving a section of the Wall – it did not view the SZDSZ as a legitimate political party. Nevertheless, Modrow was advised to grant this wish for political reasons and also since the request was being made so "pushily". However, only two pieces of the Wall were given, and not the 12 originally requested. On 6th April 1990, the newly elected GDR government confirmed the sale. The SZDSZ public festival was already over, but the sections of Wall were still transported to the Hungarian capital. There is little known about what happened after this. Gábor Demszky, member of the Free Democrats was elected Mayor of Budapest in 1990. In the same year, the sections of Wall were placed on a hill in Tabán where they remained until 1998 when they suddenly disappeared. Officials in Budapest reported that the segments had been taken away. Nobody could say exactly where and when they were taken. It has since been confirmed, with help from the German embassy in Hungary that they are in the gardens at the Malteser International relief agency. They were put there after a suggestion by Father Imre Kozma (founding president of the Hungarian charity). In 1989, Imre Kozma set up the first place of aid for GDR citizens arriving in Hungary. He is particularly well remembered for saying "the gate is open, the heart even more so". German tourists can often be found visiting the section of Wall in the grounds here.

BUDAPEST
HUNGARY

Location:
Budapest Malteser International relief agency garden

The Wall in Budapest
© Budapest Malteser International relief agency

BUDAPEST
HUNGARY

Location:
In front of the
House of Terror Museum

The Berlin Wall in front of the
House of Terror Museum
© House of Terror Museum

An original section of the Berlin Wall was put up in front of the *House of Terror Museum* in November 2010 to mark and celebrate 20 years since German reunification. State Secretary, Zoltán Balogh, was present at the unveiling. He said that the symbol of the division of Berlin and Germany should stand as a memorial to to remind us "that there must always be people who do not accept walls that divide people and worlds from each other". Other guests in attendance included former Berlin Mayor, Eberhard Diepgen and the former museum director, Mária Schmit.

The building which houses the museum was built in 1880 according to plans drawn up by architect Adolf Feszty, as a residential building. In 1937, it was occupied by the Arrow Cross Party (a Hungarian fascist party) and served as their headquarters from 1940. When the party, which was connected to the Nazis, came to power in autumn 1944, the cellars were used as prison and torture cells. The Hungarian intelligence services took over the building in 1945 after Soviet troops entered and the Hungarian Communist party returned from exile in Moscow. They also used the cellars as prison and torture cells. After the 1956 uprising had been suppressed, the intelligence services lost the building. It was used as an office building in the decades that followed.

A museum, funded by a public foundation dedicated to Central and Eastern European history, was opened in the building. The museum is dedicated to the victims of totalitarian rule in Hungary.

The exhibition looks at the far right Arrow Cross Party in 1944/5 and the Stalinists from 1945 onwards, whereas the collaboration with the Third Reich is only looked at in part.

A memorial to the Iron Curtain has been on display outside the *House of Terror Museum* since 2009. It commemorates the reality and threat of what was once a political, economical and above all military division which once spilt Europe. A division which seems incomprehensible to today's generation.

Location:
„Renzo Pezzani"
primary school,
via Quasimodo 2

The Wall in front of the school
in Albinea
© Jens Otto

On 25th March 1995, Hans Schmidt, born in the Berlin district Treptow-Köpenick, was posthumously na-med an honorary citizen of Albinea. Schmidt was stationed as an officer in Italy in 1944 and, alongside four other soldiers, made contact with the Italian resistance movement 'Resistenza'. His connections to the resistance were reported, and he was sentenced to death by a martial court.

This story was documented by photographer and hobby historian, Mario Crotti. His exhibition, 'Re-sistance in Albinea', was shown one year later in Treptow and paved the way for the town-twinning. Crotti also had other connections to the German capital. In 1963, he met three refugees from East Berlin, who informed him of the situation in the divided city. He then made his way to Germany with his camera and recorded what life behind the Wall was like. His work was met with great interest and was later shown in Italy. After the Fall of the Wall, Crotti made his way back to Berlin. His photo reportage, "Berlin – the city that was walled up" came about as result. After the exhibition had been shown in Treptow city hall, it was then shown in Italy and other European cities and even Australia. Crotti also wanted to erect a section of the Wall in the place he was born. Siegfried Stock, borough mayor of Treptow, supported the project. Crotti travelled by lorry personally to Berlin to receive the segment. It had originally stood near a children's farm on the West Berlin Adalbertstraße in Kreuzberg. Parts of the graffiti painted by Christophe Bouchet and Thierry Noir can still be seen on the section today. One year later, it was taken to its new location in front of a primary school in Albinea. The opening ceremony, on 28th October 2000, was attended by representa-

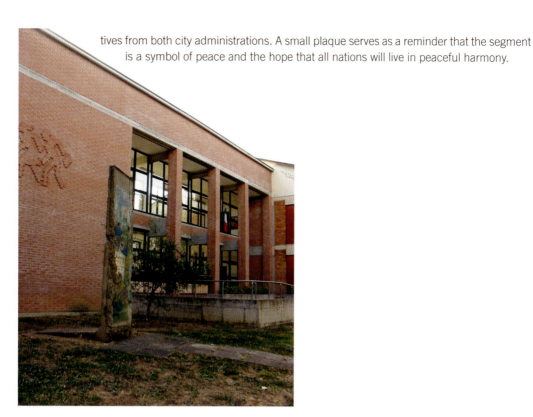

tives from both city administrations. A small plaque serves as a reminder that the segment is a symbol of peace and the hope that all nations will live in peaceful harmony.

The Wall in front of the school
in Albinea
© Jens Otto

MERONE
ITALY

The former manager from Italian cement factory 'Cementeria di Merone' was one of the many art collectors and lovers from all over the world in attendance at the biggest Wall auction in Monaco in June 1990. He bought a piece of the Wall for 20,000 D-Mark. The segment had previously been deemed "extraordinarily ugly" by 'Stern' magazine.[1] It was put on display outside the plant's own art museum in Merone. The 'Cementeria di Merone' was sold to the global building materials group, 'Holcim'. The piece of Wall still apparently exists, but the museum is no longer open. The piece of Wall, weighing tonnes, now stands in the garden of the Italian concrete factory.

Location:
Holcim (Italia) S.p.A.,
Via Volta, 1

---

1 Eine Mauer für die ganze Welt (A wall for the entire world). In: Der Stern, 46/90, p. 77

SPILAMBERTO
ITALY

Location:
Spilamberto

The sections of Wall for
Spilamberto
© Patrice Lux

S pilamberto, Northern Italy, south of Modena, is famous for its historical medieval buildings. Since 2008, there has been one further attraction. 27 year old entrepreneur and local, Carlo Accorsi, gave four brightly coloured pieces of the Wall to his home town on valentine's day 2008.

They are currently in a depot, but will soon be put on display at a suitable location, say the town fathers.

Accorsi, who has been working in real estate for years, discovered the pieces at an auction and want-ed to bring a piece of "significant world history" back home. The pieces had been brightened up before the auction on orders from Berliner art agent, Patrice Lux. Accorsi then acquired ten segments of the Wall for an undisclosed sum. He donated four to his hometown and wishes to make the others available for art and cultural purposes – until then, they stand in his garden in Spilamberto.

The sections of Wall are
prepared for transportation
to Italy
© Patrice Lux

84

RIGA
LATVIA

Location:
Kronvalds Parks,
Elizabetes iela 2

Inscription on the Wall in Riga
© German Embassy Riga

In 1990, the Baltic Republic called for the restoration of independence, lost during the USSR military occupation in 1940 – it was known as the 'Singing Revolution'. After Lithuania, Latvia was the second state to declare its independence from Moscow. Representatives of the Latvian government invited the Berlin museum, 'Haus am Checkpoint Charlie' to exhibit. The exhibition, documenting the Cold War, was a clear symbol that freedom in the Baltic States could not be held back any loner after the Fall of the Berlin Wall.

When he left, Rainer Hildebrand, director of the Berlin Museum, donated a piece of the Wall to Riga. In January 1991, when the Soviet Union government chose violent means to end the independent movement, the citizens of Riga showed resistance. Barricades were put up in the streets of the capital to stop the Soviet tanks advancing. The altercations, lasting a number of days, climaxed on 20th January 1991 when Soviet special units stormed the Latvian Interior Ministry. Violent scenes also took place around the parliament building, which was to be occupied on orders from the Soviet state and general secretary, Mikhail Gorbachev. Demonstrators used cement blocks to block access roads. The protests were a success. Latvia achieved total independence on 20th August 1991. A memorial, made from the remains of the barricades was erected a year later in front of the parliament building close to the nearby Kronvalda Park. An unknown poet wrote the following quote on one of the five concrete blocks, "the Berlin Wall separated us, this wall

unites us. Let us love one another, And pray to God for our enemy" – the words have almost completely faded away. The piece of Wall, presented in 1990, was added to the memorial in the same year. Originally, it was inscribed with 'LIN' and its counterpart in Moscow, 'BER'. Today, there is nothing left of this to see. A red altar commemorates the circumstances surrounding the donation:

The Wall in Riga
before restoration
© German Embassy Riga

„Berlines mūra fragments / Fragment der Berliner Mau-
er / Pec Berlines muzeja „Haus am Checkpoint Charlie" izstādes Rīgā 1990 gada novembri muzeja direktors Dr. Rainer Hildebrandts šo mūra fragmenty uzdavipaja Latvijas galvaspilsētaj / Nach der Ausstellung des Berliner Museums „Haus am Checkpoint Charlie" im November 1990 in Rīga hat der Direktor des Museums Dr. Rainer Hildebrand dieses Fragment der Mauer der Hauptstadt Lettlands geschenkt."
("This fragment of the Berlin Wall was presented to the capital city of Lativa in November 1990 by Dr. Rainer Hildebrand, director of the Berlin Museum 'Haus am Checkpoint Charlie' after his exhibition in Riga.")

It had been planned to restore this section of Wall for the 20th anniversary of the Fall of the Wall. The plans had to be postponed due to the financial crisis. The restoration finally took place in 2001. The memorial was said to have been sprayed with grafitti – this was removed.

The Wall in Riga
after restoration
© German Embassy Riga

SCHENGEN
LUXEMBURG

Location:
Centre Européen
Schengen,
Rue Robert Goebbels

The Wall in front of
Centre Euopéen Schengen,
Schengen asbl
© Schengen asbl

The European memorial on the banks of the Moselle commemorates the major agreement made in setting the course for free transport of passengers and freight. Schengen borders Luxembourg, Germany and France. 25 years after the Schengen Agreement was signed by Germany, France and the States of the Benelux Economic Union on 14th June 1985, a section of the Berlin Wall was unveiled in February 2010 in front of the Relais Europe Direct. It commemorates the eastward enlargement of the EU. The Berlin Senate gave the section of the Wall, weighing 2.8 tonnes, to Schengen. It originally stood at Potsdamer Platz. 3.8 metres tall and 1.2 metres wide, it was transported to Schengen on a lorry and positioned in front of the information centre with the help of a crane.

The side of the Wall that faced West Berlin between 1961 and 1989 has been preserved in its original state. The other side of the Wall, which faces the Centre Européen, has been decorated with graffiti. Alongside the section of Wall is a peace pole, donated by the Goi Peace Foundation. "May peace prevail on earth" is written on the pole in 12 languages. There are approximately 200,000 peace poles around the world, each standing as a symbol of world peace.

Location:
Monaco-Monte Carlo
railway station,
La Condamine

The Wall in front of the station
in Monaco
© Elena Codecà

Set somewhat aside from the railway station in the Principality of Monaco, is a piece of the Berlin Wall. The concrete section, set in a black metal frame and painted in blue, green and red pastel tones, is a more vague commemoration to the former border fortification. Connections to the Wall can only be evoked by a distant landscape and small dove, seen through a window. The words "Mur de Berlin" (Berlin Wall) have been inscribed along its base. Contact was made to the city administration and to the tourist information, but they were not able to tell us how and when it found its way to Monaco. Monaco hosted the first international Wall auction, where an illustrious group of collectors, artists, celebrities and businesses were able to buy a piece of brightly coloured Wall remains.

GDANSK
POLAND

Location:
Gdańsk dockyard,
Kreuzung ul. Wały
Piastowskie und
ul. Kupiecka

The Wall in Gdańsk

© Michael Lewandowski
European Solidarity Centre

Two days before the 20th anniversary of the signing of the historical Gdańsk Agreement, celebrations began to mark the 20th anniversary since Solidarność's (Solidarity) emergence. The Polish trade union emerged from a strike movement in the summer of 1980. For the first time ever, communist leaders were forced to endorse an independent worker's council and accept political freedom. Although prohibited in summer 1980 after the introduction of martial law and also still being very much underground, 'Solidarność' still had a lot to do with Poland's politics. In early 1989, representatives of the state, political parties and Solidarność opened a round table which initiated the end of the communist regime in Poland.

The Solidarność movement was a model for many other civil and human rights movements in the former East Block. The movement had a profound effect throughout Europe and for this reason heads of state and governments from many other European countries joined in the celebrations in Gdańsk. Lech Wałęsa, leader and co-founder of Solidarność and Paweł Adamowicz, Mayor of Gdańsk, held speeches from the top of an old green truck – just as had been done during the strikes in the eighties. Third to take to the microphone and make a speech was Berlin's incumbent mayor, Eberhard Diepgen. He brought a section of the Wall as a gift and and presented it to the public at the shipyard for this special occasion.

"What began with Lech Wałęsa jumping over the fence in this ship yard, made the Fall of the Wall possible", said Diepgen in his speech.

Today, the segment can be found outside the shipyard at the intersection between Wały Piastowskie ul. and Kupiecka. ul. The Wall protrudes from a rust coloured base with a relief of Europe on it.

A small plaque explains the meaning of the concrete slab in Polish, English and German:

89

„Fragment muru Berlińskiego, symbolu podziału Europy na wolna i zniewoloną, którego obalenie 9 listopada 1989 roku stało się znakiem zjednoczenia Niemiec i odbudowy jedności Europy."

"A fragment of the Berlin Wall, a symbol of Europe divided into a free and an enslaved realm. The collapse of the Berlin Wall on November 9th 1989 was a sign of uniting Germany and regaining European unity."

„Teil der Berliner Mauer, Symbol der Teilung in ein freies und in ein unterdrücktes Europa. Der Mauerfall am 9. November 1989 wurde zum Zeichen für die Vereinigung Deutschlands und den Aufbau der Europäischen Einheit."

KRZYŻOWA
POLAND

Location:
Fundacjs Krzyż
owa dla Porozumienia
Europejskiego,
Krzyżowa 7

The Wall in Krzyżowa

© Krzyżow, Fundacja Krzyżowa

20 years after the so-called "Mass of Reconciliation", an original section of the Berlin Wall and a memorial plaque were unveiled in Krzyżowa. In attendance at the unveiling were President of the Bundestag, Norbert Lammert, former Marshal of the Sejm and current Polish President, Bronisław Komorowski.

The segment of Wall stands in the centre of a small open space between the palace and surrounding agricultural buildings, which belong to the Krzyżowa Foundation.

Former Chancellor, Helmut Kohl was on a visit to Poland when the border in Berlin was unexpectedly opened on 9th November 1989. Moved by the events, Helmut Kohl and former Polish prime minister, Tadeusz Mazowiecki decided to attend a mass of reconciliation in Krzyżowa.

Krzyżowa had already played a significant historical role in 1942 and 1943 with the three meetings of the Kreisau Circle. Helmuth James von Moltke and Peter Yorck von Wartenburg were the initiators behind a Nazi resistance group made up of people from varying social, political and confessional origins. The group, which famously became known at the Kreisau Circle was made up of friends, acquaintances and trusted individuals. Together they developed ideas and plans to rebuild a democratic Germany rooted in Europe after the end of National Socialism. Many of the members, amongst them, Helmuth James von Moltke paid for their resistance with their lives. An international community centre, in grounds belonging to the Moltke family, was opened in the 1990s. The opening ceremony was attended by German and Polish heads of government.

The permanent exhibition "Living in the truth. From the history of resistance and opposition in the 20th century" in Kreisauer castle combines the commemoration of the Kreisauer Circle and the struggle against

totalitarian dictatorships in other European countries during the 20th century.

Prior to the unveiling of the segment of the Berlin Wall and plaque in December 2009, a segment of wall from the Gdańsk shipyard was unveiled on 17th June near the Reichstag in Berlin.

A bronze plaque has been put on the Wall with the words "to commemorate the struggle by Solidarność for freedom and democracy, and the role played by Poland in German unification and for a politically united Europe".

The Gdańsk Shipyard was at the centre of the Polish strike movement in the 1980s. Members of Solidarność (a Polish trade union group), and their leader Lech Wałęsa, who later became Poland's president, made their first political demands from here.

The Wall in Krzyżowa

© Krzyżow, Fundacja Krzyżowa

BIAŁA PODLASKA COUNTY
POLAND

Location:
Miedzyrec Podlaski,
Kobylany and Terespol

The sections of Wall for
Biała Podlaska are loaded.

© René Karstedt /
Landkreis Oberhavel

The sections of Wall for
Biała Podlaska are loaded.

© René Karstedt /
Landkreis Oberhavel

Since March 2009, Biała Podlaska County, a unit of territorial administration and local government in eastern Poland, has also been home to two Wall memorials, thanks to an initiative by County Commissioner of Oberhavel, Karl-Heinz Schröter. Pieces of the Wall have been put on display in both Międzyrzec Podlaski and Kobylany to commemorate the Fall of the Wall and overcoming the division of Europe, as well as being symbols of peace between nations. The district of Oberhavel went on to present a further Wall memorial to another partner after the sections they had already donated to Tampere, Finland and Hudson County, USA. Biała Podlaska's County Commissioner, Tadeusz Łazowski, hopes that the new attraction will generate more tourism in the remote area. The memorial is also one of political significance in the Polish-Lithuanian-Belarusian border zone. The heavily guarded eastern border of the Euro-

Unveiling the Wall in Terespol
with Lech Wałęsa in attendance
© Landkreis Oberhavel

pean Union runs along this area to neighbouring state, Belarus – often referred to as "the last dictatorship in Europe". The Wall is not intended to symbolise division, but spread the message of European unity to East Poland.

SOSNÓVKA
POLAND

Location:
Sosnóvka,
Voivodeship
Silesia

„Wolfshunger"

© Collection Ludwik Wasecki

In early 1990, in the Polish village of Sosnóvka (near Wrocław), a peculiar spectacle took place. A gold coloured Trabant, wedged between pieces of Wall, chugged along a meadow. Berliner dentist and art collector, Ludwik Wasecki, was inspired to begin his artwork by the Fall of the Wall. Waseckis' work was the follow-up to a previous instillation in which he had rebuilt the Wall using wood and papier-mâché. In this piece, a giant aluminium fork pierced thorough the Wall and its prongs penetrated a wooden table. Wasecki named this piece "Wolfshunger" (Wolf's hunger) and coupled his experience in East Berlin in the 1970s with the work. The aluminium cutlery from this period had stayed in his memory. Wasecki met up with his parents and friends in the GDR, who he had not been able to visit directly in Poland since his emigration to Sweden in 1973. Born in Wrocław, he studied dentistry and left his place of birth after his studies in 1972. It was only in 1977 that he was allowed to come back to visit. It was at this time that he developed an interest in art. He collected work by contemporary Polish artists including Jan Aleksiun, Józef Halas, Przybyslaw Krajewski and Anna Binkunskas. He brought their paintings back to West Berlin, where he has run a dental surgery since 1979. The editor of a Berlin based newspaper noticed the pieces of Wall art in 1990. There was big interest in such projects in the months immediately after the Fall of the Wall, and Wasecki came into contact with Rainer Hildebrandt, director of the Wall museum 'Haus am Checkpoint Charlie'. He was so thrilled by the pieces, that he wanted to install them on the roof of the museum. Hildebrand suggested that Waseckis' creations should be made using real segments of the Wall. Hildebrandt promised to help,

since the price for such a piece at the time was tens of thousands of Marks and Wasecki could not come up with the money. Wasecki was allowed to choose six pieces of the Wall in October 1990 – the pieces had already been taken from their original sites and brought to be stored before sale. After donating 7,000 marks, he had them put on the back of a lorry and transported to Sosnóvka. The start of a unique collection had begun. With help from the Wall museum and via his contact to Hagen Koch, Wasecki acquired ever more pieces of Wall. Former border soldier and Stasi officer, Koch, was named by the GDR government as special representative for the dismantling of the Wall.

Eight brightly coloured segments of Wall were amongst those bought by Wasecki – they belonged to a collection of segments that had been bought at the first Wall auction in Monaco, but not collected. Japanese buyers had already paid 40,000 D-Mark for a piece of blue Wall, decorated with an orange female head, which they subsequently decided they did not actually want. Today, it stands alongside 42 further segments in a meadow in Sosnóvka. In the following years, Wasecki completed many more pieces. A giant oversized pepper mill grinds pieces of the Wall; giant red boxing gloves hang between further segments of the Wall – the "Knockout", as Waseckis called them, of the Wall. On one of the grey segments, stick men made of wood reach out to the Wall – "looking for the exit" is the title of this piece. A selection of his work was put on public display in Germany in 1991 to celebrate 30 years since the project was started. His work also caused a stir in his home land. A Wall art exhibition was opened in the Wrocław architecture museum

Ludwik Wasecki in front of his
sections of Wall

© fernsehbüro

The Wall in the green meadow

© fernsehbüro

The Wall in Sosnówka
© fernsehbüro

in october 1992. It included works by Wasecki, which once again were received with great interest. The pieces were put on display again seven years later in Wrocław, where they could be seen on the market place in open-air.

Works by other Wall artists including Kiddy Citny, Keith Harring and Thierry Noir can be found alongside his work in Sosnóvka. Thierry Noir came to Sosnóvka to paint his famous heads on a number of blank segments. Whilst there, he took the opportunity to repaint Waseckis' bathroom and barn. Despite this great collection, many pieces of the Wall stand today, untouched on a plot of land in Sosnóvka. Very rarely do visitors make their way into the nearby village. For this reason, one of the pieces was taken and placed outside the theatre in Gniezno. A giant drill – which very much resembles a dentist's drill – pierces through two pieces of Wall, and brightens up the centre of the Polish capital.

FÁTIMA
PORTUGAL

Location:
Santuario em Fátima

About 100 kilometres north of Lisbon, lies Portugal's largest and most important Catholic pilgrimage site: Fátima. It was here on 13th May 1917, that the virgin Mary is said to have appeared to three shepherd children. She told the children she would come back on the 13th day of each month and promised to perform miracles. Despite the pledge to keep the vision a secret, more and more people gathered each month and waited for the return of the Most Holy Mother of God. According to contemporary reports, there were indeed unexplained phenomenon until 13th October 1917. More important, however, were the three secrets revealed to the three children by Maria on 13th July 1917. Years later, they were written down by Lúcia, the last surviving child and published at the request of the church as the 'Three Secrets of Fátima'. The third and last part was first published in 2000. It is said that the assassination attempt on Pope John Paul II on 13th May 1981 had been foreseen.

The first secret was a vision of Hell, the second secret predicted the start of the Second World War and the final part concerned the collapse of Communism:

"If my requests are heeded, Russia will be converted, and there will be peace; if not, she will spread her errors throughout the world, causing wars and persecutions of the Church. The good will be martyred; the Holy Father will have much to suffer; various nations will be annihilated. In the end, my Immaculate Heart will triumph."

(Official translation from the Vatican.)

The prophecy in the final part was the biggest cause for concern amongst Catholics around the world. Images of what have since become recognisable as those of 'Our Lady of Fatima', were carried through Hungary, Czechoslovakia and Poland in the 1970s.

A service was held in front of the Reichstag and in the shadows of the Wall in 1978 in honour of the Marian apparition. The fact that the Wall was built on the 13th day of the month was another sign that the prophecies had been right and when the Wall fell on the 9th November 1989, many believers considered the prophecy to have been fulfilled. Remains of the Wall made their way to the Portuguese sanctuary as pilgrimage gifts. A piece of Wall was laid into a glass goblet and wrapped in a black, red and golden ribbon and presented to the sanctuary in early 1990 by Teodoro Claudio Spiess, architecture lecturer at the Technical University of Lisbon.

Fragments of Wall in a rosary, the Sanctuary of Fátima

© Santuário de nossa Senhora de Fátima

Today, it can be found on display in the Fatiman Sanctuary. Six more pieces, which have been worked in to a rosary, were delivered by an anonymous pilgrim in July 1990. A prayer was attached, thanking the grace

Blessed by the Pope: the Wall
in the Sanctuary of Fátima

© Santuário de nossa
Senhora de Fátima

of the Most Holy Mother of God. The present was given by Casimiro Virgilio Ferreira, born in Portugal in 1953, who moved to Kaiserslautern (Germany) in 1967. He was also responsible for making sure a segment of the Wall found its way to Fátima. On 26th September 1990, Ferreira got in touch with the last prime minister of the GDR and asked him for a segment of the Wall. It should stand in Portugal and commemorate the reunification of Germany. His project was supported by the then Portuguese consulate general, Joao Carlos Versteeg. After the development of diplomatic relations between Portugal and the GDR in 1974, Versteeg worked at the embassy in East Berlin.

The Portuguese tourist board organised the transportation for the 2.6 tonne piece of Wall, which arrived in Lisbon in one piece on 4th March 1991. Pope John Paul II visited Fátima a few weeks later and blessed the segment – until now a one-off occurrence. A few years later, the Roman Catholic Diocese of Leiria-Fátima worked alongside the town administrators to begin work on a memorial. The concrete segments stand at the south entrance to Fátima in a semi-circular glass case, designed by architect José Carlos Loureiro. Alongside the case hangs a sign with the following words written on it: "Thank you heavenly shepherdess for guiding people to freedom with motherly affection", words spoken by John Paul II in Fátima, 1991.

TIMIŞOARA
ROMÂNIA

Location:

"Memorial", Memorial to the Romanian Revolution from 16th-22nd December 1989, Str. Oituz Nr. 2B

The Wall in Timişoara

© Memorial to the Romanian Revolution from 16th-22nd December 1989

Klaus Christian Olasz, representative for the Federal Republic of Germany and director of the 'Memorial' museum in Timişoara, Dr. Traian Orban, unveiled an original section of the Berlin Wall on 20th December 2012 – the anniversary day of the Romanian Revolution. The section of Wall serves as a memorial to overcoming the 'Iron Curtain' in Europe. Two further exhibitions, courtesy of the Federal Foundation for the Reappraisal of the SED Dictatorship, were also opened at the unveiling and guests at the event included the mayor of Timişoara, Prof Dr. Nicolae Robu. The exhibition entitled "The Wall – a border through Germany" was a poster exhibition which put the Wall in a contemporary context and explained the history of the Berlin Wall and the inner-German division which came to an end with the Fall of the Wall and the Peaceful Revolution.

The Romanian Revolution began on 15th December 1989 in Timişoara, Romania's second largest city. After priest, László Tőkés, publicly criticised the discrimination of the Hungarian minorities, poverty and Ceauşescu's proposed reforms, he was ordered to leave Timişoara by December 15th.

He refused, and by 15th December, thousands of parishioners gathered outside the parish prayer room and the priest's home to show their support to László Tőkés. Members of Securitate, Romania's secret police, reacted violently towards the people. The protests continued the next day in Timişoara. They spread and eventually reached the capital city, Bucharest, where demonstrators stormed the party's headquarter

building. An attempt by the Romanian dictator and his wife to escape failed. After a short trial, they were executed. With the help of his powerful secret police, Nicolae Ceaușescu had controlled the Romanian people for 22 years and oppressed freedom of speech and opinion.

The cult around Ceaușescu's persona, the poverty of the people and his own personal gain all increased over the course of the dictatorship.

Director of Federal Foundation for the Reappraisal of the SED Dictatorship, Anna Kaminsky, suggested that the Berlin Senate donate a section of the Wall to Romanian Revolution Memorial. The section of Wall sent to Romania stood on Potsdamer Platz during the German division. The "Memorial to the Romanian Revolution from 16th-22nd December 1989" houses a museum and permanent exhibition which focus on the chronology of the Cold War, Ceaușescu's cult of personality and the memorials in honour of the heroes of the revolution, all in pictures. The memorial has made it its duty to look into the events of the revolution in Romania in December 1989 and to ensure that the victims of the revolution will be remembered by future generations.

The segment of the Wall in front of the Memorial to the Romanian Revolution

© Memorial to the Romanian Revolution from 16th-22nd December 1989

Information plaque explaining the origin of the Wall segment

© Memorial to the Romanian Revolution from 16th-22nd December 1989

MOSCOW
RUSSIA

Location:

In front of the Andrei Sakharov Museum and Public Centre, Semljanoj Wal

The Wall in front of the

Sakharov Centre, Moscow

© Rainer Eppelmann / Bundesstiftung zur Aufarbeitung der SED-Diktatur

Semljanoj Wall is a park that stretches along the banks of the River Yauza. The Andrei Sakharov Centre has been on this site since 1994 in a small house, named after the Russian physicist and nobel prize winner, Andrei Sakharov. Sakharov – one of the world's greatest dissidents – died a few weeks after the Fall of the Wall on 5th December 1989. He helped pave the way for (and became one of the founding members) of the 'Memorial Society'. The society was dedicated to protecting human rights and dealing with Stalinist crimes. His wife carried on his work after his death and, in 1991, she was the driving force behind the foundation of the Sakharov Museum and Public Centre. The project also received international support. Before the end of the Soviet Union in January 1991, an exhibition by the Berlin Wall Museum (Haus am Checkpoint Charlie), was shown. The project was made possible by Elena Bonner and Rainer Hildebrandt. In summer 1990, the Soviet Artist' Union (which had also supported the Wall Museum and brought it to Moscow at the time) tried to get hold of a piece of the Wall. They intended to place it at the entrance to the Gorky Park. However, the plans were never realised. Nevertheless, five Soviet artists were able to paint a number of Wall segments in Berlin, which are currently on sale in the US.

It was only later, in conjunction with the 5th anniversary of the Sakharov Museum and Public Centre, that a piece of the Wall finally made it to the Russian capital. It was originally located around Checkpoint Charlie in Berlin. The segment was turned into a freedom memorial by Daniel Mitljanskij, Aleksej Grigorjew and Maksim Mitljanskij. It was unveiled on 21st May 1996 with Rainer Hildebrandt present. It stands in the middle of a path which leads up to the Sakharov Centre. It is cast on two iron bars which hold it at a slant giving the impression that it could fall at any second. Four blue and red butterflies flap their wings around a hole in the centre of the Wall – symbolic of the Fall of the Iron Curtain and the victory for freedom.

Location:
Cala Vadella

The Wall in Ibiza
© Olaf Stölt

A piece of the Wall, originally from Waldemarstraße, found a new home on the Spanish holiday island of Ibiza. It belongs to Olaf Stölt, who paid €7000 for it at an auction in Germany. The concrete slab, with a brightly coloured design by Kitty Cinty, was torn down by the GDR government in 1990 and was supposed to be sold to Stölt by 'Limex' and 'LeLé Berlin'. However, there was no interest at that time. It was put on sale to the highest bidder in early 2005 along with three other pieces from the same stock. Olaf Stölt saw his opportunity:

"My motivation for buying the piece of Wall was to have some kind of 'evidence' to show my children, who have been brought up in Spain. I wanted them to bring them 'closer' to history and show them how significant the Wall was as a symbol of modern German history. I didn't just mean the pre-war years and the division of Germany; the Wall was ultimately a direct result of the Nazi regime. There was a certain amount of wonder from all sides when I revealed I wanted to take the piece of Wall to Ibiza: journalists, friend and family were all amazed. If I happen to get into a conversation about the Berlin Wall and reveal that I brought a piece of it back to Ibiza, people normally think I'm talking about a little piece chipped from the Wall – not a complete segment. When they take a look at it, they are mostly astounded by its size. And every time we talk about it, the conversation is steered back to the Nazis."

MADRID
SPAIN

Location:
Parque de Berlín

The Wall in Madrid
© Fanny Heidenreich

Plaque on Wall memorial
in the Parque de Berlín
© Fanny Heidenreich

A Wall memorial had already been built one year after the Wall came down on the Parque de Berlín in Madrid. However, except for a small bronze plaque (commemorating the day the pieces were unveiled at a ceremony attended by the city mayor, José María Álvarez del Manzan), there is not much information about the history of the segments. Neither the German embassy, nor the city administrators can remember how it came to be that the three pieces of Wall ended up in the middle of the fountain. According to press reports, Madrid paid 37,500 D-Marks for the segments.

The local government wanted to have the graffiti removed in the mid-90s. They blamed the graffiti on young graffiti artists and chose to have it removed from the memorial immediately. If it had not have been for the quick intervention from town administrators, the historical graffiti would have been destroyed. The segments were later treated with an anti-vandal spray to stop such incidents in the future.

The park lies in the 'German Quarter' of the city and was opened in 1967 by the then West Berlin mayor, Willy Brandt. German schools, kindergartens and the German embassy are all nearby. A Berlin bear by Spanish artist, Álvaro Iglesias and a bust of Ludwig van Beethoven both stand alongside the Wall memorial.

The first world exposition to take place after German unification was in 1992 in Spanish Seville. Two pieces of the Berlin Wall were put up inside the German pavilion to represent the Fall of the Berlin Wall.

"No-Europe" is scrawled along the two pieces, which are supposed to have come from Potsdamer Platz.

A hole had already been made underneath by Wall Peckers (people who took to the Wall with hammers shortly after the Fall of the Wall). Through the hole, the iron reinforcements that ran through the cement can be seen. Interest in the Wall was still big the world over two years after its fall. The organisers of the exposition saw this as an opportunity to sell small pieces of the Wall to visitors. More than 600,000 D-Mark were made and donated to a national park in Andalusien.

The two larger pieces were not for sale and were supposed to be brought back to Germany. They ended up staying on the exposition grounds, as the costs for transporting them back to Germany were too high. Building work started on the amusement park 'Isla Magica' at the start of the 1900s. Famous tourists attractions are depicted in numerous themed areas: a 16th century Spanish village, a pirate's nest and the Amazonian jungle. Today, the two pieces of Wall stand somewhat secluded at the entrance.

SEVILLE
SPAIN

Location:

Next to the entrance at 'Isla Magica' amusement park

The Wall in Sevilla
© Matthias Lutz

Inscription on the Wall in Sevilla
© Matthias Lutz

UTRERA
SPAIN

Location:

In front of Santuario de Consolación, Paseo de la Consolación

The Wall in Utrera

© Margarita Castillo Grijota

There are two pieces of Wall on the north-west border of the Andalusian town, Utrera. The segments are on a square surrounded by orange trees.

Standing in the shadows of the church, they are badly damaged, but the local tourist information assures us that they are real. Clues to the meaning or significance of the

installation are not available. They have stood in the square since the end of the 90s and are visited mostly by church-goers and tourists.

Location:
German Embassy,
Kiev, Bohdana
Chmelnytzkoho 25

The Wall segment is
ceremoniously unveiled
at the embassy in Kiev
© German Embassy Kiev

The following words are those of Hans-Jürgen Heimsoeth, former German ambassador in Kiev, upon unveiling a section of the Berlin Wall in the grounds of the German embassy in November 2009 – the 9th November was not just a significant date for Germany, but also for Europe and Ukraine:

"To commemorate 20 years since the Fall of the Berlin Wall, we want to unveil an original piece of the Berlin Wall as a permanent memorial. It was taken from Potsdamer Platz. Let it stand as a symbol of overcoming the division of Europe and may it further unite us Germans and Ukrainians in the shaping of our continent."

Another memorial was also unveiled in Kiev just in time for the celebrations taking place to mark 20 years since the Fall of the Wall. This second memorial stands to commemorate the Fall of the Iron Curtain which ran through Germany and Europe.

The Wall segment is
ceremoniously unveiled
at the embassy in Kiev
© German Embassy Kiev

This section of Wall originally stood on Potsdamer Platz, which was also divided by the Wall. A deadly border regime ruled on what was once one of the most congested places in Europe. By 1989, Potsdamer Platz had become a fallow area between East and West Berlin. Today, there are only a few remains of the Wall left for the public to see. Sony, which celebrated the opening of the Sony Center in June 2000, donated a number of segments from the Wall at Potsdamer Platz to Berlin.

This section of Wall in Kiev is one such piece. Berlin then donated it to Kiev and plans by the former German ambassador in Kiev for a memorial were made possible. Before it was transported to Ukraine, it had been stored in the 'Gardens of the World' in Berlin Marzahn.

Location:
North of the
Vatican City Gardens

From West Berlin to the Vatican
– the Wall in the Holy See
© Archiv Bundesstiftung Aufarbeitung,
Coll. Rosmarie Gentges, No. 122

P ope John Paul II received a very special present from Italian businessman, Marco Piccininni. Piccininni had purchased a 2.6 tonne concrete segment at a Wall auction in Monaco in 1990. According to the auction catalogue, entry 75 included the remains of a historically significant painting.

Barriers were also put up in front of Berlin's St. Michael's church on the former Luisenstadt Canal when the Wall was built in August 1961. Only the upper half of the East Berlin church could be seen from West Berlin. Architect, Bernhard Strecker requested Iranian artist Yadegar Asisi to paint the Wall in front of the church from the western side. In 1986 Asisi painted the bottom half of the church on the Wall, giving the illusion that the church was accessible from the West. When the Wall fell in 1989 and work to dismantle the Wall commenced, it was possible to save one of the pieces Asisi had used as a canvas to paint the bottom half of the church. It was put on sale

The Wall in the Holy See,
Vatican
© German Embassy to the Holy See

at the auction in Monaco and from there, it fell into Piccininnis' hands. Reports from the time claim that the piece of the Wall arrived in the Vatican City as early as autumn 1990. For a short time it was on display on the outskirts of the Vatican Gardens and the official opening ceremony followed in August 1994.

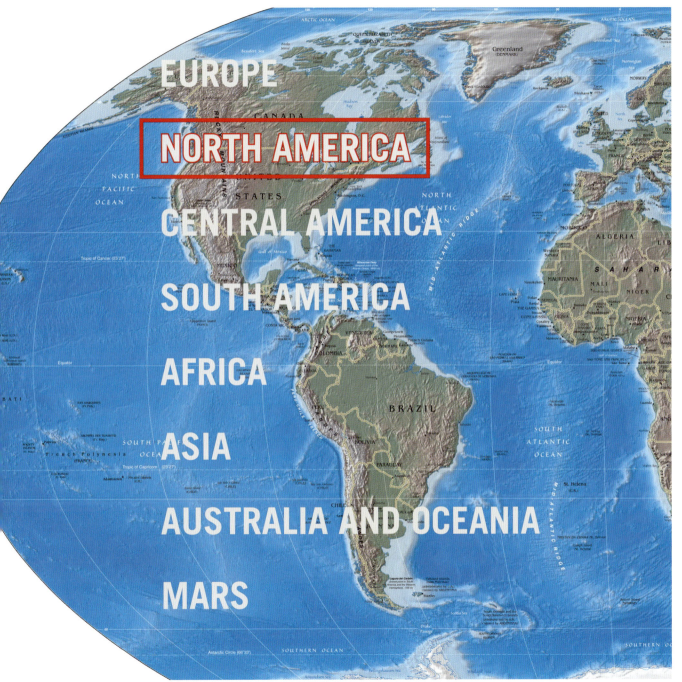

EUROPE

NORTH AMERICA

CENTRAL AMERICA

SOUTH AMERICA

AFRICA

ASIA

AUSTRALIA AND OCEANIA

MARS

Six sections of the Berlin Wall have been displayed outside since 2000 on an undeveloped plot of land west of Truro, Canada. The sections have been somewhat weathered and it is now difficult to make out the graffiti which was once sprayed on these pieces. It is also plain to see that these sections suffered considerable damage at the hands of Wall Peckers. No sign, nor plaque, has been displayed alongside them to explain their history.

Due to was a disagreement between owner, Martin S. Young and town officials and the future of the sections is uncertain. Young loaned the segments to the town in spring 2000 whilst he tried to find a suitable place to display them. The city treasurer granted the project 2,500 Canadian Dollars. After a year, a suitable site and use for the sections of Wall had still not been found and the sections remained where they were. Plans were put forward by town officials to put them on temporary display in the so-called "Diefenbaker Bunker" in nearby Debert. The bunker was built at the start of the sixties during John Diefenbaker's time in office and was one of the many bunkers designed to offer protection from a Soviet nuclear attack. These plans never came to fruition as no permission was granted by Martin Young. In summer 2008, Young said that the sections of Wall would more than likely stay put, although he did say he would be willing to donate one or two sections to a museum or private collector. City officials campaigned for them to be put up at a different location and they found their way to Bible Hill in January 2011. They can now be found on-campus at Novia Scotia Agricultural College.

The pieces already had a story to tell when Young acquired them from an anonymous source. They had been shipped from Germany to Long Beach, California, by "Price Air Freight" in September 1990, where they spent some time in storage. They then made the 7,000 km journey through America and over the border into east Canada where Young claims to have seen them for the first time. He bought them in spring 2000 and they were shipped from Greenfield to Truro. Town officials paid the transportation costs.

BIBLE HILL, NOVA SCOTIA
CANADA

Location:
Outside the Haley Institute, Dalhousie University Agricultural Campus, 62 Cumming Drive, Bible Hill

HALIFAX, NOVA SCOTIA
CANADA

Location:
World Peace Pavilion,
Dartmouth Waterfront

Pieces of the Wall for the World

Peace Pavilion in Halifax

© Nova Scotia – Halifax Regional
Municipality Archives, CR 1257

The World Peace Pavilion in Halifax, East Canada was founded in 1995 by the Foreign Ministers of the USA, Russia, France, Canada, Japan and Italy to mark the 21st G7 summit. The summit, based on political cooperation and peace were unthinkable just six years earlier. The Cold War had entered its final phase when young people met for a conference in Halifax, but it was still very much dominating world politics. Those taking part in the meeting came up with the idea to build a World Peace Pavilion which should serve as a meeting point for all states and nations. They requested that all embassies in Canada take part in the project and a symbolic piece of stone was to be brought from every country.

When the preparations for the G7 summit began a few years later, the plan was put into action. In Dartmouth, building work began on the World Peace Pavilion. A triangular shaped conference centre was built, and the donated pieces of stone from over seventy countries were put out in the surrounding parks.

China donated a piece of the Great Wall of China and Uruguay is represented by a piece of amethyst. Former GDR embassy counsellor in Canada, Günter Cawein, brought four smaller pieces of the Wall (weighing a total of 75 kilos) from Germany, which are now on display in the park. Even a piece of moon rock is on display in the World Peace Pavillion, highlighting the idea that peace and justice are not just concepts that should prevail on Earth.

LUNENBURG, NOVA SCOTIA
CANADA

Location:
Foundry Lunenburg

Fishing and ship building have been the main sources of income for the citizens of Lunenburg since the it was founded. German and Swiss settlers make up a large number of the Founding Fathers. It was not until 1750 that people settled in the surrounding villages on the south coast. Architectural remnants from this time can still be found today in the historic part of town, which is also a listed area. There is also another tangible part of German history in the town: a segment of the Berlin Wall has been standing in front of the local foundry since 2001. The following text was added to explain the significance of the concrete to visitors.

"This is a section of the Berlin Wall. Erected 13. August 1961, thrown down 9. November 1989"

By the time the segment of Wall made it to Lunenburg, it had been on an incredible journey through North America. It was bought by a German entrepreneur and shipped from Hamburg to Long Beach, California, in 1999. From there it was transported across the United States to Fredericton on the east coast of Canada, where it was on public display alongside six other segments. In 2000, Canadian businessman, Martin S. Young, bought six of the segments which are now on display in Truro. The seventh piece should have originally been put on display in Fredericton's Hotel Sheraton, but the hotel was forced to close down and the piece landed in John James Kinley's hands (former Lieutenant Governor of Nova Scotia and Governor General). He had visited the divided city twice in the 1970/80s and these visits had made a lasting impression on him. When he saw the pieces of Wall in Fredericton and later heard it was possible to buy one, Kinley

The Wall in Lunenburg

© Lunenburg Foundry

decided to bring one to Lunenburg – back to the place where German settlers had first settled in Canada. The municipal authorities in Lunenburg were less excited about the prospect of the Wall due to the costs and they were unable to offer any funding to display the Wall on a suitable public site.

When the second biggest city in Canada celebrated its 250th birthday, Berlin donated a bright piece of the Wall to Montréal. It was put on display in the local World Trade Center, where, according to local press it stood "as proof for the return of Berlin to the global community of free states". Simultaneously it should serve as a reminder to the people of the Canadian metropolitan of how "precious and fragile peace really is". Information boards stand on both sides of the Wall in French and English with information about the history of division and the Cold War.

MONTRÉAL, QUEBEC
CANADA

Location:
World Trade Center

The Wall in the World Trade Center Montreal

© Centre de commerce mondial de Montréal

OTTAWA, ONTARIO
CANADA

Location:

Canadian War Museum,
1 Vimy Place

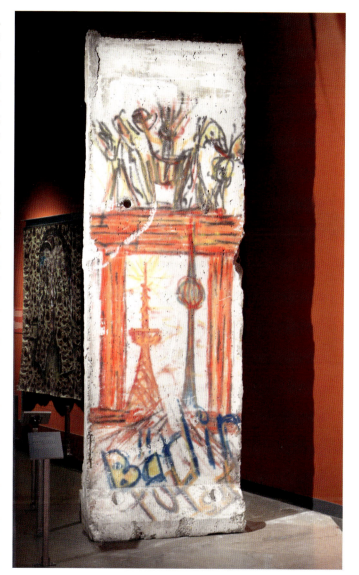

The Wall in

Canadian War Museum, Ottawa

© Canadian War Museum,
CWM 20110041-001,
Photo: Bill Kent

As part of the *Open Skies Conference* in Ottawa (12th-24th February 1990) which aimed to negotiate disarmament efforts, and was attended by all NATO and Warsaw countries, the four victorious powers (USA, Soviet Union, Great Britain and France) concluded talks on the "Final Settlement with Respect to Germany". The treaty, published on 13th February 1990, marked the beginning of the *Two-Plus-Four Agreement* between the Federal Republic and the GDR – they smoothed the path to reunification between the two German states on 3rd October 1990, on an international level.

Former German foreign minister, Hans-Dietrich Genscher, presented Ottawa with a piece of the Wall on 27th September 1991 to commemorate the memorable event. It is located on the historical site in the Ottawa Conference Center, where the victorious powers had met a year before. It still stands on the same site today, inside the entrance, framed by a German and a Canadian flag and is accessible to visitors.

The painting on the piece of Wall (probably designed and painted especially for Ottawa), shows the Brandenburg Gate in front of the TV tower and West Berliner Funkturm. The word "Bärlin" (Bear-lin) is painted along the bottom and there is an English/French information board with details about the historical events that took place on 13th February 1990.

Location:
The Great Passion Play

The Wall memorial in
Eureka Springs
© The Great Passion Play

None other than Emmet Sullivan, a sculptor born in 1895 in Montana (who, amongst other things, was involved with designing the monumental president head sculptures on Mount Rushmore), was able to win over conservative Evangelical clergyman Gerald L. K. Smith for his 'Great Passion Play' in Eureka Springs.

'Christ of the Ozarks', the largest statue of Jesus in North America, was completed in 1966 according to plans by Sullivan. The giant marble statue is almost 20 metres tall, weighs around one million tonnes and stands above the Victorian spa town.

Eureka Springs has been famous for its spas for hundreds of years. Under Smith's direction, the 'Christ of the Ozarks' became the focal point for an open-air event at which thousands of tourists watched a reenactment of Jesus' story of suffering. The location was filled with reconstructions of locations along the way of the cross. Museums, churches, chapels and countless means of entertainment were set up.

In 1992, as part of an exhibition, a number of pieces of the Berlin Wall (pieces from the so called 'hinterland-mauer') were put together at the foot of the statue as a memorial. The sections have been neatly framed with ornamental stones and completely painted over so that it is hardly recognisable as a piece of the Berlin Wall.

It was a gift from the Elna M. Smith Foundation, wife of deceased Gerald L. K. Smith, has stood since then as a tribute "to the souls of all people, who have risked their lives for the belief in and practicing of Christianity". In accordance with this, a bible quote has been added to the Wall by 'an East Berlin artist' "Und geht es auch durchs dunkle Tal, ich habe keine Angst. Psalm 23" (When life goes through dark valleys, I will not be afraid). Whether or not this was already on the Wall when it was in Berlin is not clear.

CULVER CITY, CALIFORNIA
USA

Location:

The Wende Museum,
5741 Buckingham
Parkway, Suite E

The Wall in front of the
Wende Museum, Culver City
© The Wende Museum, Culver City, California

© The Wende Museum, Culver City, California

The 'Facing the Wall' exhibition was opened on 29th September 2007 in Culver City, southwest of Los Angeles in Santa Monica Bay. The unique project was initiated by Justinian Jampol, founder and manager of 'The Wende Museum'. He aims to give young Americans an understanding of the Cold War and division of Germany. His idea to present the history of the GDR in the US stems back to his time spent in Germany as a student. To date, more than 100,000 exhibition objects have been collected which document everyday life and politics in the former East Block. The collection includes a large collection of posters and newspapers, a GDR bugging system, memoirs from both the GDR state and party leader Erich Honecker (written during his incarceration from July 1992-January 1993 in Berlin Moabit), as well as numerous exhibits documenting the inner German border.

'The Wende Museum' was opened in summer 2002.

In 2006 Jampol was able to get hold of an original section of the Berlin Wall. He convinced well-known Wall artist, Thierry Noir to paint the segment with his famous face designs. Noir had already painted a similar image together with Christophe Bouchet on the Wall at Postdamer Platz in 1998. The brightly painted piece of Wall has since stood at the entrance to the museum. To mark the opening of the 'Facing the Wall' exhibition, Jampol had a further 15 reconstructed pieces of the Wall made which were then painted by students from the local art college, the Los Angeles Girl Scouts and young members of a Christian and a Jewish community. The young artists were asked not only to focus on the Cold War in their work, but to also include modern problems. The results showed that the Cold War was, in their eyes, on a level with the war in Iraq and migration/environmental issues.

The Loyola Marymount University (LMU) in Los Angeles is the largest Catholic university on the west coast of the United States and has been in possession of a segment of the Berlin Wall since 1997. Dirk Verheyen, political scientist from the Netherlands and former university lecturer got in touch with the reigning mayor of Berlin in summer 1996 whilst on a research trip. Eberhard Diepgen supported the project which aimed to send a piece of the Wall to the twin city of Los Angeles. Verheyan selected a piece of the Wall from the Berlin senate stock which had been painted by renowned Wall artist Thierry Noir in 1987. Originally situated on Waldemarstraße in Berlin Kreuzberg, it belonged to the 360 segments of Wall assigned for resale by the GDR government.

Furthermore, the piece of concrete – already drenched in symbolism – had another story to tell. The segment can be seen in Wim Wenders' film 'Der Himmel über Berlin' (Wings of Desire) which had been filmed in the divided city.

Back in the USA, preparations were underway at the university to display the segment. The heavy load was shipped from Germany to Long Beach, California, and then loaded onto a lorry which brought it to the campus. The unloading was overseen by LMU vice president, David Trump and sponsors, Guy Fox and Mr. Moses Cordova. A platform was made and a canopy erected to protect it from rain and sunlight.

The ceremonial unveiling took place on 8th May 1997. Alongside representatives from LMU, consulate general Hans Alard von Rohr made a speech on behalf of the reigning mayor of Berlin. Erber recalled the twinning between Los Angeles and Berlin which had taken place thirty years earlier "to the chimes of the Freedom Bell". He went on to say that the "disgrace of Communism" had now become symbol of the successful fight for freedom.

Richard Riordan, president at the university shared a similar sentiment: "The Berlin Wall was a symbol of everything that was wrong in the world. A piece of the Berlin Wall in open surroundings is a symbol of what is right in the world".

LOS ANGELES, CALIFORNIA
USA

Location:
Loyola Marymount University, 1 LMU Drive

The Wall at
Loyola Marymount University,
Los Angeles
© Dirk Verheyen

MOUNTAIN VIEW, CALIFORNIA
USA

Location:
Mountain View Public
Library, Franklin Street

The Berlin Wall in front of the
library in Mountain View
© Norbert von der Groeben,
Daily News

In 1931 Frank Golzen, having just turned 15 years of age, boarded a ship in Frankfurt/Main which brought him to America. He wanted to make his dream of a better life a reality. His home, back then economically and politically in ruins, could not offer him this chance. Frank Golzen went to California where, for the next few decades, his work as a building contractor brought him considerable prosperity.

He later began building office blocks along the highways. One of the first to be completed was on the picturesque San Francisco Bay. Countless single/two-storey office blocks today stand between expansive parking lots between Japanese-style gardens. Similar business parks can also be found on the outskirts of California. In May 1991, Golzen had two segments of the Berlin Wall erected on one of the parking lots. In gratitude for the realisation of his American dream of success and prosperity, he devoted the concrete segment to 'American Resolve', which eventually had brought about the Fall of the Wall:

"The period after the Second World War divided western Democratic and eastern Communist ideologies by what was known as the Iron Curtain, which stretched from the Baltic Sea to the Black Sea. Within East Germany, part of the Communist sphere of influence, West Berlin was an island of freedom surrounded by a sea of oppression. In August, 1961, the East German government built a wall dividing the city to prevent the flight of its citizens from East to West Berlin. For 28 years the Berlin Wall was the Rubicon for East and West until 'Glasnost' became the new thinking in the Communist world. Between November, 9 and 12, 1989,

the Wall was breached, not with bombs and bullets, but from within by the sound of freedom and the vision of a better life that had drifted over the Wall.

The world must not forget that it was America's resolve and its political and economic ideals that made this bloodless revolution and incredibly significant historical event possible."

For a great number of people in the East, the sound of freedom was music. Elvis Presley, King of Rock'n'Roll,

The Berlin Wall in front of the library in Mountain View
© Norbert von der Groeben, Daily News

adorns one of the segments of the Wall and opposite, the words 'We love you', framed in a black, red and golden heart.

After Golzen's death, the family offered both segments of the Berlin Wall to the city. In March 2013 the city of Mountain View decided upon a new location for the segments. A budget of 50,000 Dollars made it possible to move and erect the pieces in front of the library in Mountain View. This also took into account and covered costs for later maintenance. Don Bahl was one of the residents of Mountain View who had wished for a more prominent place for the Berlin Wall as a symbol of overcoming the Cold War: "Proudly put these pieces of the Berlin Wall in a place of prominence, not tucked away in some obscure location, but a location where people will ask, 'What do these pieces of concrete mean?'" The segments were finally unveiled on at their new location in November 2013.

ORANGE, CALIFORNIA
USA

Location:
Chapman University,
1 University Drive

The Wall at Chapman
University, Orange
© Chapman University

James L. Doti, president and professor in science at Chapman University in Orange, California, was thrilled on his visit to the Nixon Presidential Library in Yorba. There he saw a piece of the Wall and wanted to get a section for his university, too. He got in touch with the Berlin senate and requested a section of the Wall. After two years of negotiations and a search for a sponsor who would pay the transport costs, the senate agreed. A section of Wall was taken from the reserves and shipped via Hamburg to Long Beach, California, in September 1998. Both sides of the Wall had been decorated with graffiti. British band U 2 had been immortalised on the former eastern side with the words 'U 2 Slays', on the other side the words 'Fuck you' had been graffitied. Despite this slogan being somewhat underpinning of the state, the section of Wall was unveiled at a public ceremony at which German vice consul, Anne Wohlleben was also present. Today, it stands in the centre of an oval water feature. One of Abraham Lincoln's famous quotes can be read on the outside, "A house divided against itself shall not stand". Originally coined during the American Civil War, the quote was used in this context to highlight the division between East and West. A replica of the chair found at the Lincoln Memorial in Washington is a further reference to Lincoln. The construction as a whole was given the name 'Liberty Plaza'. Numerous plaques have been put up around it with quotes relating to democracy and freedom by George Washington, Patrick Henry, Woodrow Wilson and others.

Location:
Defense Language School,
Korean Department,
Building 610

Wall memorial in front of Defense Language Institute Foreign Language Center
© Sal Marullo, Presidio of Monterey

When the military conflict between Japan and the USA was becoming more and more serious in autumn 1941, the American army prepared itself for war. As part of these preparations a language school was set up in Presidio of Monterey where soldiers were to learn Japanese. Especially the Nisei (American citizens with Japanese roots) were prepared for deployment. Almost two weeks later, the Japanese air force attacked the naval base at Pearl Harbour, and the USA were brought into the Second World War.

The Military Intelligence Service Language School (MISLS) was moved in land as a consequence. More than 6,000 were trained at the school by the time the Second World War came to an end in 1945.

When in 1945, during the fight against Hitler's Germany, the former consolidarity between the allies was transformed into a face off between the western allies and the Soviet Union, the language school was given new tasks.

Prospective military personal and secret agents were now taught Korean, Russian, Chinese and Arabic in order to prepare them for their duties on the Cold War stage.

The school was later renamed the Defence Language Institute (DLI) and played a significant role during the Vietnam War. 20,000 soldiers attended classes, many of whom did not survive their deployment. The DLI continued its work even after the collapse of the Iron Curtain. Today they teach approximately 4,000 candidates, who are taught in more than 30 languages.

A Wall monument was unveiled on 3rd November outside the Korean Centre to commemorate the services of those who had served during the Cold War. The three segments were funded by Walter Scureo, a Berliner who had resettled in America. They stand today in a semi-circle in the centre of a large plaza. The

section in the centre is decorated in bright graffiti, whilst the two surrounding sections delivered to Presidio of Monterey are still plain grey. They were discovered by Skip Johnson, an employee at DLI, during a visit to Scureis' resident city of Phoenix (Arizona). Scurei was willing to donate the three segments to the DLI, which he had also come across by chance. In 1990 he rented a storage warehouse and found to his surprise numerous sections of the Wall inside. The owner of the warehouse was in arrears and had to hand it over. It seemed there had been no money left for him to pay for the transportation of the segments.

German magazine 'Stern' reported in 1990 that the segments of Wall belonged to Irvin Dyer. The Texan haulage contractor had made his way to East Berlin in 1990 hoping to set up a business. Here he bought a number of large and small segments of the Wall for an unknown price and had them brought back to Phoenix. The plan had been to resell the segments at a large profit. However, it seems he could not ged rid of his stock. The three largest segments, which Dyer had seen photographs of, finally landed in a storage warehouse. It was here, ten years later, that Scurei had them moved and taken them to his home where they were then seen by Skip Johnson. His suggestion to have them put on display was met with approval by his superiors. However, the attacks on the 11th September 2001 prevented the project from being realised. It was only four years later that the unveiling could finally take place.

Peter Robinson, former speech writer for ex-president Ronald Reagan made the ceremonial speech. He had accompanied Reagan when he visited Berlin in 1987.

Just as Churchill had seemingly predicted the building of the Berlin Wall during his speech about the 'Iron Curtain' that had been drawn across Europe, Reagan's famous "Mr. Gorbachev, tear down this Wall" was also prophetic of the Fall of the Berlin Wall.

Robinson claimed the wall today was "no longer a monument of evil, but for the American vocation".

Further speeches were made by the chancellor of the DLI, Donald Fischer, who was stationed in West Germany as a young soldier. Christian Seebolde took part in the ceremony representing the German consulate, where he told the gathered veterans and students of his experiences in the Prague Embassy in 1989.

„General Secretary Gorbachev, if you seek peace, if you seek prosperity for the Soviet Union and eastern Europe, if you seek liberalization: Come here to this gate! Mr. Gorbachev, open this gate! Mr. Gorbachev, tear down this wall!"

Ronald Reagan at the Brandenburg Gate 12th June 1987

Located atop the Santa Ynes Mountain range on the pacific coast is Ranch de Cielo, or 'Heaven's Ranch', bought by former American President Ronald Reagan for him and his wife in 1974. The property was sold in 1998 to the 'Young Americans Association', a conservative group who set up an educational centre and preserve it today along with Republican values and Reagan's memory.

The 'Reagan Ranch Centre' in downtown Santa Barbara is at the centre of the group's work. There is an exhibition about Reagan's life and work. Curator, Marilyn M. Fischer, wanted a segment of the Berlin Wall to display alongside original furniture, cars and paperwork. She appealed to the senate of the Allied Museum in Berlin, which was happy to support her. She selected a segment of the Wall during a visit to Berlin in summer 2002. The segment had taken a beating by Wall-Peckers, but still had some of its original graffiti on it. It was this imperfection that made Fischer choose this particular segment as "it reflected the eventful history of the Wall".

The 10,000 US Dollars needed to transport the segment were donated by the 'Young American Association'. It left Berlin in December 2002 and arrived in the harbour at Long Beach on the Californian coast on 6th January 2003. From there it was taken by lorry to Reagan Ranch. Before it reached its final resting place, it was stored in an old barn alongside the harvest from the previous year, and a number of tools used

to cultivate the ranch. A few months later, when the basic structure for the new Reagan Ranch Center was almost complete, the 2.6 tonne section was lifted to its new location by crane. It stands today in the atrium in front of a flight of stairs, along which the words "Mr. Gorbachev, tear down this wall" are painted.

Installing the Wall at the
Reagan Ranch Center

© Young America's Foundation and
The Reagan Ranch

Location:
Ronald Reagan
Presidential Library
and Museum,
1 Presidential Drive

The Wall in front of the Ronald
Reagan Presidential Library,
Simi Valley

© John Martorano /
Ronald Reagan Presidential Library

The Wall segment with the most impressive view probably has to be the segment located outside the Ronald Reagan Presidential Library. Standing on a mountain above the Californian city of Simi Valley, it has spectacular views over Californian coast and the Pacific Ocean. The impressive building was still under construction when Reagan accepted the piece of Wall on 12th April 1990. At a cost of over 55 million Dollars a museum and library, dedicated to the life and work of Ronald Reagen were built. Five US presidents were in attendance for the unveiling on 4th November 1990: Richard Nixon, Gerald Ford, Jimmy Carter, George Bush sen. and Ronald Reagan himself opened the memorial. The speech in which Reagan called for state and party leader, Mikhail Gorbachev to tear down the Wall has become one of the most famous in history. For this reason the Wall should be displayed prominently. Along with a exact reconstruction of the Oval Office, it is the most visited attraction at the Reagan library. The segment which had been decorated on the western side with a butterfly was bought by the Berlin Wall Commemorative Group in New Jersey.

In contrast to much of the graffiti on the Wall, the painting on Reagan's segment was commissioned. Young spray paint artist, Denis Kaun, was employed in spring 1990 by the West Berlin Wall marketing company, 'LeLé Berlin' to decorate the plain piece of Wall. It has not been disclosed how much the Reagan Library paid. The fact that one side of the segment remains grey has a political meaning for the museum staff. The grey side faced into the red communist state, an area the butterfly of freedom could not reach.

A layer of protective paint was added in 1999 to protect the segment from wind and sunlight, it was also placed on a plinth to help prevent it soaking up damp from the ground. This famous piece of the Wall should be preserved as a memorial for future generations.

STANFORD, CALIFORNIA
USA

Location:
Hoover Tower, 434
Galvez Mall, Stanford
University

Brought to life in 1919 by the then still to become president, Herbert Hoover, the Hoover Institution on the Stanford University Campus is one of the largest think tanks in the USA to deal with 20th century history.

It was originally set up to serve as an archive for documents from the First World War, but today it is home to one of the largest collections of material regarding political, social and economic change in the world. A few small pieces of the Berlin Wall have made it into the German history section.

A larger section of the Wall is also on display in the Hoover Institution's exhibition hall. It was bought by the Berlin Wall Commemorative Group, who had been commissioned by the GDR government to take over the sale of the Wall in the USA.

YORBA LINDA, CALIFORNIA
USA

Location:
Richard Nixon
Presidential Library
and Museum,
18001 Yorba Linda
Boulevard

Information board about German
division in the Richard Nixon
Presidential Library

© Richard Nixon Presidential
Library and Museum, NARA/Eric Figge

„We have seen here a wall. A wall can divide a city, but a wall can never divide a people."

Richard Nixon during his visit to West Berlin on 27th February 1969

A piece of the Berlin Wall can be found in the Richard Nixon Presidential Library in Moscow, standing amongst brightly painted onion towers, which are a symbol of the Moscow Kremlin. Both pieces commemorate the change in US foreign policy during Nixon's time in office.

He was working towards a policy of détente between the East Blocks and was the first US president to tour the area in 1972 as well as the Soviet Union and the People's Republic of China. His change in foreign policy was also of significance for the divided Germany. It offered support to Willy Brandt's efforts to converge the two German states. Despite his successes in foreign policy, Nixon's time in office was overshadowed by the Vietnam War and ended in domestic political fiasco in 1974, with the Watergate Scandal.

The private and political lives of Nixon, who came from a humble background, have been portrayed in his presidential library in Californian Yorba since 1990.

The small wooden house, built by Nixon's father, is the focal point of the memorial which today consists of a museum, library and conference rooms. A piece of the Wall, donated by owner and founder of the Californian fast food chain 'Carl's Jr.', was added to the exhibition in 1992.

Buying the piece of Wall from the 'Berlin Wall Commemorative' was made possible by a generous donation from Carl Karchers. The segment once stood on Leuschnerdamm in Kreuzberg and was painted with

The Wall in the Richard Nixon
Presidential Library

© Richard Nixon Presidential
Library and Museum, NARA/Eric Figge

a design by Jürgen Große (alias 'Indiano'). Unfortunately, not much of this design is left to see after it was mysteriously painted over. Luckily, you can still see a friendly waving bear in the bottom right-hand corner.

The largest Hard Rock Cafe in the world is located in the heart of Florida's Universal Film Studios. Built as a Roman Coliseum of rock and roll this outlet, by its own admission, is home to the company's biggest collection of Rock 'n' Roll memorabilia. The items include a suit worn by Paul McCartney in the film 'A Hard Days Night', a Mustang, once belonging to Jimi Hendrix, a tracksuit worn by Elvis during his military service in Korea and countless mementos from 50 years of music history.

A memento of another kind stands under the palm trees outside the Hard Rock Cafe; a piece of the Berlin Wall stands here as a reminder of the Cold War and the victory of the free world over Communism. There is, however, a musical connection to be made. On top of the section there is a fist with a hammer on an area of red ground. This emblem was used by British rock bank, Pink Floyd for their album 'The Wall'. At the same time the emblem was also seen in Berlin in the summer of 1990. However, it remains unknown how and when the piece of Wall made its way to Florida.

ORLANDO, FLORIDA
USA

Location:
Hard Rock Cafe Orlando,
6050 Universal Boulevard

SAINT PETERSBURG, FLORIDA
USA

Location:

Saint Petersburg
Clay Company,
420 22nd Street South

Wall memorial in
Saint Petersburg
© Courtesy of
www.outdoorartsfoundation.com

Wall art by the
Outdoor Arts Foundation
© Courtesy of
www.outdoorartsfoundation.com

The Outdoor Art Foundation planned to celebrate 20 years since the Fall of the Wall by building 100 Wall memorials. They were to be built across North America, which is already home to the largest collection of Wall segments outside Germany. Any town which was able to raise 50-100 thousand Dollars should have been able take part and claim a piece of the Wall as their own. In July 2007, around 350 sections of the so-called 'hinterland' Wall were delivered to Tampa bay for the realisation of these plans. The Outdoor Art Foundation bought a further 115 pieces of the Wall which had been painted by Russian artists Tamara Dubinowskaja, Andrej Aksenow and Wladimir Smatschin. The works of art had been sold to American collector, Cal Worthington and were considered missing. They are now on sale in Florida.

These plans, however, were never realised. The foundation concentrated instead on their exhibition and the sale of the sections of Wall painted by the Russian artists. A large proportion of the exhibition is currently on tour and can be seen all around North America.

Saint Petersburg, which was named after a Russian railway entrepreneur at the end of the 19th century, was the first community to buy themselves a section of the Wall in Florida. It was put up in the grounds of St. Petersburg Clay Company and can still be found there today.

Two pieces of the Wall have found a new home inside the grounds of the largest training centre for US Army Signal Corps in Fort Gordon. The two pieces have been placed side by side to create a memorial. One piece with the letters 'demo', the second with the letters 'cracy' (together: Democracy).

An old sign, once at display at the border, stands between the two pieces and warns (in German) that you are about to leave the American sector. Another section of the Wall is on display in the Signal Army Museum behind glass. How and when the pieces of Wall made their way to Fort Gordon is not known. They were supposedly brought back to Fort Gordon from Berlin by American troops in the early 1990s, along with other mementos. The majority of the items brought back were given to the National Museum of the United States Army Museum in Fort Bevoir, Virginia. The Museum is currently being upgraded.

FORT GORDON, GEORGIA
USA

Location:
Signal Army Museum

HONOLULU, HAWAII
USA

Location:
Hawaii Community College

Honolulu University

© Kevin W. Smith
kevinwsmithphotographie.com

Shortly after the Fall of the Wall students and professors at the Hawaii Community College in Honolulu wanted to acknowledge the historical event with a memorial on the island. The college directors got in touch with the Berlin senate who sent a piece of the Wall which made its journey oversees in October 1991. The German relief association Honolulu organised the transportation of the segment which arrived safely in late 1991. By this time the college had already hired the American Institute of Architects Honolulu to design the memorial. In order to give the people of Hawaii an impression of the sheer scale of the border fortification, the segment was put up alongside two artificial pieces of Wall. The bright graffiti was placed under glass to protect it from the weather. The memorial was officially opened after two months of construction work on 10th February 1992.

The following text was put on an information board alongside the memorial:

The Wall in Honolulu/Hawaii

© Kevin W. Smith
kevinwsmithphotographie.com

„BERLIN WALL FREEDOM MONUMENT/ DEDICATED FEBRUARY 10, 1992/ To freedom, peace and understanding/ among all people of the world./ HONOLULU COMMUNITY COLLEGE WISHES TO THANK/ THE FOLLOWING FOR THEIR CONTRIBUTIONS:/ THE STUDENTS OF HONULULU COMMUNITY COLLEGE/ THE GERMAN SENATE; FEDERAL REPUBLIC OF GERMANY/ THE GERMAN BENEVOLENT SOCIETY OF HONOLULU/ FLETCHER PACIFIC CONSTRUCTION COMPANY, LTD./ ARCHITECTS HAWAII, LTD."

The Wall in Honolulu/Hawaii

HOPE, IDAHO
USA

Location:
David Thompson Road

The Wall in Hope/Idaho
© Klaus Groenke

One hundred and eighty years before the Wall fell in Berlin, the first white settlement was founded in what is now Idaho in 1809. Picturesque and situated on the edge of Lake Pend Oreille, Hope became a popular destination for artists and art lovers from allover the world in the mid 20th century.

Ed Kienholz, one of the most prominent American object and concept artist of modern times, chose this place as his summer residence. His controversial and widely discussed works quickly found an audience in the USA. Berlin became Kienholz's second home in 1973, when he took part in an exchange programme. West Berlin real estate agent and owner of TrigonInvest, Klaus Groenke was a fan of Kienholz's work and supported the artist who was still relatively unknown in Europe. Groenke also acquired a large summer residence in Hope.

In 1991 Groenke had an original piece of the Berlin Wall erected between David Thompson Road and Kienholz Drive. The concrete structure was a present from his staff. The graffiti has been partly covered with acrylic glass to protect it from rain and snow. One of the images is of Donald Duck with a chef's hat and red flag. Another artist painted a man wearing jeans and a green jacket climbing over the Wall.

On the morning of 22nd January 2008 around 160 people gathered in ice-cold weather at the metro station on Lincoln Square, Western Avenue, Chicago. They had come to see the unveiling of a piece of the Berlin Wall. Today, countless passengers flock past it on their way to the station. The 'Berlin Wall Exhibit' next to the piece of Wall gives a brief history of the German division.

Lincoln Square and the surrounding streets have always been shaped by people of German descent who have settled here since the middle of the 19th century.

It was the German consulate's idea to erect a piece of the Wall. Due to the local connection with Germany, numerous German societies along with Gene Schulter, alderman of Chicago's 47th ward, were very open to the suggestion. The Berlin senate received the application in 2004 and supported the project. Lufthansa flew a piece of the Wall over, which had previously stood on the grounds of the Sony Center at Potsdamer Platz. However, it would take a further two years until a suitable site was found to display it. The McCormick Freedom Museum (founded by owner and publisher of the 'Chicago Tribune'), wanted to have the piece of Wall for their exhibition. Unfortunately, the building was not suitable to support the weight of the 2.6 tonnes of concrete and the plans were subsequently scrapped.

Gene Schulter had already envisaged Lincoln Square as the new location. Ron Hubermannn, president of the mass transit corporation, CTA was also taken by the idea. A place was to be found in West Avenue station. Hubermann hoped that that it would attract more people to use the metro line which was in financial trouble and Schulter was convinced that the piece of Wall would attract more tourists to his area and made 240,000 US Dollars available for the realisation of the project. German consulate general, Wolfgang Drautz, represented governing mayor of Berlin, Klaus Wowereit at the unveiling. Schulter thanked Germany and Berlin for the section of Wall, which stands for "freedom after repression".

J.D. Bindenagel was Deputy Chief of Mission at the US Embassy in East Berlin and had experienced first hand the Fall of the Wall on 9th November 1989. He recalled the dramatic scenes during a speech made at the unveiling. Representatives from the former protecting powers of France and Great Britain were also present at the ceremony, as well as diplomats from Belgium, the Czech Republic and Poland.

Location:
Western Avenue Station, Lincoln Square

The Wall in Chicago

© Generalkonsulat der Bundesrepublik Deutschland in Chicago

The Wall in Chicago

© German Consulate General Chicago

EUREKA, ILLINOIS
USA

Location:
Ronald Reagan Peace Garden at Eureka College, 300 College Avenue

Former US President, Ronald Reagan made the so-called "Eureka Speech" at Eureka College in Illinois on 9th May 1982. In his speech he called for control and prevention of the use of nuclear weapons by the US and the Soviet Union. This speech is seen by many as the beginning of the end of the Cold War. Furthermore, the fact that Reagan had also studied at the college was all the more reason to set up the Ronald Reagan Peace Garden at the college. The garden was a present to the college from Anne and David Vaughan. The Peace Garden was opened in 2000, 18 years to the day since Reagan had made his "Eureka Speech". Busts of Ronald Reagan and a piece of the Berlin Wall make up the focal points of the garden.

The piece of Berlin Wall, 1.5 metre-high and 1.2 metre-wide, was a present from the Federal Republic of Germany and arrived just on time for the opening of the Peace Garden. It symbolises overcoming the Iron Curtain between East and West – something Ronald Reagan had worked hard to achieve during the Cold War.

Section of Wall in the Ronald Reagan Peace Garden
© Eureka College, Illinois

When the USA joined the First World War in 1917 and declared war on Germany, Herbert Hoover (who would later become president) organised the food supply for the allies on the Eastern Front. Hoover managed the American Food Administration after the end of the First World War, which also supplied supplied those suffering from hunger in Germany until the start of the 1920s. He was elected 31st president of the USA in 1929 at the height of the Great Depression. Hoover stepped back from public life after his term in office, but maintained his connections to international economic crisis. The American government sent Hoover to Germany in 1946 to send back reports on the supply situation. Responding to the desperate situation in post-war Germany, Hoover set up an aid programme as he had done twenty years previously.

So called 'Hooverspeisung' or Hoover meals were introduced to schools in the western occupation zone in April 1947. The meals saved hundreds of thousands of young people from malnutrition and starvation. Germany was by now divided and the roll between the two nations, once enemies at war had changed. At a speech made in Bonn, Hoover said

"The only hope for our safety is the building up of arms and of a united front among free nations which will deter Communist aggression against us... The German people have before now been the bastions of western civilization... My prayer is that Germany may be given the unity and full freedom which will restore her to that mission in the world."

These hopes were, however, not fulfilled in Hoover's lifetime. He died in 1964 and was buried in West Branch, eastern Iowa, where the Presidential Library is today located and named after him.

The Herbert Hoover library was radically renovated after the Fall of the Wall in 1989. Further presidential libraries, such as John F. Kennedy, Gerald Ford, Ronald Reagan and Richard Nixon also secured pieces of the Wall as 'prize trophies' of the Cold War. Richard Norton Smith, former director of the Hoover Library endeavoured to get a piece of the Wall in recognition of Hoover's services to Germany. Since there was no adequate space for an entire section of the Wall, the 'Berlin Wall Commemorative Group' (who had originally taken over the job of selling the Wall in the USA on behalf of the GDR) bought a small section of the interior Wall.

It was delivered to the library on 2nd April 1992. It was decorated by an unknown artist and depicts a red and green landscape in front of white clouds. It can be found today in a metal frame at the end of an exhibition on Hoover's life.

Alongside it are the following words:

„Herbert Hoover did not live to see the Berlin Wall crumble but he never doubted the ultimate triumph of freedom."

WEST BRANCH, IOWA
USA

Location:
Herbert Hoover
Presidential Library
and Museum,
210 Parkside Drive

THE
BERLIN
WALL

The Wall in the Herbert Hoover
Presidential Library,
West Branch
© Herbert Hoover Presidential
Library

Location:
Fort Leavenworth,
Grove of Regiments

Wall memorial in
Fort Leavenworth

© Leavenworth
KS Convention & Visitors Bureau

For many people in the US the name Fort Leavenworth has unpleasant connotations. The notorious military prison of the same name was here until 2002, where members of the US army, who had been sentenced to death, were executed.

Although the complex, in use since 1974, is now closed, there is still a small prison in which those sentenced to death await their punishment. The United States Penitentiary, Leavenworth, built by prisoners can be described as having only a slightly better reputation.

Fort Leavenworth is also home to numerous military units, the National Simulation Center and a graduation school for officers. The graduates have an important role in the military which must have been a contributing factor leading to a section of the Berlin Wall finding a new home here.

The three pieces of the interior Wall were donated by president Ronald Reagan, who had received them from Raymond E. Haddock, commander of the US armed forces in West Berlin. They have stood on the Grove of Regiments since 1990. The position in which they stand is symbolic: one slants, falling towards the ground and represents the Fall of the Wall, next to it, another section standing upright represents democracy's victory. The symbolic images painted on them was probably added later – the Statue of Liberty is painted on the upright piece, and Reagan's famous "tear down this wall" quote. The piece laid on the ground next to it is decorated with the word 'freedom'.

WICHITA, KANSAS
USA

Location:
Museum of
World Treasures,
835 E 1st. Street,
Altstadt von Wichita

BerlinBrats' section of Wall
in the Museum of World
Treasures, Wichita

© American Overseas Schools
Historical Society Archives

NORTH AMERICA – USA

In summer 2005, members of the BerlinBrats Alumni Association got hold of a segment of the Berlin Wall for 5,000 US Dollars via internet auction site e bay. The former pupils from the West Berlin American High school wanted to secure a piece of their own, as well as of world history. The children of thousands of American soldiers attended the school in Berlin Zehlendorf, which was open until the withdrawal of the US troops in 1994.

Jeri Glass, who graduated in Berlin in 1972, was made aware of the online offer by the president of the former American High school Alumni Association Stuttgart, Patricia Hein.

After short consultation with other members, it was decided to buy the segment and then donate it to the American Overseas Schools Historical Society (AOSHS) in Wichita, Kansas. The money to buy it was quickly found, but the BerlinBratz wanted to make sure that they were getting an authentic piece of the Wall. They made contact with the seller and then went personally to take a look at the segment. Tom, the owner, took the opportunity to tell the story of how he came to have a piece of the Wall.

In the 1990s he ran a fitness club in Washington D.C. which was used by businessmen from allover the world. He got into conversation with a Russian businessman who was expecting a cargo of four Wall segments.

Two of the valuable segments were lost during transport, the third was kept by the unnamed businessman, and he gave the forth section to Tom. He had been storing it ever since in Rockville, Maryland, as the transport costs to Washington were too expensive.

Tom moved to the Pacific coast after retirement and chose to sell the segment to make some money.

The BerlinBratz wanted to be sure of its authenticity and sent photographs of the segment to Germany to be checked. The Berlin Wall Memorial on Bernauer Straße, the Berlin Wall Museum on Checkpoint Charlie and the Allied Museum all gave positive feedback and the sale was made.

The 2.6 tonnes of concrete were loaded in July 2005 and arrived in Wichita on 1st August. Since the AOSHS did not have its own museum, the segment was first displayed in the Museum of World Treasures. The official unveiling took place on 12th August 2005 and was attended by representatives from Berlin-Bratz, the AOSHS, the museum and the city administration. Further exhibits around the Wall include a border soldier dummy (donated by Bonner American High school) and a swastika flag which was secured by US troops when they liberated Nuremberg in April 1945 (donated by Nuremberg American High School).

FORT KNOX, KENTUCKY
USA

Location:

General George Patton Museum, 4554 Fayette Avenue

The Wall in General George Patton Museum, Fort Knox

© General George Patton Museum, Fort Knox

More than 4,500 tonnes of gold reserves are stored at Fort Knox – famous for being home to the most secure safe in the world. The entire site is secure guarded and off-limits to the public. Since 1949 a small area at the southern end of the site has been home to the General George Patton Museum. The exhibition, which depicts life in the army, is one of the largest army exhibitions in the United States. Patton is widely known in Germany as the commander of the 3rd US army, which played an important role in the liberation of Southern Germany in 1945. He later became military governor of Bayern before his death in Heidelberg on 21st November 1945.

Shortly after the Fall of the Wall, three pieces of the Wall were offered to the US Army Armor School at Fort Knox by major general Raymond D. Haddock (former commander to US forces in Berlin). The pieces were then to be put on display in the Patton Museum. The general justified transporting the heavy sections of Wall by saying that "this monument would serve as an eternal warning" and as a reminder of the fact that "ideas, based on human values are stronger than walls".

Transporting the pieces was not an easy task. The foot of the L-shaped pieces of Wall were taken off in Berlin and the pieces put on a new stand in order to make the transportation easier. To make up for the loss of the foot, the US army sent a round section from the top of the Wall which had originally been designed to prevent people climbing over the top. The sections arrived on 21st February 1991.

They were put on display within a week and can still be seen in the exhibition 'From the Berlin Wall to Operation Free Iraq'.

Since then, they have stood as a symbol of the end of the Cold War. Also in the exhibition is a statue of Iraqi dictator, Saddam Hussein. The statue was pulled down after US troops entered in 2001. There is graffiti on the segments of Wall, presumably painted on after it fell. The Wall, with the words 'freedom' and 'democracy' symbolise what the US stands for. Under the graffiti is the famous quote (cited incorrectly) from Ronald Reagan's speech in front of the Brandenburg Gate in 1987, "Tear the Wall down".

Location:
„DiMillo's On the Water"
Restaurant,
Long Wharf 25

Section of Wall in front of
"DiMillo's On the Water"
Restaurant
© Steve DiMillo

D iMillo's On the Water" Restaurant 25 claims to not only be the home of the Berlin Wall, but also the best lobster on the East coast. In fact, three sections of the Berlin Wall are actually on display at the entrance. The impressive, albeit faded, graffiti was added after this piece of the Wall was taken down.

The first shows the US and Soviet flags inside a wreath. Above the flags are the words 'time for peace', as well as the Russian word 'Мир' (peace). The second, in the colours of the German flag, reads 'party is over' and the communist hammer and sickle is in flames. Old signs which once warned people not to enter the area around the Wall can be found screwed on the back of the segments.

Current owner, Steve DiMillo knows little about the history of the pieces. His father, Tony DiMillo opened the restaurant at the beginning of the 1950s. His skill as a businessman meant he owned many areas around the harbour by the time he died in 1999. In 1996 Tony DiMillo was offered three segments of the Wall – the identity of the individual who made the offer and where the segments came from are still unknown. Shortly after this, the segments were brought to the harbour in Freeport where they had been in storage to the restaurant at a cost of 300 Dollars. According to Steve DiMillo, the unknown gentleman who

Original border signs on Wall
segments in Portland
© Steve DiMillo

supplied the segments got in touch a short while later to say he had to visit his son in Florida – and was never heard from again. The segments are well received by guests and DiMillo says he plans for a local artist to restore the graffiti to its former glory.

Bill Clinton's missing piece
of Wall

© Oliver Wia / Patrice Lux

American President Bill Clinton also nearly acquired a segment of the Wall. The idea stemmed from the Berlin-based agent Patrice Lux, who liaised with graffiti artists and the West Berlin company 'LeLé Berlin' – given the task of marketing the Wall – as early as 1990. The graffiti artists were commissioned to brighten up the grey concrete with their artwork. The most famous Wall art can be found right outside the Ronald Reagan Presidential Library in Simi Valley, California. Lux thought it was about time to honour not only the legendary Republican president with a segment, but also to bestow the Democratic faction with a piece.

This time, however, the gift section of Wall was supposed to be something really special. Consequently, Lux had Denis Kaun paint the segment for Reagen just as he had done in 1990. It was then conserved for eternity in a perspex cylinder, altogether the piece weighs 5 tonnes and is 4 metres in height. Supporters were found for the ambitious project: the Dresdener Bank granted sponsorship and the American presidential administration took a fancy to the gift. The glass container was manufactured in Berlin, where the piece of the Wall was located. It was completed right on time for the President's visit to Berlin in May 1998 and the US Embassy put the official presentation of the Wall on the itinerary for the visit. But Clinton did not appear for the function at the Dresdener Bank. The tour of Sanssouci Palace having took longer than expected and the

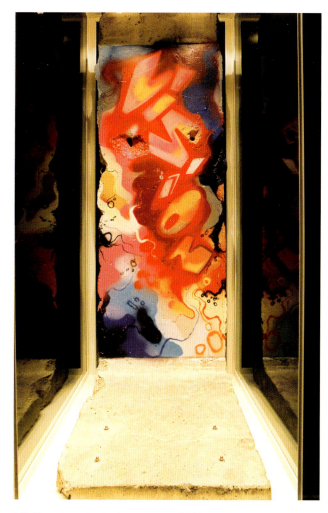

Bill Clinton's missing piece
of Wall

© Oliver Wia / Patrice Lux

President sped to the Schauspielhaus, where he gave a speech to be followed by a meeting with the Federal President of Germany. Despite the fact that the meeting was called off, Lux and the embassy agreed to present the gift – however, in the US. The Wall gift was brought from Berlin to Hamburg via a heavy goods transporter and then shipped to Baltimore on the MS Faust to arrive in the autumn of 1998. Alas, a meeting with Clinton once again failed to take place.

In the mean time the impeachment proceedings against the president had been initiated due to the Lewinsky scandal. The interest in the piece of the Wall declined more and more. Even having travelled to New York, Lux's endeavours to finish the project on the spot remained unsuccessful. Eventually the Dresdener Bank pulled back their sponsorship and Lux was left to pay 50,000 Dollars for transportation himself. Defeated, he travelled back to Europe and the pricey segment of the Wall remained in a depot in Baltimore. Some time later, it disappeared without a trace. The American owner of the depot was unable to comment on the disappearance of the 6 tonne present. A Clinton Presidential Library enquiry, opened in 2004 in Arkansas, revealed that the segment of the Wall had still not arrived. Lux thinks the slab of concrete complete with the glass container were stolen. At some point, or so he insists, it will reappear somewhere in the USA to find its way to Clinton after all.

Location:
John F. Kennedy
Library and Museum,
Columbia Point

„All free men, wherever they may live, are citizens of Berlin. And, therefore, as a free man, I take pride in the words: Ich bin ein Berliner."

John F. Kennedy in front of Schöneberg City Hall in West Berlin, 26th June 1963

The Wall in the John F. Kennedy Presidential Library

© Joel Benjamin/ John F. Kennedy Presidential Library and Museum, Boston

Two years after the Berlin Wall had been built, former US president John F. Kennedy spoke to hundreds of thousands of West Berliners who had gathered outside Schöneberg City Hall. His speech had great symbolic significance as it secured absolute support of the US to the citizens in West Berlin sector who were walled in. The Soviet Union had already tried to cut off supplies to West Berlin during the Berlin Blockade in June 1948. West Berlin was given supplies by the allied air forces, most of which were from the US army. In light of the Wall, Kennedy repeated the promise not to leave the citizens of West Berlin in their hour of need.

Jean Kennedy, sister of the former US president tried to secure a piece of the Wall 26 years later when the Wall fell.

It was to be put on display in the JFK Presidential Library in Boston. The last GDR government supported this request and sent a piece a few weeks before reunification. 'Limex', the company responsible for selling the Wall, organised the delivery. The section of Wall was loaded in Berlin on 19th September, taken to Hamburg and shipped from there to New York. It arrived at the JFK Library in Boston on 5th October 1990.

The segment had stood at the Brandenburg Gate. The word 'fear' or 'tear' can be read on the side which once faced West Berlin, this was the reason that moved Jean Kennedy to choose this segment of Wall. Another important piece of stone can also be found on the same exhibition room at the end of the tour through the JFK library and museum. In 1961, the same year the Wall was built, Kennedy announced that man would soon set foot on the Moon. The Soviets had been successful in sending a satellite into orbit three years earlier. The race to the moon was finally won by the USA, when John Glenn landed there on 20th July 1969.

To commemorate Kennedy's involvement in the project, a piece of moon rock was presented to the museum.

Location:
EF Education First
Boston,
One Education Street

A section of the Berlin Wall has stood in front of 'Education First' (international education company) since the 1990s. Even the round section along the top, designed to prevent people climbing over the top and which is missing from most other sections of the Wall, can be seen on this piece.

The Wall in Boston
© Manuel Steinbrecher

An unknown artist painted a little man with a blue hat, green T-shirt and a red jacket which is clearly a jacket by the Italian sportswear company 'Fila'.

It has not been possible to find out how or when the piece of Wall made its way to Boston, despite seeking information at sister offices of the company in Germany. 'Education First' claim to have sent millions of school children and students to language courses in Europe and the USA in the last forty years. In doing this, they claim to have helped heal division around the world through exchange programmes.

GRAND RAPIDS, MICHIGAN
USA

Location:
Van Andel Museum
Center, Grand Rapids
Public Museum,
272 Peral Street

An original piece of the Berlin Wall has been on display at the entrance to the Van Andel Museum since 1994. Management at the Rapids Public Museum, who are affiliates of the Van Andel Museum came into possession of the concrete relic three years previously.

Fred Meijer, a millionaire businessman of Dutch decent and owner of supermarket chain 'Meijers' bought the segment along with two others in 1991. His attention was drawn to the segment standing in the Van Andel Museum by an article in 'The Times'. On 13th November 1989, the English newspaper reported that the first border at Potsdamer Platz had been opened. Numerous sections of the Berlin Wall were torn down whilst press from allover the world took frenzied pictures. One segment remained and upon it the word 'Meijer' could be clearly seen. Fred Meijer saw it and wanted 'his' piece of the Wall. He got in touch with the 'Berlin Wall Commemorative Group' who had taken over marketing the Wall in the US from the GDR company 'Limex'. Meijer travelled to New York where he was able to find the piece he wanted. He bought two further pieces which he later presented to the Gerald R. Ford Presidential Library and the Grand Valley University in Grand Rapids. The cargo, weighing tonnes, was brought to Grand Rapids and presented to the museum. The city did not just have to thank Fred Meijers for the three segments of Wall, but also for the Fred Meijers Garden and Sculpture Park, a Fred Meijers campus at the Grand Valley University and obviously, a street named after him.

The Wall in the Van Andel Museum, Grand Rapids

© Collections of the Public Museum, Grand Rapids, Michigan

Information board about the history of the Berlin Wall

© Collections of the Public Museum, Grand Rapids, Michigan

Throughout his life, Fred Meijer, a businessman worth millions and owner of supermarket chain 'Meijers', rendered outstanding services to Valley State University. Many new institutes were founded with his generous support as well as a whole campus in his home country of the Netherlands. After Meijers had purchased a number of sections from the 'Berlin Wall Commemorative Group', he presented one to the university. The section was put on display in a base outside the James H. Zumberge Library on campus in Grand Rapids.

It was presented to the public during a University general meeting on 1st September 1992 by the former chancellor Arend D. Lubbers und Fred Meijer, who himself had never been able to attend university. A bronze plaque in German and English explains the historical significance of the concrete block:

„Section of the Berlin Wall

We, the students and faculty of Grand Valley State University, dedicate this section of the Berlin Wall to the German people's strength, determination and desire to be free. May this wall remind us all of the precious gift of freedom which we possess and which all humans desire. This section of the Berlin Wall was donated by Frederik C. H. Meijer."

GRAND RAPIDS, MICHIGAN
USA

Location:
James H. Zumberge
Library, Grand Valley State
University,
Allendale Campus

GRAND RAPIDS, MICHIGAN
USA

Location:
Gerald R. Ford
Presidential Library
and Museum,
303 Pearl Street

The Helsinki Declaration was signed by the leaders of 35 European countries in Helsinki on 1st August 1975.

Talks about collaborations between nations and observing human rights had been going on for the previous four weeks between the USA and Canada, as well as the Soviet Union and all members of the Warsaw Pact. The GDR signed the pact, and in doing so made significant steps forward in their foreign policy and to become a recognised state. However, signing the pact also obligated the GDR state and its leader Erich Honecker to adhere to laws regarding freedom of speech, opinion and religion. Furthermore, the GDR was now required to ease restrictions on travel to the West.

Although the pact was legally binding, very little changed for the people of the GDR.

Travel to the 'other side' was prevented by the authorities and the deathstrip continued to make escape attempts almost impossible. Those caught trying to escape faced severe punishment. Nevertheless, the people of the GDR kept coming back to the terms of the pact the state had signed. It became the basis for many protests and movements which in turn led to the Fall of the communist dictatorship in Europe.

The Helsinki Declaration was the most significant and successful part of Gerald R Ford's foreign policy. According to Henry Kissinger, the former US foreign minister, the thing had "laid the basis of the changes in Eastern Europe today", which in turn led to the Fall of the Wall.

Ford was symbolically given a piece of the Wall on 6th September 1991. A number of Ford's former colleagues turned out to attend a ceremony to mark the 10th anniversary of the Presidential Library. Guests included former chancellor Helmut Schmidt, who had signed the treaty alongside Honecker and James Callaghan, who was in office at the British foreign ministry in 1975. The piece of the Wall was bought by museum curators for 35,000 Dollars from the 'Berlin Wall Commemorative Group', who had been given the job of promoting and selling the Wall in the US. The piece with its bright graffiti can still be seen today in the Meijer lobby at the presidential library.

A small plaque next to the segment explains its significance.

„The people of Eastern Europe have sought freedom and national independence since the end of World War II. After it was built in 1961, the Berlin Wall came to symbolize their oppression. It is a great irony that man's response to the Wall: escape, became one of the most meaningful and important actions to all freedom-loving men and women.
This section of the Wall is a gift to the American people who, for over forty years, have supported their country's efforts to promote independence for Eastern Europe.
Gerald R. Ford 38th President of the United States September 6, 1991"

Ford's domestic politics were not as successful, as America was facing one of the worst economic crises since the great depression. Nevertheless, he did achieve some milestones: he signed a bill in 1974, which officially made it legal for cash machines to pay out bank notes. One of the oldest cash machines in the US can be found in the presidential library as a result of this. Until recently, another smaller piece of the wall could be found next to it. Admittedly, a little out of place it has been put in storage, until a better place can be found. According to officials at the museum its new home has yet to be found.

FULTON, MISSOURI
USA

Location:
Westminster College,
501 Westminster Avenue

"Breakthrough" in the National
Churchill Museum, Fulton
© The National Churchill Museum

„A shadow has fallen upon the scenes so lately lighted by the Allied victory. Nobody knows what Soviet Russia and its communist international organization intends to do in the immediate future, or what the limits, if any, to their expansive and proselytizing tendencies. (…) From Stettin in the Baltic to Trieste in the Adriatic, an Iron Curtain has descended across the continent. Behind that line lie all the capitals of the ancient states of Central and Eastern Europe. Warsaw, Berlin, Prague, Vienna, Budapest, Belgrade, Bucharest and Sofia, all these famous cities and the populations around them lie in what I must call the Soviet sphere, and all are subject in one form or another, not only to Soviet influence but to a very high and, in many cases, increasing measure of control from Moscow."
Winston Churchill, "Sinews of Peace",
Speech at Westminister College, Fulton (USA), 5th March 1946

Former British Prime Minister Winston Churchill made the famous speech in Fulton in March 1945 and warned of a separation in the West between east and west. The anti-Hitler-coalition had fallen apart not even a year after the end of the Second World War. Great Britain, the USA, France and the Soviet Union had all been members. The countries who had once stood united against Hitler now stood against each other in a confrontation between the two blocks which led to the Cold War. Churchill's speech was a massive media event. More than 30,000 people made their way to Westminster College to listen. The event was also broadcast via radio. His term 'Iron Curtain' was to become synonymous with the looming Cold War.

The GDR government presented Edwina Sandys, Winston Churchill's granddaughter, with eight pieces of the Wall in 1990 in recognition of Churchill's political legacy. The artist and sculptor who was then living in New York with her architect husband Richard Kaplan, travelled to Berlin in February 1990. She had an idea

for a freedom memorial which should consist of pieces of the Wall. However, the GDR government lead by Hans Modrow had recognised the symbolic worth of the former GDR border fortification and had decided to put sections of it up for sale. Sandys, however, could not afford the asking price of 60,000-200,000 dollars per segment. It was only when Sandys revealed plans to display her art work in the National Churchill Museum in Fulton (est. 1969), that the GDR officials were willing to agree to hand over segments of the Wall. Modrow's government finally agreed to let Sandys chose eight sections of the Wall during a meeting on 8th March 1990. She chose a number of bright segments which had once stood in front of the Brandenburg Gate. The word 'unwahr' (untrue) was repeatedly sprawled across the segments, and this fascinated Sandys.

A short while later the pieces of Wall arrived on a ship in New York. Sandys began work in her Queens studio. Two giant silhouettes, one male and one female, were to be etched out of the Wall and symbolise the 'breakthrough' of the Iron Curtain, this was also the title of her piece. The piece then went on a US tour. It was on temporary display in front of the IBM building in New York, as well as in Washington.

'Breakthrough' was then officially unveiled at a ceremony at Westminster College on 9th November 1990, to coincide with the one year anniversary of the Fall of the Berlin Wall. For Sandys, it was a dream come true.

At the unveiling she said "I had always dreamed of making a sculpture for the National Churchill Museum, and now seemed like the right time to me."

Former US president Ronald Reagan was also present at the ceremony. Two years earlier, he had ordered Mikhail Gorbachev, head of the Soviet Union, to tear down the Wall. He claimed that with the unveiling of 'breakthrough', the time had come for a world free of walls.

Once enemies, they came together in the following years in front of the sculpture, almost ten metres wide and three metres high. Mikhail Gorbachev, by now awarded the Nobel Peace Prize, spoke on 6th May 1992 in Fulton.

The Soviet Union had collapsed only two months previously and Gorbachev has retired from his post.

"An era has ended and another one has begun. Nobody knows right now how concrete it will be", he said in his speech in front of 'Breakthrough'. The final part of his speech, held in English, alluded to concrete Berlin Wall

British Prime Minister Margaret Thatcher visited 'Breakthrough' as the last head of state at the end of Cold War. However, she only posed for photos in front of the remains of the Wall.

The pieces of the Wall that had been carved out to make way for the silhouettes were assigned to a US president.

Ronald Reagan standing in front of "Breakthrough"
© Rich Sugg / Kansas City Star

"Breakthrough" in the National

Churchill Museum, Fulton

© The Winston Churchill
Memorial & Library in the USA

They can be found today in the Franklin D. Roosevelt national historic site in Hyde Park, New York.

Mikhail Gorbachev in front of

"Breakthrough"

© Rich Sugg / Kansas City Star

Location:
Banks of the Hudson
River, Jersey City,
Hudson County

The Hudson County pieces of
Wall are loaded
© Lutz Busse / Landkreis Oberhavel

The distance between the two metropolitan cities of Berlin and New York is bridged by the German district of Oberhavel and the American district of Hudson County. They are linked economically and by the ever growing number of tourists they attract each year.

It was on this basis that the partnership between Jersey City and Oranienburg was cemented with the presentation of four complete (unpainted) sections of the Berlin Wall on 30th June 2007 in Germendorf. County commissioner Karl Heinz Schröter also presented Tampere in South Finland with sections of the former inner German border. They all came from a company called Recyclinghof, owned by Klaus Grunkse who had been given the task of demolishing the Wall in North Berlin. In comparison to others who found themselves in possession of parts of the Wall, Grunske did not make a business out of them. He gave the pieces free of charge to the district as he deemed it a good cause. The costs of shipping the pieces of Wall, weighing in at over 7 tonnes, were covered by Sparkasse, a German bank. They arrived on the American east coast in late 2007.

Exactly where the sections of Wall were to be put on display in Jersey had not been finalised by this point in time. Hudson County freeholder, Thomas Liggio, wanted the "symbol of victory and democracy" to be put on display for the American public. There were plans in spring 2009 to display the four sections on the banks of the Hudson River. They were to be arranged in a rectangular formation at the centre of a circular plaza. The memorial would be erected at a site overlooking the Freedom Tower, which has since been renamed 'One World Trade Center' and built on the site of the towers destroyed on 11th September 2001.

The opening was due to take place on 9th November 2009. However, there were still no sufficient funds available in 2010 and eventually the exact whereabouts of the sections was not known anymore and plans for the "Berlin Wall Memorial For Peace" were put on hold.

HAMILTON, NEW YORK
USA

Location:
Colgate University

The Wall at Colgate University, Hamilton

© Colgate University / Andrew Daddio

An original section of the Berlin Wall was put up on campus at Colgate University. The opening ceremony took place at the university in 1995 to mark the 25th anniversary of the introduction of the 'Peace Studies Programme'.

Scores of former Colgate University students made their way to the event, many who had been forced to end their studies when they were enlisted to the armed forces.

Today, the segment of Wall stands not far from the West Hall, which is built on a hill and is the oldest university building. The graffiti has been weathered and can now hardly be seen.

The Franklin D. Roosevelt Library in Hyde Park (New York) was opened in 1941 and is also the house in which the former president was born. The US declared war on Germany in the same year and it ended four years later with the allied victory over the Nazi dictatorship. It was Roosevelt who founded the anti-Hitler coalition alongside Stalin and Churchill. When he died in April 1945, the final phase of the war unfolded in Europe. The Four Freedoms he laid down in the Atlantic Charter – freedom of speech, freedom of worship, freedom of want, and freedom of fear – would radically shape the foreign politics of the US. Even more so when the increasing bond between the great powers changed into the beginnings of the Cold War after the end of the Second World War.

Roosevelts legacy was the reason for the 'break free' sculpture that was placed in the Presidential Library gardens in 1990. It was made by sculptor and granddaughter of Winston Churchill, Edwina Sandys. The four figures made from parts of the Berlin Wall are the leftovers from 'Breakthrough', another sculpture by Sandys. This second sculpture can be seen today at the National Churchill Museum in Fulton, Missouri.

Location:
Franklin D. Roosevelt Library and Museum, 4079 Albany Post Road, Hyde Park

BreakFree sculpture in front of the Franklin D. Roosevelt Library
© Edwina Sandys

NEW YORK CITY, NEW YORK
USA

Location:
United Nations (UN),
North Lawn,
1st Avenue, E 42nd Street

The Wall at the United
Nations, New York City

© Patrick Gräfe / German
Consulate General New York

Former secretary General of the United Nations Kofi Annan was not only given an honorary doctorate by the Freie Universität (Free University) Berlin on his visit in 2001, the city also presented him with three sections of the Berlin Wall complete with graffiti art by Kani Alavi.

The sections of Wall were amongst the last standing on Leipziger Platz in Berlin Mitte. The presentation of the segments was, however, controversial. Erich Stanke, who had bought the area of land, and thereby the pieces of Wall standing on it, wanted to prevent them from being taken down. He was not interested in being paid to hand over the sections of Wall. Stanke was more interested in keeping the few remaining pieces of the former border in place and putting them under monument protection. According to the Senate Chancellory, the pieces of Wall and their symbolic image, 'two people hug each other over the Wall', would be better preserved in New York. An agreement was reached that the remaining pieces of the Wall, along with the watchtower would stay put on Leipziger Platz. Now, nothing else stood in the way of handing over the section of Wall to Annan on 13th July 2001. President of the Bundestag, Wolfgang Thierse, and Berlin mayor, Klaus Wowereit, presented the pieces to Kofi Annan from their original location. They were delivered to New York and the words "Trophy of Civil Rights" can be seen along the top.

This quote belongs to another piece of graffiti on Potsdamer Platz by Thierry Noir.

Until recently, only the left half of Kiddy's heart painting, which decorated two segments of the Wall, could be found onboard warship USS Intrepid New York. In summer 1990, artist Peter Max presented the second segment of the Wall with the missing half of the artwork to the open-air museum. In 2007, the modernisation of the ship began, and, thus, the remaining segment of the Wall was given back to Max, according to the curator of the museum.

The history of the two segments, which were once deemed the beginning of a major business idea, ends here for now. In early 1990, Max had obtained the two segments with a painting by Kiddy Citny on them from the "Berlin Wall Commemorative Group". They had organised a "Wall happening" at New York Harbour. The event marked the beginning of marketing the Wall in the US, which, the GDR government hoped, would produce a substantial foreign exchange revenue. Max added two doves to the painting and said it was his entirely his own artwork. He painted one of the doves where the mounting of the barbed wire had preserved the grey colour of the concrete. The other was made by Max himself out of concrete and put on the top edge of the concrete slab. With the new piece of art complete, 250 copies of it were to be recast and sold at a price of 7,000 US-Dollar per piece. However, it seems this idea was never realised. The dove on the piece of Wall on the USS Intrepid had to be removed after visitors tried to steal it. The other segment of the Wall disappeared in the following years and can now be found in the Marbles Kids Museum in Raleigh.

As for the rest, the piece of the Wall that remained on the warship is supposed to have been a present, not a purchase, to him from entrepreneur Donald Trump, who had not wanted the piece of the Wall anymore. Whatever the truth of the story, since 2008 both segments of the Wall have disappeared from New York.

NEW YORK CITY, NEW YORK
USA

Location:

Jerry Speyer Building,
523 Madison Avenue

The Wall in front of the
Jerry Speyer Building,
New York

© Patrick Gräfe / German
Consulate General New York

Five original pieces of the Berlin Wall can be seen outside the Jerry Speyer Real Estate Building on Madison Avenue. In the summer, guests from the nearby burger restaurant can sit and enjoy the view of the segments which were painted by Kiddy Citny and Thierry Noir. Efforts to find out exactly how the pieces of Wall made it here have been unsuccessful. It is presumed that they were bought in the early nineteens by Jerry and Rob Speyer, owners of the largest real estate company in New York to put on display at their headquarters. Another possibility is that they came from the Museum of Modern Art (MoMa) in New York. GDR company 'Limex' sold the sections of the Wall, painted by Citny and Noir, in 1990 for 500,000 D-Mark to the museum. However, none of the museum's management were able to recall such a transaction.

The five pieces of Wall were already famous when they stood at their original site on Waldemarstraße in Berlin. Citny and Noir painted them in 1984 at the border between Kreuzberg and the East Berlin district of Mitte. They were then photographed by Liselotte and Armin Orgel-Köhne in 1985 and eternalised as a series of posters. The pictures were also published in other forms and on other occasions, notably in 1987 when Berlin celebrated its 750th birthday. Wim Wenders filmed his famous film in the same year at the Berlin Wall. The graffiti painted by Citny and Noir and which has now found its way to New York can also be seen in the film 'Wings of Desire'.

Bausch&Lomb was founded in 1853 by two German immigrants and today is one of the biggest manufacturers of eye health products. In 1996, Berlin based sister company, Dr. Mann Pharma, presented the headquarters in Rochester with an original segment of the Wall. It can be seen today in a lunch room next to the entrance hall.

The company was also to move into new buildings in the same year. To mark the occasion all branches were asked to commission a

Location:
Bausch&Lomb

The Berlin Wall in
Rochester, New York
© Sabine Strübing

piece of art, typical to its country. It was clear to the then Dr. Mann Pharma management that it had to be a segment from the Berlin Wall.

Members of staff also met the idea with enthusiasm. Executive Assistant at Bausch&Lomb, Hannelore Lamoth: "I remember it well, as I saw the piece and was happy about the fact that it had my daughter's name 'Andrea' written at the top of it."

Having the piece shipped over was, however, a little problematic. "It was a massive piece, and transporting it was harder than we had expected. It had to be packed up safely in a container and then painstakingly loaded onto a low-loader, which then brought the gigantic piece to Bremerhaven. It was a ceremonious event when the "slab of concrete" left us", remembers Jürgen Kannegießer, member of staff at the Berlin subsidiary. In order to present the gift in an adequate light, it had to undergo a little cosmetic treatment beforehand. Werner Gesang, another member of staff at the Berlin branch, looks back: "The 'paintings', or rather daubing on the segment had faded since they had been exposed to wind and weather for years. Later, an unknown artist refreshed the colours a little and enhanced the contours – it was restored in a way." Ready for the journey, the 2.6 tonne slab of concrete left for Toronto and was then transported to Rochester in a lorry.

Next to the piece of Wall is an information sign on which you can see the segment in its original location, shortly after the Fall of the Wall on 9th of November 1989. A provisional border crossing was set up next to Brandenburg Gate. "Every wall falls at some point" had been scrawled across several parts of the Wall by an unknown artist, and finally it has come true.

172

COLUMBUS, OHIO
USA

Location:

Capital University,
Blackmore Library,
Drexel Campus

The Wall in the
Blackmore Library, Columbus

© Blackmore Library,
Capital University

In America, preparations to mark the 500th anniversary of Christopher Columbus' discovery of America were already underway in 1989. From Alaska to Chile, scores of events were to take place in 1992, the jubilee year. The planning committee made plans for a great horticultural show to celebrate the arrival of Columbus. However, the preparations were drawn out over many years. The event itself was to take place in Columbus, Ohio – a town named after the explorer.

Under the supervision of former First Lady, Barbara Bush, 36 hectares were filled with flower arrangements from allover the world.

Further exhibitions were also organised in an attempt to bring in more tourists. One such exhibition focused on Germany and was organised in part by German entrepreneur, Günther Tukay. The owner of a large plant construction and recycling company had expanded into further German territories after the Fall of the Wall. According to Tukay, his business 'Hansa Consulting GmbH' was doing very well and secured work places during times of economic difficulty. In an attempt to get American businesses interested in working with the new eastern states of Germany, Tukay gave financial support to the German exhibition. One of the main attractions was a section of the Wall, brought in especially for the occasion. In 1992 Capital University offered to house the piece on campus on permanent loan.

With support from Huntington Bank, the 2.6 tonne section of Wall was taken to the university and put up in the Blackmoore Library where it stands today as "symbol of the triumph of human will in insurmountable circumstances".

The remains of a devil, some brightly coloured snow flakes and the number '89' can be found on this section – mainly on the side of the Wall which faced east. It was quite rare for the Wall to be painted on this side. In contrast, the side which once faced the West remains completely grey. A sign was put up alongside the section asking students not to mark or graffiti the Wall, so that it may remain in its original state.

A collection of over 300 planes which span the history of military aviation can be visited by guests to the US Air Force Museum near Dayton.

The development of aerial warfare is documented in three giant hangars. Two of the three exhibition rooms are designated to the Cold War. From bombers and how they came to be used in the Korean War in 1950/51, to Stealth bombers and reconnaissance aircraft and further to rocket science.

Two Wall installations have been on display here since 2000. They have been integrated into the exhibition to highlight the significant role of the US Airforce in the Cold War. The first four sections of the Wall arrived in Ohio from Frankfurt/Main in exchange for two planes: a Douglas C-47 and a Douglas C-54. The planes had been used during the Berlin Air Blockade in 1948.

William J. Begert, commander of the US Air Force, travelled to Frankfurt/Main to receive the pieces of Wall on 23rd December 1999. The sections of the Wall were so heavy (16 tonnes), that a jumbo jet (a C-141 Starlifter) was needed to fly them back to the US. They were finally unveiled to the public almost a year later on 11th November 2000. The mu-

Location:
US Air Force Museum, 1100 Spaatz Street, Wright-Patterson Air Force Base, near Dayton

seum planners thought that presenting museum visitors with plain grey sections of the Wall would not be enough. They placed the sections of Wall behind a Trabi which had been painted to resemble military camouflage. A woman can be seen standing on the roof and waving over the Wall. Her passenger has already climbed over the Wall and can be seen cheering on top of it. They are both holding on to a German flag – symbolic of the reunification of Germany and the end of the Cold War.

The Wall in the
U.S. Air Force Museum
© U.S. Air Force Museum

Two more sections of the Wall made their way to Dayton in 2000. The museum claims they were a present from the Berlin Allied Museum.

The famous brightly coloured heads were painted on these sections especially for the museum by renowned Wall artist, Thierry Noir.

CHALK HILL, PENNSYLVANIA
USA

Location:
Kentuck Knob

British art collector and architect, Lord Peter Palumbo, first visited Kentuck Knob (ca 70 kilometres south of Pittsburgh) in 1985. He later bought it from the former owners, I. N. and Bernadine Hagan. In 1935, architect, Frank Lloyd Wright, began work on Fallingwater. The house was to be built on a remote spot at the bottom of Chalk Hill. It became one of the most architecturally significant buildings and was made using only natural materials from the surrounding area. The building was closed off from the public until 1996, when it was opened to visitors who have been fascinated by the building ever since.

Palumbo used the surrounding forest as a setting to display works of contemporary art. He put up two sections of the Wall alongside works from Andy Goldsworthy, Ray Smith and Sir Anthony Caro. He bought six pieces of the Wall at an auction held at the London Fischer Fine Art Gallery. One of these segments now stands in front of the Imperial War Museuem in London, a second piece in Yorkshire Sculpture Park and a further piece is now in a private collection.

The two sections at Kentuck Knob are covered in graffiti by Jürgen Große ('Indiano'). Both are from the 'Global Messages' series, which Große had painted on the Wall in November 1989. The slogans 'Save the Planet' and 'Create Live' can be seen on the sections at Kentuck Knob.

The Wall in Kentuck Knob
© Kentuck Knob

NEMACOLIN, PENNSYLVANIA
USA

Location:
Nemacolin Woodland Resort

The Wall in Nemacolin
Woodlands Resort, Farmington
© Nemacolin Woodlands Resort

The luxurious Nemacolin Woodlands Resort is situated in idilic woodland in South West Pensylvania. Top class hotels and restaurants await high class guests who come to the area to relax in the parks and health farms or play a round of golf. An original piece of the Berlin Wall can be found in the grounds. How and when it got there is not clear. The balck and white graffiti was painted by Jürgen Große ('Indiano') in 1990. 'Change myself' and 'Wake up' are part of the 'Global Messages' which were painted on numerous sections of the Wall. This piece, weighing 2.6 tonnes was a present from Joseph Hardy from Pennsylvania. Hardy had obtained the section from Lord Peter Palumbo, who had bought it alongside five other sections in 1994.

SPARTANBURG, SOUTH CAROLINA
USA

Location:
Menzel LP

Students from Oakbrook Preparatory School in Spartanburg and Menzel LP manager Alois Krussig in front of original sections of the Berlin Wall
© Thomas Koenig

Spartanburg appears as though it could just as easily be in the German provinces and not in South Carolina. In 'Gerhard's Cafe', guests can order a piece of black forest cherry cake, or once a month, take part in a round of 'Skat' (a German card game). Spartanburg has 230,000 inhabitants and a large German community. Around 2000 German managers and skilled workers live here with their families – Jochen Menzel, owner of Menzel Machinery is one of them. He had the 3.6 metre-high section of the Berlin Wall put up outside his factory when he took over the company in 1992. Radio stations were giving away pieces of the Wall after it fell in 1989. This is how his idea took shape. He asked friends to apply for both pieces of Wall and had them sent to the USA in containers. He already lived in South Carolina before the Fall of the Wall.

Each section of the Wall has a quote by American President on it and together they make up the collective memory of the Cold War: "Ich bin ein Berliner" (John F. Kennedy) and "Mr. Gorbachev tear down this wall" (Ronald Reagan). According to Jochen Menzel, these two US presidents made German unification possible and his two sections of the Berlin Wall are a symbolic thank you from his family to the US. Groups of school children often make their way to see the sections of Wall and learn about the history of the Wall.

Two pieces of the Berlin Wall have been on display near Mount Rushmore National Memorial since 1996. Mount Rushmore is also home to the monumental heads of American presidents George Washington, Thomas Jefferson, Theodore Roosevelt and Abraham Lincoln. They were carved into the black hills in 1930.

The sections of Wall are situated on Mt. Rushmore Highway in Rapid City next

RAPID CITY, SOUTH DAKOTA
USA

Location:
South Dakota
Memorial Park,
Mt. Rushmore Highway

to the Rushmore Plaza Civic Centre car park. On either side of the Wall are two anti-tank obstacles which are presumed to have been taken from the former border crossing 'Checkpoint Charlie' in Berlin.

The South Dakota School of Mines and Technology was home to a 1993 exhibition entitled 'Break Through: Fight for Freedom at the Berlin Wall. The exhibition triggered a massive response from the public and the idea to erect a Wall memorial in Rapid City was born.

An organisation committee was drafted and sponsors were searched for. A section of the Wall was donated to Vermillion in South Dakota by Ernst Dietrich, mayor of Ratingen, North Rhine-Westphalia. Ratingen and Vermillion are twinned-towns. The second section of Wall was put up by US airforce military chaplain, H. W. Reinke, in memory of all American military chaplains. A sign tells visitors that the segment was supposed to have originally stood between Checkpoint Charlie and the Brandenburg Gate. One of the anti-tank obstacles was also donated by the US military. It was donated by the Ellsworth Air Force Base in South Dakota in memory of all soldiers who "stood loyally to protect the world in times of war and peace".

The second anti-tank obstacle arrived in Rapid city with help from the German city of Potsdam – twinned with Sioux Falls, South Dakota. However, this one does not serve as a memorial to the German division, but to the edict of toleration issued on 29th October 1685 by Frederick Wilhelm, Elector of Brandenburg and Duke of Prussia. He offered oppressed Huguenots refuge and benefits in Potsdam. The piece was officially unveiled on 5th October 1996 in the park next to the Rushmore Plaza Civic Center, which is today officially called Dakota Memorial Park. The pieces were completed with a number of plaques that inform visitors about the division of Germany and the Cold War. The memorial grabs the attention of visitors with a huge sign on the street upon which people are warned that they are leaving the American Sector (in English, Russian and French).

COLLEGE STATION, TEXAS
USA

Location:
George H. W. Bush
Presidential Library
and Museum

The Wall in the
George Bush Presidential
Library, College Station

© George Bush Presidential Library
and Museum

„Well, I don't think any single event is the end of what you might call the Iron Curtain, but clearly this is a long way from the harshest Iron Curtain days – a long way from that."

George H. W. Bush auf der Pressekonferenz zum Mauerfall am 9. November 1989 in Washington D. C.

W hilst tens of thousands of euphoric people made their way over the border to West Berlin on the evening of 9th November 1989, American President, George H. W. Bush, made a press appearance at the White House. Surprised by the events unfolding in the GDR, the president was noticeably cautious. The public reacted with anger to his lack of emotion. He admitted himself that this moment in word history was passing him by. He told the press "I'm just not an emotional kind of guy".

Even if his Bush's reaction to the Fall of the Wall was seen to be unsatisfactory, his part in the Fall of the Wall and the reunification of Germany can not be disputed. A small piece of the Wall was given to Bush by former foreign minister, Hans-Dietrich Genscher, on 21st November 1989 in recognition and thanks for his work. He was given another section by the Berlin senate at the end of his time in office on 21st April 1993.

It was supposed to become part of the George H. Bush Presidential Library in College Station, north of Houston. The cost of transporting the 2.6 tonne piece of Wall was sponsored by the Axel Springer Verlag and Krone AG. It was put up at the A & M University in Texas whilst the 80 million dollar building project

Location:
James A. Baker III.
Institute for Public
Policy, Rice University,
6100 Main Street

Helmut Kohl and James Baker
in front of the Wall at
Rice University, Houston

© 2003 Rice University,
photo courtesy of James A. Baker III
Institute for Public Policy

O n 10th November 1999, former American secretary of state, James A. Baker, received an original section of the Berlin Wall – ten years after its historic fall. Whilst almost all presidential memorials in the US (of presidents in office since 1945) are homes to sections of the Berlin Wall, James A. Baker was the first non-president to be bestowed the honour. This honour was in recognition of his efforts during his term (1989-1992) to bring about German reunification. These efforts had already been recognised by Rice University, Texas. Before Baker stepped back from his post as secretary of state in summer 1992, political scientist and professor, Richard J. Stoll, had made an appeal to the presidents at Rice University. His request to set up the 'James A. Baker Institute for Public Policy' was granted and the plans completed a few months later. The institute was opened on campus in 1995 and the section of Wall was unveiled four years later. German ambassador, Jürgen Chrobog, was in attendance at the unveiling alongside many prominent university figures. The section of Wall itself is relatively plain: there is no graffiti on it. There is merely a heart, pierced by an arrow, the words 'Love He' and, fittingly, the words 'Salut mes amis' (hello my friends).

Former Federal Chancellor, Helmut Kohl, also paid a visit to James Baker in Texas. On his visit in September 2003, he talked of transatlantic relations and was photographed with Banker in front of the Wall.

NEWPORT NEWS, VIRGINIA
USA

Location:
Virginia War Museum,
9285 Warwick Boulevard

The Wall in

Virginia War Museum

© Virginia War Museum

2009 marked 20 years since the Fall of the Berlin Wall. The Virginia War Museum used this anniversary as the basis for its special exhibition "Turned Upside Down. The 20th Anniversary of the Fall of the Berlin Wall", which looked at how the Berlin Wall divided not just a city, but above all the people of Berlin.

The museum was founded in 1923 and is situated in Huntington Park. The exhibitions focus on the history of the American military from 1755 to the present day. On display are weapons, military vehicles, uniforms and posters from different periods in American history.

German-American history is represented by a part of the exterior wall from the concentration camp in Dachau, as well as two sections of the Berlin Wall. Both sections of the Wall are complemented by newspaper articles and uniforms of the National People's Army.

American, Tie D. Sosnowski – who today is a member of the museum board – bought the original Berlin Wall segments on one of his visits to Berlin. After having been transported from Berlin to Bremen, they were loaded on the Orient Overseas Container Line and made the rest of the journey to Norfolk, Virginia. Tie D. Sosnowski donated them to the museum in 1992. He thought it important to maintain pieces of the Berlin Wall in order to highlight how precious and valuable freedom is. According to Sosnowski, these sections of the Wall once stood somewhere between Checkpoint Charlie and the Brandenburg Gate. Both segments are approximately 1.5 metres wide and 3 metres high. Both sections of the Wall are decorated along the top with the German national colours and are upside down – accordingly, the words "Auf den Kopf gestellt" (turned upside down) can be read. Dick Hoffeditz, curator of the museum, says that this is perhaps symbolic of the feelings felt by many who were so surprised when the Wall fell.

The German armed forces are working closely alongside the US armed forces as a result of the transatlantic Nato alliance. The German armed forces are represented at the German Armed Forces Command in Reston, Virginia. A 3.2 metre high section of the Wall greets guests. It was brought to the United States by the German Air Force in 1991 to mark the opening of the new service building. General Gero Schachthöfer, Senior Military Academe of the German Armed forces, spoke of the significance of the section of Wall:

"The Berlin Wall stands everyday as a symbol for the soldiers and civil servants who work in this building.

For our American guests, this piece of the Berlin Wall stands for the Cold War, for the overcoming of German and European division as a piece of history."

This section was originally in the Berlin district of Kreuzberg on Waldemarstraße and was painted by graffiti artist Thierry Noir. At its base is a plaque which explains the significance of the segment of Wall.

RESTON, VIRGINIA
USA

Location:
German Armed Forces Command Reston, 1150 Sunrise Valley Drive

The Wall in front of the German Armed Forces Command, Reston

© German Armed Forces Command USA and Canada

"The Division of Berlin ended in November 1989. This original segment of the former Berlin Wall attests to the spirit of German-American Friendship."

REDMOND, WASHINGTON
USA

Location:
Microsoft Art Collection,
One Microsoft Way

The former eastern side of the
Wall at Microsoft, Redmond

© With permission of the
Microsoft Art Collection

Until the Wall fell in 1989, the death-strip ran directly across Potsdamer Platz and divided East and West Berlin. Potsdamer Platz pulsated with traffic before the Second World War. After the war, it became a barren wasteland. Daimler-Benz began to buy pieces of land in this area along the border from the West Berlin senate at the end of the 1970s. When the Wall fell in 1989, the company decided to build offices here. Large sections of the Wall from this area, which had been painted on both sides by Wall artists, were torn down and most of them crushed.

A few remaining pieces were presented to Daimler-Benz's business partners around the world. Whilst visiting Daimler-Benz in spring 1996, Bill Gates, founder of Microsoft, was given a section of the Wall. The 2.6 tonne section of Wall was presented to him by Klaus Mangol, a member on the board of supervisors at Daimler-Benz. A picture of a rainbow and the word 'happy' had been painted on the side of the Wall that used to face East – presumably by someone caught up in the joy when the Wall fell.

The western side of the Wall is also brightly painted. The many layers of paint make it clear that many generations of Wall artists had been at work on this section.

The concrete section arrived in Redmond on 15th August 1996 – almost 35 years to the day since the Wall had been built. Today, it can be found at the entrance to the cafeteria. There is no public access, and only Microsoft staff have the pleasure of admiring it. Microsoft have, however, set up a page on their website which documents the history of this section of Wall as well as information about Wall art and the construction of the Wall.

The former eastern side of the

Wall at Microsoft, Redmond

SEATTLE, WASHINGTON
USA

Location:
Seattle Center,
305 Harrison Street

In 1990, Achim Becker, businessesman and successful coin dealer from Hamburg, attended an international coin conference in Seattle and had a very special gift in his luggage.

He had a section of the Berlin Wall shipped to the West coast of America. It was originally brought over to advertise the sale of German reunification coins, but the 2.6 tonne concrete section remained in the USA. Becker was talked into leaving the section as a 'symbol of freedom' by Seattle's former consul general, Hans con Beesten. Seattle's mayor, Norm Rice, was delighted to accept the piece and had it put up in the Seattle Center. It was given the name 'Bloddy Erich' and can still be visited here today. It was originally part of the border at Potsdamer Platz and has some notable graffiti on it: a ladder is propped up against the Wall and leads the way to freedom – behind it are the watchful eyes of the GDR state and party leaders.

"Bloody Erich" in
Seattle Center, Seattle
© Stacey Warnke, Metairie

Two sections of the Berlin Wall have been on display in the north-west city of Seattle since March 2003. They were presented to History House of Greater Seattle – a museum devoted to the history of the town and its people. It was donated by Australian businessman, Carl Asmus, who had bought the pieces of Wall in the early 1990s for an estimated 500,000 US dollars.

They were originally intended to accompany a controversial statue of Lenin in Westlake Park. The statue had been bought from the town of Poprad in Slovakia in 1993 by Lewis E. Carpenter for 13,000 US dollars. Carpenter had gone to Slovakia at the start of the 1990s to work as an English teacher. He came across the statue, which was designed and made in 1998 by Emil Venkov and torn down only a year later. For him, it was not just a political statue, but a work of art, and for this reason he paid for it to be taken to Seattle.

SEATTLE, WASHINGTON
USA

Location:
History House of Greater Seattle, 790 N. 34th

The Wall in
Seattle History House, Seattle

© Tom Hood, Owings Mills, Maryland USA

Many people in Seattle did not consider the statue just to be an artistic relic of the fallen East Block and it caused a lot of controversy before it was finally put up in the artist's quarter in Fremont. The massive bronze statue still stands here today, not as a memorial, but as a piece of art, and it is often decorated to mark special occasions. For example, a red star is placed on Lenin's head at Christmas and he is dressed up in women's clothing for the annual gay pride parade. Nevertheless, it still remains a source of controversy. It was not only Carl Asmus who wanted to use the sections of Wall for his Lenin memorial. There were also plans to use them as part of a memorial for the American pilots who flew during the Berlin Air Blockade. Since none of these plans could be realised, the pieces remained in front of the historical museum.

WASHINGTON D.C.
USA

Location:

U.S. State Department, Harry S. Truman Building, Exhibition Hall, Ecke 23rd Street und C-Street

Bill Clinton in front of the cardboard Wall in the State Department, Washington

© picture-alliance/dpa

On 11th February 1998, former US president, Bill Clinton, made a press appearance. The meeting was called as part of the Enlargement of Nato which saw the inclusion of Poland, Hungary and the Czech Republic. The decision to include these nation was made during a Nato-summit in Madrid 1997 and was a significant step towards the end of the divisions throughout the world at the end of the Cold War. Clinton had spoken from the Benjamin Franklin room on the eight floor of the State Department. After signing the protocol, Clinton then went on to answer questions from the press whilst he stood in front of supposed pieces of the Berlin Wall upon which the word 'freedom' could be clearly seen.

Despite critique from a number of NATO-members – above all from Russia, Clinton claimed that the goal to create an "undivided democratic and peaceful Europe" with the enlargement of NATO was irrefutable.

This message was symbolically signed with the supposed pieces of Wall in the background. The US Senate agreed a few weeks later to the enlargement and Hungary, Poland and the Czech Republic joined Nato on 12th March 1998.

Since the conference, the State Department belongs to scores of US institutions who have a piece of the Berlin Wall to call their own.

However, an enquiry to the State Department revealed another story. Nobody could remember anything about the pieces of the Wall. It was now claimed that it was unlikely that the sections of Wall, weighing hundreds of tonnes, would have been hauled up to the eighth floor. The sections of Wall seen on the photos were actually deceivingly good cardboard replicas. One of these replicas ended up in one of the Department's offices. It is not clear where the other sections ended up. There is, however, a genuine piece of the Wall at the State Department – albeit smaller. Since 1996, the Diplomacy Center has been home to an exhibition on US foreign politics. The exhibition consists of more than 300 exhibits from impressive presents given by guests to official documents. American diplomat, Douglas R. Keene, donated a small piece of Wall which can be found at the entrance to the exhibition.

From the moment visitors set foot in the Newseum in Washington, they are faced with a 12 metre-high watch tower once used by GDR border soldiers to get a good view over the deathstrip on Stallschrei-berstraße in Berlin Kreuzberg. Eight segments of the Wall can also be found next to it and are presumed to have come from the corner of Bethaniendamm/ Leuschnerdamm – also in Kreuzberg. This Wall-ensemble is the biggest of its kind to be found outside Germany, and

Location:
Newseum,
555 Pennsylvania
Avenue

Pieces of the Wall being put up
in Newseum in Washington
© The Freedom Forum

staff at the museum have been collecting the segments since 1994. The first piece in the collection was the watch tower, which was reported to have been saved from demolition by Rainer Hildebrand, founder of the museum 'Haus am Checkpoint Charlie'. When the land where the watch tower stood went up for sale, Hilde-brand wanted to save the tower. He then offered the tower to anyone willing to use it for non-profit purposes. There was, however, one condition: the costs to transport the tower had to be met by the new owner. Chris Wells, vice president of Freedom Parks, (which at the time were still under construction) jumped at the unique chance.

She travelled to Berlin and with cooperation from the Wall Museum, organised the dismantling and load-ing of the exhibit which weighed many tonnes. It was transported to America by haulage company Heilmann, which ownes numerous other sections of the Berlin Wall. Wells took the opportunity to buy a further 12 sections of the Wall, which had all been decorated by Wall artists like Thierry Noir and Jürgen Große (alias 'Indiano'). The cost of these segments (36,000 US dollars), was almost as much the price paid to transport them: it cost 40,000 US dollars to have them shipped to Baltimore. The precious load finally arrived in July 1994 and was taken the final 100 km to Arlington by lorry. Four of the sections were damaged in transit or deemed not fit for display in the exhibition. For this reason, only eight of the original 12 found a home in the exhibition. When Freedom Park was opened in 1997, the watch tower and Wall segments became the main attractions of the Newseums.

The museum and park hark back to the Freedom Forum. They combine history with the present day and presents the two in an impressive interactive theme park and museum. It focuses on the problems of managing freedom of speech, press and expression, but also tells the success stories of free and independent media, which has helped to make the importance of democracy and human rights abundantly clear. Other significant and unique exhibits in Freedom Park, which stretched out around Newseum, included a decapitated statue of Lenin, a ballot box from South Africa, a bronze casting of a boat used by Cuban refugees and the Berlin Wall with its watch tower. A new exhibition was opened to mark ten years since the Fall of the Wall. There were many prominent political figures in attendance. Former US Secretary of the Treasury, James Baker, and Marianne Birthler, former Federal Commissioner for the Stasi Archives in Berlin were both at the opening ceremony.

A series of pictures depicting the German division and a documentary about the roll of the media in both German states were added to the section of Wall which once made up part of the former border.

In 2006, the park closed its gates in Arlington and reopened at a new location in the heart of the American capital. The watch tower and segments of Wall, which had been on open-air display for almost ten years, were treated with great care as they were moved inside the museum and out of the wind and weather.

Pieces of the Wall in
Newseum Washington
© Maria Brik/ Newseum

Original border watch tower in
Newseum Washington
© Maria Brik/ Newseum

The massive Ronald Reagan Building and International Trade Center soars above Pennsylvania Avenue and is just a stone's throw away from the White House and the Capital. Plans for the enormous building were finalised in 1987 during Ronald Reagan's time in office. Today it is a place of work for many US government officials and international businesses. It was opened on 5th May 1998 after eight years under construction. A majority decision to name the building after Reagan had already been made three years earlier by Congress. A section of the Wall was donated by Daimler-Benz to mark the official opening. The segments were originally part of the border at the Brandenburg Gate. The plaque next to the segments explains that this section of the Wall was sprayed with graffiti on 11th November 1989 – two days after the Fall of the Wall:

„*Original section of the Berlin Wall*

At the conclusion of World War II, Berlin was administratively separated into four sectors, each controlled by one of the allies. Russia controlled the entire eastern half of the city, placing it firmly within the sphere of influence of the Communist Bloc. Over the years, the divided city of Berlin became the focal point of tension between East and West and a symbol of the continuing Cold War.

In August 1961, East Germany's ruling Socialist Party constructed a 103 mile-long wall surrounding West Berlin, which had remained „free" since the end of World War II. The wall's purpose was to prevent eastern Germans from leaving the east, in search of freedom in the western parts of the city.

On June, 12, President Ronald Reagan visited West Berlin, stood before the Brandenburg Gate and sent a message to the General Secretary of the Soviet Union:

„Mr. Gorbachev, open this gate! Mr. Gorbachev, tear down this wall!"

Less than two and on-half year later on November 9, 1989, the Berlin Wall was opened and the city of Berlin was free to unite once again. Over the 28 years the wall stood separating east from west, hundreds of east Berliners were killed to escape to the west by climbing over the wall.

This section on display was cut from an inner city section of the wall very near the Brandenburg Gate. The graffiti is original and appears as it did on November 11, 1989, when the eastern part of the city was reopened.

From the employees of Daimler-Benz and the citizens of Berlin, Germany"

Location:
Ronald Reagan Building and International Trade Center,
1300 Pennsylvania Avenue

The Wall in the Ronald Reagan
Building, Washington
© Kelly Cutchin

Location:
John Hopkins University, School for Advanced International Studies, 1740 Massachusetts Avenue

Jackson Janes, President of the American Institute for Contemporary German Studies at the Johns Hopkins University in Washington, made his way to Berlin in summer 1994 to find a piece of the Berlin Wall for his university. Janes had been in contact with the Berlin senate who had agreed to his request for a piece of the Wall. Janes had to change his plans when there were no small pieces of the Wall available, only complete segments. Plans to display the piece of Wall in a conference room were not viable due to the weight of the segment (2.6 tonnes). Janes did not let this ruin his plans and he went about choosing a piece of the Wall from the senate reserves.

The Wall in the School für Advanced Interntional Studies, Washington
© Kelly Cutchin

He chose a section which bore the letters 'FR'. Convinced that the letters made up the word 'frei', Janes organised for the section to be shipped to the US. Upon closer inspection back in Washington, it was clear to Janes that 'frei' was actually 'fred'. However, this was to have no impact on the segment's historical significance. The task of shipping the extremely heavy freight back to the US did not come without its problems. Arrangements still had to be made for the transportation costs and its assembly on the university campus. The University's dean, Paul Wolfowitz (who later became President of the World Bank) and Ted Baker, a university administrator, both offered financial support to the project. Despite this support, the cost of transporting the segment was still too expensive and the university asked the armed forces for help to bring the segment to the USA. It took years before Janes was given an answer. He eventually received a phone call from a military Attaché who informed him that his segment of Wall had arrived at a military airbase in Virginia. Plans to put the Wall on display in Washington could finally come to fruition and it was finally unveiled on 5th November 1997 – four days before the eighth anniversary of the Fall of the Wall.

LANGLEY (VIRGINIA), WASHINGTON D.C.
USA

Location:
CIA Headquarters

The Wall in front of the CIA
© fernsehbüro

One of the entrances at the CIA headquarters in Langley, Washington D.C., has been blocked by three segments of the Wall since December 1992. The US foreign intelligence service's website even points out that staff have to make a detour around the Wall memorial to access the premises. After all, these segments had prevented movement between East and West Berlin for almost three decades. Using them to block an entrance aims to give a new generation a sense of what the Wall actually meant. They were the first sections of Wall to be unveiled in the American capital in winter 1992.

They were a present from the Federal Republic of Germany and had previously stood at Potsdamer Platz. Two quotes have been painted in bright colours on them and supposedly date back to when the Wall stood in Berlin: "The wind cries freedom" and Ronald Reagan's famous line "Tear down the Wall".

General Haddock, commander of the US forces in Berlin, helped with the realisation of the project and was present at the unveiling. Director of central intelligence, Robert Gates, took the opportunity at the unveiling to explain why the sections of Wall were suitably placed at he CIA headquarters. In the same year the Wall was built, the CIA moved into its new buildings in Langley. Furthermore "it was in Berlin, where we worked to tear down the Wall. The names of those who worked there, took risks and fought for freedom, belong to some of the most famous names in CIA history. (…) America's secret services were prepared well for the challenges of the Cold War, in which military action was too severe and friendly diplomacy too mild. We helped our leaders to navigate through these precarious waters. We informed them of the danger of war and of the possibility for peace." Ultimately, the American secret services played a "key role in preventing a third world war and the triumph over Communism", as Gates remarked.

The Wall in front of the CIA
© fernsehbüro

Vernon A. Walters, Top-Agent, former Deputy CIA Director and US diplomat in Bonn when the Wall fell, recalled his impressions of Berlin on 10th November 1989 when he himself experienced the Wall being opened together with Haddock on Glienicke Bridge. For him, overcoming the Iron Curtain was also a personal victory which all members of the CIA could accredit to themselves. To close, he addressed his former colleagues: "So, I would just like to take this opportunity of coming back here to thank Director Gates, previous directors, other superiors of mine including the Secretary of the Army, and FBI Director Sessions for manning the battlements of the besieged citadel that never fell. It never fell because of you. Thank you."

EUROPE

NORTH AMERICA

CENTRAL AMERICA

SOUTH AMERICA

AFRICA

ASIA

AUSTRALIA AND OCEANIA

MARS

One segment of the Wall has made its was to Paradise Island in the Bahamas. It can be found on private land in the affluent neighbourhood of Lyford Cay, the capital of Nassau. The exclusive residential area, home to scores of millionaires from allover the world, is cut off from the outside world. It is not known who owns this section of Wall, nor how it made its way to the island. The island is a popular holiday destination for many Americans and there is no other country in the world where interest in such segments of the Wall is so great. One thing is for certain, this section of the Wall was bought during the first Wall auction in Monaco on 23rd June 1990. The 2.6 tonne section of Wall was orgionally on Potsdamer Platz and was sold as lot number 16 for 40,000 Francs. The words "Hello Virgin" can be read on one side. The rest of the brightly coloured graffiti is by anonymous artists.

NASSAU
BAHAMAS

Location:
Lyford Clay

SAN JOSÉ
COSTA RICA

Location:
Foreign Ministry, Costa
Rica, Avenida 7 y 9,
Calle 11 y 13

The Wall at the Federal Foreign
Office in Costa Rica
© Federal Foreign Office of Costa
Rica

S ince 1994, a section of the Berlin Wall has been on display in the gardens of the famous 'Casa Amarilla' (yellow house). The house is home to the Costa Rican foreign office. It was donated by former German foreign minister and honorary Latin American citizen, Hans-Dietrich Genscher. He donated it in response to a request for a section of the Wall from former Costa Rican foreign minister and personal friend, Bern Niehaus. Costa Rica was to be the first Latin American country to be in possession of an original section of the Wall.

The 2.6 tonne section of Wall was shipped to San Jose by haulage company, Hapag Lloyd. It was supposed to be put on display in a 'Garden of Freedom'. However, these plans were never realised and the section of Wall stands today in the foreigner ministry's garden in the centre of a fountain. Members of the public are not allowed on site, but the memorial can can be seen from the street.

The Wall at the Federal Foreign
Office in Costa Rica
© Federal Foreign Office of Costa
Rica

Location:
Plaza de Berlín

Plaza de Berlín in
Guatemala City
© German Embassy Guatemala

B erlín por la Libertad' (Berlin for Freedom) is a Wall memorial in Guatemala and can be found on 'Plaza de Berlín' (Berlin square). It was unveiled on 23rd May 1995. Those in attendance at the unveiling of the three segments included German ambassador Joachim Neukirch, mayor of Guatemala City, Oscar Berger Perdomos, and president of the German-Guatemalan Chamber of Commerce, Eugenio Bosch. The segments have been on display since then in a water feature over ten metres long. The intention of this memorial was to convey the importance of the victory over oppression and the core values of democracy to the citizens of Latin America. A small plaque in Spanish reminds us that this victory was even possible in divided Germany: "La fé del hombe por la libertad es más fuerte cualquier muro" ("The human belief in freedom is stronger than any wall").

The idea for the Wall memorial originally came from the German-Guatemalan Chamber of Commerce and had been put forward to the Guatemalan City mayor by the chamber's former chairman, Manfred Kratz. The project won ground after talks were held with the Berlin Senate and the election of Oscar Berger as Guatemalan City mayor. The decision to send three segments of the Berlin Wall to Guatemala was granted by the Berlin Senate in August 1991. The seven tonnes of Wall were shipped with the help and support of haulage company Schenker und Hapag Lloyd. They arrived in Santo Tomás de Castilla on 2nd September 1991. The construction costs were, however, higher than originally thought. The ambitious plans by architect Fidel Roberto Reyna envisaged a pond filled with water and decorated with mosaics. A three-metre concrete wall, covered in abstract images, rose from it. At the centre of the wall was a statue

The Wall memorial on Plaza de Berlín in Guatemala City
© German Embassy Guatemala

of Alexander Humboldt in between two maps, one of divided Berlin and one of divided Germany. The actual segments of Wall stand to the right on three bases of varying height. One of the sections is on its side to commemorate the Fall of the Wall. The construction work was finally completed in spring 1995 after four years of planning and construction. Plaza de Berlín, which had previously been quite unspectacular, now had a new attraction. The history of the square itself is also an interesting one. Former borough mayor Arturo Sandoval Soto first suggested turning the area – back then a waste tip – into the Berlin Square in 1965. His idea, however, was met with little enthusiasm. Soto's wife was a native German and he himself was on the committee at the Alexander von Humboldt Foundation. Despite protests from the local council, he took his idea to Francisco Montenegro Sierra, mayor of Guatemala City. He in turn spoke to his colleague, Willy Brandt, in Berlin who welcomed the idea. Critics in Guatemala City were won over with the idea that the unification of Berlin and the unification of Latin America were historical duties. Plaza de Berlín was opened in November 1965 by Guatemalan President Enrique Peralta Azurdia and Berlin Senator Klaus Schultz was also in attendance.

EL MURO

Gran Evento Histórico:
Develación del *Muro de Berlín*

Miércoles 3 de octubre de 1990

COLEGIO ALEMAN TEPEPAN

Av. México 5501 Col. Huichapan
(Noria) Tepepan, Xochimilco
México D.F.

Organizado por:

ASEGURADORA
CUAUHTEMOC, S.A.
Blvd. M. Avila Camacho No. 164
Col. Chapultepec Morales
C.P. 11570 México D.F.
Tels: 250 9800 / 395 3055
Telex: 1772617
Fax. 540 3204

ALLIANZ AG
Koniginstraße 28
Postfach 440124
D-8000 München 44
Telephon: 089 / 380 00
Telex: 5 230 110 a m d
Fax: 089 / 34 99 41,

Location:
German School,
Paseo Alexander von
Humboldt No.2 – III,
Sección Lomas Verdes,
Naucalpan de Juárez

German School,
Av. México 5501,
Col. Huichapan
(La Noria),
Del. Xochimilco

Unveiling ceremony at the
northern school on
3rd October 1990 (left)
© Colegio Aleman
Alexander von Humboldt /
Peter Thomann

Invitation to unveiling ceremony
in Mexico City (right)
© Colegio Aleman
Alexander von Humboldt

Two sections of the Berlin Wall were erected in Mexico City to commemorate German reunification on 3rd October 1990. A single segment can be found at both of the 'Alexander von Humboldt' schools – one in the southern borough of Xochimilco and one in the northern neighbourhood of Lomas Verdes. The 'Alexander von Humboldt' schools, founded in 1884, belong to the largest German schools abroad. The unveiling of the sections of Wall took place to the sounds of Mexican folk music and the school choir singing Beethoven's 'Ode to Joy' in German.

Philipp Fabry, former headmaster originally from the Eifel made the official opening speech. Present at the ceremony were guests including Mexican President Carlos Salinas de Gortaris, Secretary of Public Education Manuel Bartlett Díaz and acting East Berlin Mayor, Hartmut Hempel. The idea to put up sections of the Wall on this site came to school chairman Gerhart. E Reuss whilst reading the 'Economist' at the start of the nineties. West Berlin company 'LeLé Berlin' had been given the task of selling the Wall, the proceeds for which should be used for charitable purposes in the GDR.

Reuss, who is also on the board of directors at the insurance company 'Allianz', was able to gain support for the project from German businessmen, Erich and Kurt Vogt. Reuss travelled to East Berlin to oversee the sale of the Wall segments personally. He recalls his experience with 'Limex', the company responsible for selling the Wall like this:

The piece of Wall in front of the southern German school in Mexico City
© Ludwig Johannsen

"100,000 was the asking price for two sections of the Wall, each one 3.6 metres high and each weighing two and a half tonnes. However, due to the fact that the buyer was a German school, a price of 30,000 Marks would be accepted. The proceeds would go to the Charité and a certificate confirming the authenticity (presented upon transaction) was promised. But you were allowed to pick out your own piece. Come back tomorrow and a police official will take you to the storage area. The money had been raised by Reuss and the Vogt brothers. And, true to their word, a man arrived on time and we went in his car to the People's Police barracks just outside the city. I was still at this time inclined to think that East Germany was still some sort of dictatorship, albeit one in decline.

This opinion quickly changed when I was chauffeured past the guards and into the barracks. The Guards, with loose ties, their uniform hats pushed back on their heads and cigarettes hanging out of their mouths, waved us through. In that moment it became clear to me: this state is no more. Hundreds of sections from the Wall were standing on a filed behind the bar-

From West Berlin to Mexico City – the piece of Wall in the northern school

© Archiv Bundesstiftung Aufarbeitung, Coll. Rosmarie Gentges, No. 8

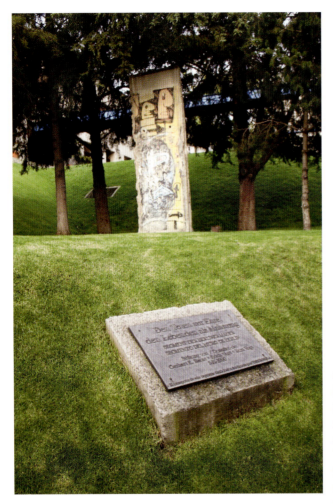

racks. Just as you would say to a child in a sweet shop, my officer told me, Mister Reuss, just take your pick. You have my word that you will get the pieces you choose. And that's how it happened. The segments were then shipped back to Mexico after a generous donation was made by a German-Mexican shipping company."

A small plaque in German was put on the segment in the south school:„DEN TOTEN ZUR EHRE, DEN LEBENDEN ALS MAHNUNG" (IN HONOUR OF THE DEAD, A WARNING TO THE LIVING). The bits of graffiti seen on this section are leftovers from the famous wall heads painted by Thierry Noir, in the mid-80s, on Waldemarstraße.

The section at the north school was placed next the main entrance. The Graffiti, also by Noir, on this segment is protected by a metal frame. The sections that originally stood to the left of these sections in Berlin can now be found in Paris under the name 'König Buffo'.

EUROPE

NORTH AMERICA

CENTRAL AMERICA

SOUTH AMERICA

AFRICA

ASIA

AUSTRALIA AND OCEANIA

MARS

Location:
Palacio San Martín

The Wall in the Argentinean
Foreign Ministry in
Buenos Aires
© Federación de Asociaciones
Argentino-Germanas

San Martín palace has been home to the Argentina foreign ministry since 1936 and its grand gardens are home to an original section of the Berlin Wall. It is situated between two palm tress the remains of graffiti can still be seen on it. A plaque at the site has the following text on it:

„… este fragmento pone de manifiesto la amistad entre la Republica Federal de Alemania y la República Argentina; el mismo une simbolicamente al pueblo Argetino con la istoria de la Capital Alemanna y nos recuerda que la libertad, la democrazia y los derechos humanos nunca se enconraran asegurados si los ciudadanos de cada nacion no se esfueerzan por su defensa y hasta luchan por ellos.."
(Acta de donation de senato de Berlín al Ministerio de relaciones exteriores de la República Argentinia)
En ocasion del 10 aniversario de la caida del Muro de Berlín, el 9-XI 1999
Ignacio Guido di Tella / Cancaler
Dr. Adolf Ritter von Wagner / Embajador de Alemanna"
"…this fragment is testament to the friendship between the Republic of Argentina and the Federal Republic of Germany: it symbolically combines the Argentinian people with the history of the German capital and reminds us that freedom, democracy and human rights cannot be secured if a nation's people do not stand up for their rights, or even fight for them…"
(Donated to the Foreign Ministry of the Republic of Argentina by the Berlin Senate)
To commemorate 10 years since the Fall of the Wall on 9th November 1999
Ignacio Guido di Tella / Foreign Minister
Dr. Adolf Ritter von Wagner / German Ambassador"

The segment of Wall from the Berlin Senate was presented to the Argentinian government in February 1999 as part of Roman Herzog's state visit.

BUENOS AIRES
ARGENTINA

Location:
Foyer at Editoria Perfil,
Chacabucco 271

The Wall in the entrance area
today at Editoria Perfil
© Editoria Perfil

The discovery of America by Christopher Columbus in 1492 was no less significant to world history as the Fall of the Berlin Wall was in 1989. When Argentinian capital Buenos Aires prepared the festivities for the 500th anniversary of Columbus's expedition in 1992, both events were to be at the centre of attention. A replica of the ship in which the Spanish sailor had once found his way into the New World was put on display in the old harbour of Buenos Aires. The exhibition grounds at "America 92" were filled with a replica of a Maya pyramid, several pavilions of American countries, a dolphinarium and other attractions to represent the diversity of both American continents. Thematically and visually, the Berlin Wall seemed slightly lost in this ensemble. Artistic director of the exhibition Rafael Jijena Sánchez tried his best to display the segments of the Wall. Supported by the largest hispanic publishing house, Editoria Perfil, 20 running metres of the boundary wall were shipped to Buenos Aires. Ironically, the ship that transported the 50-tonne freight across the Atlantic Ocean in 1991 was called "Leningrad". Once they had crossed the Atlantic, the concrete slabs were loaded onto 20 lorries, which brought them to the exhibition grounds. There, visitors welcomed two segments of the Wall at the beginning of the exhibition, suspended high up in the air from a crane. On the inside of the of the pavilion, images of the divided Berlin were shown on a wall made from sections of the Berlin Wall. For the more courageous visitors, there was also the possibility of re-enacting an attempted escape through a tunnel under two of the segments. Naturally, this took place under the watchful eyes of the border guards – rubber dolls dressed as border guards at least. Accompanied by Richard Wagner's 'Tannhäuser', visitors left the pavilion over a ramp. On the last metres of the exhibition to both

Pieces of the Wall arriving in
Buenos Aires in 1992
© Editoria Perfil

sides, visitors could read the names of 195 people who were killed attempting escape from the GDR. The Checkpoint Charlie Museum provided support and advice for the exhibition.

After the festivities, eight of the segments shipped to Buenos Aires were then taken to the Editoria Perfil Centre, where the flaking concrete slabs were placed in the entrance hall. Between marble, glass and steel in the entrance hall, they seem somewhat out of place with "Fuck you" graffitied along them. Editoria Perfil's management, however, are proud of the pieces from the Berlin Wall. The publishing house, which is linked to several influential newspapers and TV channels advocates independent and critical journalism.

SUCRE
BOLIVIA

Location:

Casa de la Libertad,
Plaza 25 de Mayo Nr. 11

One hundred and eighty years before the Fall of the Berlin Wall, South and Latin American colonies rose up against Spanish rule. Ecuador was the first country to claim independence on 10th August 1809 and Bolivia soon followed suit after their first calls for freedom began on 25th May 1809. 1809 marks the prelude for the Spanish American wars of independence which ended with the break up of the colonies. Many of the Latin American revolutionists were educated at the Jesuit Missions of Chiquitos. It was here that the leaders of the first free Bolivian government met in July 1825 after the country's independence had been declared. The Bolivian government still met in the rooms of the university which now has the name "Casa de la Libertad" (House of Freedom). Today there is a museum dedicated to the independence movement. Three sections of the Wall were presented to the 'House of Freedom' at the start of the 1990s by German ambassador, Hermann Saumweber – they can still be found there today. Whilst carrying out research for the book, it was revealed, however, that they are no longer on display in the exhibition. Considerations are, however, being made to put them back on public display.

Location:
In front of the German Embassy in Vitacura of Santiago de chile, Las Hualtatas 5677

The Wall in front of the German

embassy in Santiago de Chile

© German Embassy Santiago de Chile

In early 1990, students from Universidad de Chile asked the GDR government for a section of the Berlin Wall. They had been inspired by the massive interest in the construction, steeped in history. They wanted to put up the section of Wall in the Chilean capital and then auction it. The proceeds made at the auction would then go towards a social project in Pudahuel – a commune of Chile located in Santiago Province.

The German Embassy in Chile report that a section of the Wall was indeed given for free by "Mauergesellschaft e.V". Chilean students who were studying in Berlin at the time took the piece of Wall into their care, but were then faced with the problem of how to get the 2.6 tonnes of Wall back to Chile. Thanks to help from Wiegand Pabsch, former German ambassador in Santiago de Chile, the project could be realised. Ultramar shipping agency, whose director, Albert von Appen, was born in Hamburg, transported the section of Wall free of charge once it had been brought via train from Berlin to Hamburg.

In 1991, it arrived in the Chilean seaport of Valparaiso. An offer was made to buy it by the German Embassy and the students were given a donation in the name of the Federal Republic of Germany towards the social project. The Wall was finally put on display at the embassy on 3rd October 1991 – Day of German Unity.

In spring 1992, the students worked together with the German embassy to organise a competition to paint the piece of Wall. Chilean artists were called upon to take inspiration from the Fall of the Wall and Ger-

Moving the Wall section

© German Embassy
Santiago de Chile

man reunification. Famous artists including José Balmes, Gracia Barrios, José Basso and Carmen Aldunate all took part and the fifty best works were showcased in an exhibition. Wiegand Pabsch recalls the opening:

"With Doña leonor (wife of the Chilean president Patricio Aylwin Azócar at the time), Minister for Education Ricardo Lagos and 1500 guests, I presented both sides of the Wall – barren ugliness towards the East, where bleakness reigned, and the vivid colours on the West where the steadfast ideal "Think Global" provided a solution. As it happened, the architect who had designed this prison wall now lives as a sheltered guest at the Chilean embassy. The applause was immense, the message had been heard."

The fact that GDR party leader Erich Honecker had sought refuge in the Chilean Embassy in Berlin was nothing more than a historical coincidence. It was not long before Honecker was handed over to the German authorities and, charged with issuing the order to shoot at the inner German border. He was released shortly after due to his state of ill health. Honecker then travelled to Chile where he died in Santiago de Chile in 1994.

G erman colonists settled on the Uruguay River, not far from the Argentinean border around 1850. Brothers Karl and Richard Wendelstandt created a settlement called 'Nueva Melhem', which, thanks to successful agricultural cultivation, grew and thrived economically. 20 years later, the brothers bought further areas of land around Nueva Melhem and brought in an architect, Fridolin Quincke, to plan a town. In 1875, Nueva Melhem became 'Nuevo Berlín'. The original settlement, made up prominently of Germans, grew further thanks to good trade. Locals and people from other countries became integrated into the society in the following decades.

It was thanks to trading contacts that a section of the Berlin Wall found its way to Uruguay. A *Freedom and Wall Memorial* was unveiled on 9th March 1991 in the centre of Nuevo Berlín and was the result of a German- Uruguayan chamber of commerce cooperation. In attendance at the unveiling were representatives from local government, the German embassy and "Los Alpinos", a group from Montevideo who sings in traditional Bavarian folk style.

The group provided Bavarian folk music to which the section of Wall was handed over to the public. A small plaque reminds residents about the significance of the Fall of the Wall:

"trozo del muro de Berlin echado abajo el 9.11.1989. Simbolo del ansia de libertad del hombre. La camara de comecio Uruguayo – Alemana al pueblo de nuevo Berlin"

"Piece of the Berlin Wall, torn down on 9.11.1989. Symbol of the people's longing for freedom. Presented by the German- Uruguayan Chamber of Commerce to the people of Nuevo Berlin"

The president of the local government of Rio Negro was also presented with two lime trees. The lime trees make up the first part of a copy of the Berliner boulevard "Unter den Linden" (under the lime trees). A few years later, the name of the local school was also changed to "República Federal de Alemania" (Federal Republic of Germany).

Location:
Crossing at avenida romay and allee "alemania"

Unveiling ceremony
in Nuevo Berlín
© Dr. W. Forker

A group of folk dancers
at the unveiling ceremony
© Dr. W. Forker

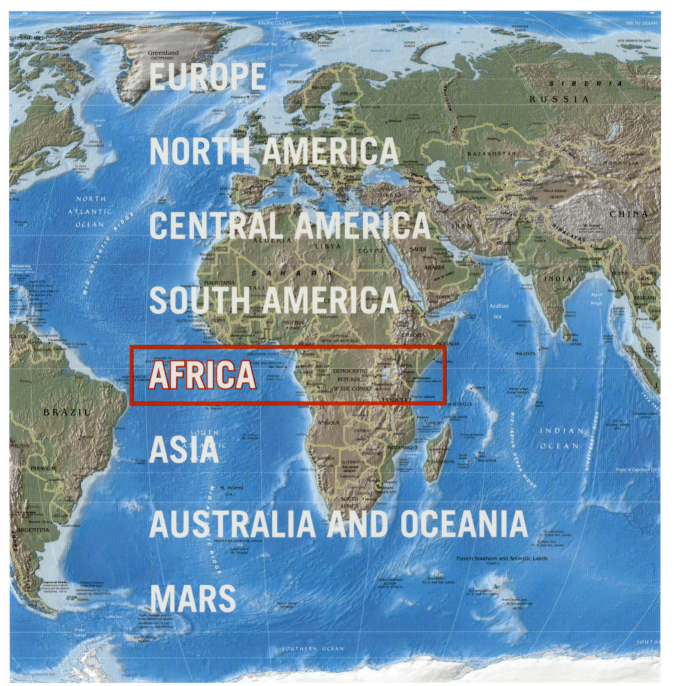

EUROPE

NORTH AMERICA

CENTRAL AMERICA

SOUTH AMERICA

AFRICA

ASIA

AUSTRALIA AND OCEANIA

MARS

Location:
St. Georges Mall

The Wall in Cape Town
© Marco Schmitt

The Fall of the Berlin Wall and the release of Nelson Mandela from prison were more than historical coincidences." These are the words of the German Ambassador in South Africa, Dr. Uwe Kästner upon receiving a segment of the Berlin Wall which can still be seen today in the harbour of the capital city. He was presented with the segment by the city of Berlin during a state visit by Nelson Mandela in May 1996. Mandela and Köstner had picked out the piece personally in Berlin. It was brought to South Africa in summer 1996 by the German Federal Navy from Wilhelmshaven, a coastal town in Lower Saxony. The handing over of the segment coincided with the Day of German Unity on 3rd October 1996 and brought with it a new chapter in German-South African relations. South Africa, which had been isolated for so long by its apartheid regime, agreed to a cooperation agreement with the German Armed Forces.

The Mayor of Cape Town, Theresa Solomon, accepted the piece of Wall and promised to find a suitable location for it. Amongst the suggested locations was 'Waterfront', an amusement centre in Cape Town. Ships had once left here on their way to Robben Island where Nelson Mandela was imprisoned for 28 years. He was released following international pressure on 11th May 1990. President Frederik Willem de Klerk was elected as head of state in September 1989. In February 1990, he called for the ANC (led my Mandela) to be unbanned and, thus, led the end of the apartheid regime.

In 1993, he and Nelson Mandela received the Nobel Peace Prize for their roles in bringing an end to apartheid.

Mandela was elected as South Africa's President four years later in the first free elections. Cape Town's famous 'District Six' was also considered as a location for the section of Wall. The district, which is populated mainly by people of colour, gained upsetting fame when the South African government ordered the forced displacement of people in order to make a settlement for "whites". All citizens were forced to move to other districts and 'District Six' was levelled to the ground.

A decision was made in favour of Waterfront. However, it was put up almost at the end of the harbour promenade near to the BMW Pavillon. Very few people make their way to this remote location. When BMW sold its Pavillon in 2010 (which had not only been used as a sales house, but also an exhibition space), there no longer appeared to be an apparent connection between the Wall and its former location. Since then, the piece of Wall has been on display on St. George's Mall, the inner-city's pedestrian zone. More people visit the new location which is near to the St. George Cathedral, the parliament and the famous Company's Garden

There is a small plaque at the bottom of the Wall section which commemorates the history of division and the building of the Berlin Wall.

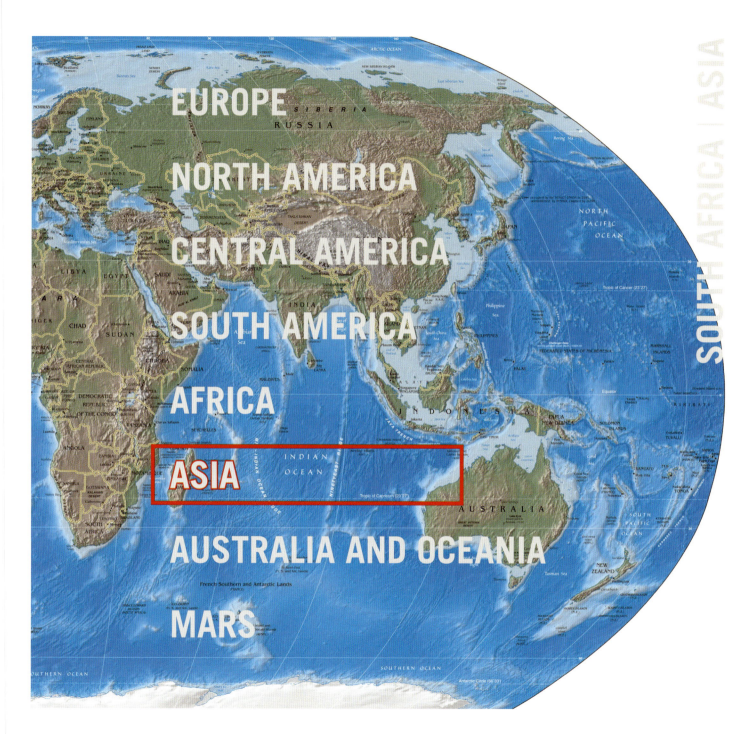

EUROPE

NORTH AMERICA

CENTRAL AMERICA

SOUTH AMERICA

AFRICA

ASIA

AUSTRALIA AND OCEANIA

MARS

Remains of the Wall in Teguh
Ostenrik's garden, Jakarta
© Teguh Ostenrik / B. Haryanto

raised, however, the plans were scrapped. There was renewed hope in 1994 when Berlin and Jakarta became twin towns. In return for economic assistance, the government of the Indonesian capital promised to
set up a Berlin Square, where the segments of the Wall would eventually find a new home. But the plans
were once again scrapped. The economic crisis in the 1990s hit the island state hard – so bad that the
funding ran dry. The Berlin Senate was also unable to help out with the project.

Today, the four segments of the Wall are situated outside the artist's studio on open-air display alongside
the first human steel sculptures Ostenrik had made at the beginning of the 1990s. He cannot expect any
support from the Indonesian government. According to the artist, it lacks "the ability for abstract thinking".
Hoping that he will be able to go ahead with his plans in Berlin, the artist would even go so far as to take
the segments of the Wall back in order to finish off the project.

EIN HOD
ISRAEL

Location:
Janco-Dada-Museum

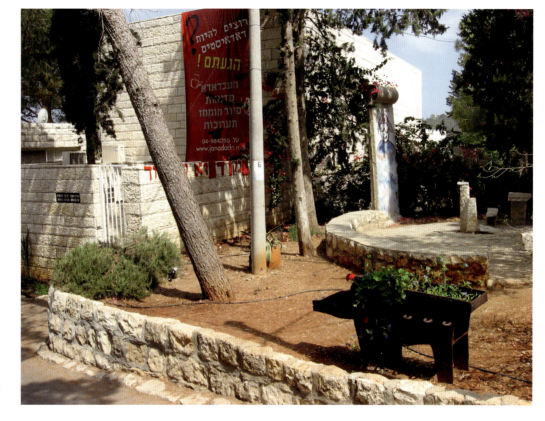

The Wall in front of the
Janco-Dada-Museum, Ein Hod
© Ein Hod Visitors Centre

Since 1992, a brightly painted piece of the Wall has stood in front of Marco Janco's museum (founder of Dadaism). West Berliner, Patrice Lux, sprayed the segments with an image of a little boy wearing a red baseball cap and sunglasses. It is meant to be a memorial for the victims of the Holocaust. A small plaque with Hebrew inscriptions can be found at the bottom of the piece:

"A piece of the Berlin Wall. Purchased and erected thanks to the donation of a member of the board of trustees of the Janco-Dada-Museum in memory of his mother, Perl Jablonka and his sisters, Chaja and Dwora, who were killed behind the walls of the Warsaw ghetto in 1943."

This dedication goes to show that the Fall of the Berlin Wall was not symbolic of freedom and justice for the whole world. In Israel, it stirred up traumatic memories amongst survivors of the Holocaust. The division of Germany was considered appropriate punishment for the genocide of European Jews in Hitler's Germany. Nevertheless, Raya Zommer, the curator of the Janco-Dada-Museum at the time, was thrilled by the enthusiasm she experienced on a visit to Berlin in 1991. A friend had told her about the museum at Checkpoint Charlie. The exhibition there about the inner-German border had been shown in many places within the former Eastern Bloc. It was brought to the artists' village, Ein Hod South, south of Haifa in Northern Israel and called "Beyond the Wall". It was put on display in the Janco-Dada-Museum. The museum had been cleared especially for the exhibition in 1992. The exhibition gained international attention: even a

high-ranking representative of the German Embassy was present at the opening. Survivors of the Holocaust did not have any understanding for the intentions behind it. For them, the separation of Germany was an "appropriate punishment", and the idea of a reunified Germany instilled fear. For the curator, however, it was about something entirely different: in the face of the horror of the Cold War and the inhumane Berlin Wall, she wanted to spark a debate about human rights.

When the exhibition came to an end, the curator of Checkpoint Charlie Museum, Rainer Hildebrand, presented the piece of the Wall to Janco-Dada-Museum. Several years later, it was on sale. Fortunately, a member of the board of trustees purchased the concrete slab and it remained in Ein Hod. The new owner, Zeev Yalon, and his wife eventually decided to put up the plaque in memory of his mother and sisters. In doing so, he bridged the gap between the darkest chapter in German history and the Fall of the Wall.

HIKONE
JAPAN

Location:
Maruho Co. Ltd.

The Wall in Hikone
© Maruho Co. Ltd.

Jiro Takagi was director of pharmaceutical company, 'Maruho Co. Ltd.' in Hikone in Central Japan. In November 1989, whilst watching the events in Berlin unfold on his TV, he decided his company should make a contribution to world history. Takagi wanted to get hold of a segment of the Wall for the company in an attempt to enlighten his younger members of staff. It was supposed to stand here as a symbol of freedom and to make people think about the most recent events in Japanese history during World War II.

The sale of the Berlin Wall had begun in early 1990 in the GDR, and Takagi got in touch with his partner company in Berlin Kreuzberg 'Dr. Kade'. Both companies are connected by a long history. Founded at the end of the 19th century in Berlin, the pharmaceutical company had an international breakthrough in 1922 by launching the world's first haemorrhoid compound. Just one year later, they became business partners with Maruho in Japan.

The benefactor of the Wall in
Hikone: Jiro Takagi
© Maruho Co. Ltd.

Arthur Felix Sackler, owner at the time, granted Takagi's wish immediately. In April 1990, Segment 28 from Checkpoint Charlie was bought from 'Limex', the company tasked with selling the Wall by the GDR. Intended as a gift for Jiro Takagi's upcoming 70th birthday, the segment of the Wall arrived at Kobe harbour in June 1990 just in time. Japanese customs, however, denied the delivery of the freight at first, as they were not sure how to tax it: as art, or as debris. As a result, the segment of Wall could not be officially unveiled until 20th November 1990 in the garden of Maruho Co. Ltd. To prevent further damage from wind and rain, it was soon placed in the entrance hall.

This is where it can still be found today with a map and a Japanese description of the course of the Wall from Brandenburg Gate to Checkpoint Charlie. Limex certificates of authenticity in Japanese and German have been put up alongside it.

NAGOYA
JAPAN

Location:

Protestant Congregation
Nagoya-Tenpaku,
Umezato 2-82-1,
Midori-Ku, Nagoya-Shi,
Aichi-Ken, 458-0001

Cross made from segments
of the Wall at the community
centre in Nagoya
© Dankmar Hottenbacher

At the inauguration of the protestant community centre in the Japanese city Nagoya between Tokio and Osaka, the congregation was presented with four different crosses: one on the roof, one in the prayer room, the third next to the entrance of the church and a fourth wooden cross was given to each member of the congregation. The cross next to the entrance, made from small pieces of the Berlin Wall, has been inset in the Wall and is intended to serve as a symbol of freedom and remind people of the opening of the border. The idea came

from Protestant missionary, Erhard Hottenbacher, who had been the head of the parish council for many years. He remembers the Fall of the Berlin Wall and how the pieces of Wall made their way to Japan:

Friedemann Hottenbacher
at the Berlin Wall
© Dankmar Hottenbacher

"In autumn 1989, we had our charity bazar in our chapel in Nagoya (back then the chapel was small and made of wood). Due to the large amount of 'proper German' things in the area it was well received. It was easy to get Japanese people interested in all things German. German lessons, German-themed nights and concerts were all ways in which we drummed up interest. The Wall had fallen just a few weeks before the bazar. We saw a picture in the papers of Genscher presenting a piece of the Wall to the President of the United States. That's how we came up with the idea of asking our son, Friedemann, who studied in Berlin at the time, to send some stones and fragments over, so we could sell them at the Bazar in smaller pieces. The crowd of interested people was overwhelming. All profits went to a Christian charity for Africa."

OSAKA
JAPAN

Location:
Temple of Toukokuji,
Ten-nouji,
chausuyama 1-31

Memorial stone next to the Wall
in Osaka
© Takahisa Matsuura

The Toukokuij-Temple is in the heart of the Japanese metropolitan city of Osaka. It was founded by settling immigrants from Baekje around the 7th century. Legend has it, that the first priest had a tumulus built north of where the temple is today. It is now part of a different sanctuary. Since then, the Toukouji Temple has had strong ties to the Korean Peninsula. Two members of the congregation presented the house of worship with two pieces of the Wall in 1998. They are meant to be an expression of the longing for reunification of North and South Korea. A small Memorial stone with Korean and Japanese inscriptions reminds visitors of this.

The Wall in Osaka
© Takahisa Matsuura

TOGITSU
JAPAN

Location:
Nihon Bisoh,
3788 Hinami, Togitsu,
Nagasaki 851-2108

Staff at Nihon Bisho
in front of the Wall
© Nihon Bisho Co., Ltd.

The only segment of the Wall outside Germany complete with its own door found its way to Japan in 1990. Nihon Bisoh, member of the executive board of a company that maintains façades, purchased it from GDR company 'Limex'. The unconventional piece of Berlin Wall originally stood at the Brandenburg Gate. Today's owners were unable to tell us how much was paid for the piece. Together with a certificate of authenticity and two 'Limex'-seals, segment 'B008' arrived along with the keys to the door in summer 1990. Plans had originally been made to use it as the founding piece for a museum, "Outside Walls". Nihon Bihon's board of managers saw moral obligations in this: the company, who mainly produced cars for ladder lifts, would need to think about the more profound meaning of walls. The idea for the museum has not yet been realised. The segment of the Wall found a new location in the Nihon Bisho factory in Togitsu and it is pointed out to all visitors and members of staff on tours around the factory building. The owners are particularly proud of the door and its keys, and it is always made clear to guests how rare these pieces are.

In the 1970s, upon orders from the GDR government, the border installations to West Berlin were modernised. Instead of the varied types of the Wall seen up until then, the well-known L-shaped concrete components were to be erected. Three years after the work on "Grenzmauer 75" (Border Wall 75) had started, the East German border troops found it hard to gain access to the border strip where the Wall should be erected. This was especially so in inner-city areas and it resulted in a small strip of East Berlin being easily accessible from the West. Whilst trespassing the Wall from the West was made impossible by Border Wall 75, this was also the case for the East German border troops from the other side, who could no longer secure all of the GDR's territory. The chief commander of the Berlin Mitte commando brought

The Wall with the door arriving (left)
© Nihon Bisho Co., Ltd.

The Wall at Nihon Bisho (right)
© Nihon Bisho Co., Ltd.

people's attention to this predicament. To prevent nasty surprises, and, moreover, to enable the removal of graffiti on the West Berlin side of the Wall, it was decided in autumn 1978 that doors should be fitted in these sections of the Wall. As well as the technical problems this posed (the concrete elements were made centrally and it was hard to make any adjustments when unforeseen problems arose), the East German border guards were mainly worried about possible escape attempts through the doors. Two different locks were to be installed, and the keys were to be kept safe in order to prevent such escape attempts. In spring 1980, the first door was tested in the Berlin Mitte segment of the border. A further 35 doors were to be installed by 1983 at different sites along the Wall. Two doors were installed at the Brandenburg Gate in 1982, one of which is now in Japan.

UENO, MIYAKO-JIMA
JAPAN

Location:
German cultural village
Ueno, Miyako-jima,
Prefecturer Okinawa

The Wall in German
cultural village, Ueno
© Takahisa Matsuura

On 2nd July 1873, a massive typhoon smashed German trade ship J.R. Robertson to pieces just off the Japanese Island of Miyako-jima. Despite the stormy sea, residents from the coastal village of Ueno used their own boats to come to the aid of the Germans on board the ill-fated ship. All of the men on board the ship were rescued. The Germans were taken in by the fishermen and one month later, they were able to sail back to the main land and travel home. German emperor, Wilhelm I, was deeply impressed by the help the German sailors had been offered. To say thank you, he donated a memorial stone which can still be seen today at the port in Hirara.

120 years on, these events were the inspiration for the founding of a German cultural village in the small fishing village of Ueno. The idea came in 1987. Ancestors of the fishermen who had saved the German

Location:
Jeju April 3 Peace
Memorial Park,
53-5 Bongae-Dong

The Wall in front of the
Jeju Peace Institute
© Jeju Peace Institute

On the morning of the 3rd of April 1948, enraged farmers and fishermen started an uprising on the Korean Island of Jeju. They attacked police stations and the authorities of the central government in Seoul. The poorly-armed rebels managed, for a short period of time, to get the island under their control, until the South Korean secret services and the army struck back ruthlessly.

The cause of the uprising was the military regime on the island at the time. Liberated from the Japanese occupation in 1945, most people on Jeju hoped for a better future. Oppression and exploitation were to be replaced by self-administration that would provide for better subsistence of farmers and fishermen. Among them were followers of a socialist movement, who had returned to the island after imprisonment and forced labour. Opposing them were the police, who had collaborated with Japan previously, and were now taken on to work for the Korean secret services. Furthermoe, there were anti-communist refugees who united to work against the alleged leftist islanders. For the population of the island, one occupying power had been replaced by the other. Assaults, blackmail and attacks ruled the day on Jeju. The American occupying power did not interfere and tolerated the politics implemented by the government in Seoul. In spring 1948, 30,000 people demonstrated in the islands capital Jeju-si. The police fired their guns into the unarmed public and killed six people. Just a few weeks later, the uprising began.

A piece of the inner German
border on Jeju
© Jeju Peace Institute

The response from the South Korean police and security services was brutal. More than half of the settlements were burned down and its inhabitants were displaced or shot. Between 25,000 and 30,000 islanders became victims of this unprecedented massacre in the following months. Special military services were deployed to Jeju whilst the American military watched the murders without interfering. One year later, and the last remaining rebels had been killed. When North Korea attacked the South of the country in 1950, alleged rebels were arrested and shot once again. What followed was 50 years of silence – the events were not recognised. It was not until 1992 that the silence was broken and permission was given to lay some of those to rest who had been buried in mass graves. Eight years later, the government in Seoul passed a law to throw light on the events on Jeju in 1948. The inquiry panel produced a report in 2003 in which all guilt was acknowledged. President Roh Moo-Hyun offered an official apology to the inhabitants of Jeju. To commemorate the victims, the April 3rd Peace Park was built in 2003. Alongside a large memorial and an altar for the victims, a museum was also opened.

Today, there also are two segments of the Berlin Wall, which arrived on the island as gifts from the city of Berlin in 2007. Former ambassador in Berlin and chancellor of the Jeju Peace Institute, Youngmin Kwon, tried to obtain the segments together with the administrators of the island. According to Jae-hawn Kim, the

Wall art by
Jung Hyun Kim in Jeju
© Jeju Peace Institute

Planning and Coordination Officer from the Jeju Peace Institute, the Berlin Wall and the uprising in Jeju in 1948 were results of the block confrontation. Both were eventually overcome peacefully, and the island is an eligible location for the segments. They were originally located on the Sony site at Potsdamer Platz and were given to the Berlin Senate in 2005. Marked with a plaque to show that they are a present from Sony to the capital, they are now on open-air display.

The Borderlandmuseum Eichsfeld in Thuringia donated a further section of the inner-German border. A two-metre-wide section of metal fence – like those found along the former border – was put on display at a Memorial Park in 2007.

Two years earlier, Sylvestre Verger's exhibition about the Wall was hosted in Jeju-si. Works by international Wall artists were exhibited and entitled 'From the DMZ to the Berlin Wall'. Korean artists were given sections of concrete from the Wall to mark the exhibition and they can still be seen in Jeju-si today. Jung Hyun Kim mounted a whole piece of the so-called "hinterland Wall" in a bracket and marked it with the letters "DMZ". The abbreviation stands for the de-militarised strip of border separating North and South Korea since 1953. Hoping for a reunion of the two states, Suk Won Park connected a black and a white piece of the Wall with an inscription reading 'one'. Upon a final piece of the Wall, Sung Mook Choi painted a left-facing swastika, which is a symbol of love in Korea.

"Love" by
Sung Mook Choi in Jeju
© Jeju Peace Institute

SEOUL
REPUBLIC OF KOREA

Location:
Between Sanghuh
Memorial Library and
Konkuk University
Hospital, Konkuk
Universtity.

The Wall on Campus at
Konkuk University Seoul

© Konkuk University, Seoul,
South Korea

In 1946, one year after the Korean liberation from Japanese occupation, the Chosun Political Science School was opened. The school was dedicated to the education of scientists who were to help build an independent state. Despite the Korean War and the separation of the peninsula, the university grew and was re-named Konkuk University in 1959.

The campus in the South Korean capital boasts a large collection of stones from all across the world, which have been collected over many decades. A very special stone was provided by the Berlin Senate in 1991. Former president of Konkuk University, Seung-yune Yoo, together with the Pacific State University in Los Angeles tried to obtain a segment from the former border fortification. Overcoming this border was supposed to be an inspiration to the separated Korean peninsula. The Pacific State University purchased a piece of the Wall, 1.2 metres-high and formerly located at Brandenburg Gate, and had it shipped to Seoul. There is a plaque to certify its authenticity.

The ceremonial presentation of the segment as a memorial to the reunion of both Korean states followed on 30th November 1993 at Konkuk University. On the front of it, an inscription in Korean and English reads:

233

제2차 세계대전의 패전국 독일은 1949년 동독과 서독으로 양분되었으나,
1990년 8월 30일 통일조약으로 게르만 민족의 염원인 통일독일이 이루어지고,
그동안 동·서독을 갈라 놓았던 베를린 장벽이 철거되었다.
베를린 장벽의 일부인 이 콘크리트 구조물은 학교법인 건국대학교 명예 이사장 유승윤 박사가
게르만 민족의 통일문제에 깊은 관심을 가지고 미국 Pacific States University로
하여금 교섭하게 한 결과 베를린 시장으로부터 기증을 받은 것으로
한반도의 통일을 기원하는 상징적인 의미로 이곳에 세운다.

1993년 11월 30일
학교법인 건국대학교
이사장 현 승 종

Lost in World War II, Germany is divided into East and West Germanies in 1949.
Under the Unification Treaty on August 30, 1990,
the two Germanies are unified and the Berlin Walls are demolished.
Asked by Dr. Seung-yune Yoo in his consideration of the meaning of the unification
of Germany, the Former Chairman of the Kon-Kuk University Foundation,
cooperated with Pacific States University, and donated by the mayor of the Berlin City,
this monument, a part of the Berlin wall, is installed as symbol
to represent our wish for the Korean Unification.

November 30, 1993

Dr. Soong-Jong Hyun
Chairman
Kon-Kuk University Foundation

Informaiton board on the Wall
at Konkuk University Seoul
© Konkuk University, Seoul,
South Korea

„This concrete structure is an important portion of
the Berlin Wall which once separated East from West
Germany. Hoping that the peaceful unification of our
country will come true at the earliest possible date, we
should ruminate on the significance of the fence."

Certificate of authentication
on the Wall at
Konkuk University Seoul
© Konkuk University, Seoul,
South Korea

234

SEOUL
REPUBLIC OF KOREA

Location:

Cheonggyecheon,
at Samilgyo Bridge

The Wall on "Berlin Square"
in Seoul
© Seoul Metropolitan Government

Since 28th September 2005, three segments of the Berlin Wall, a blue Berlin 'Buddy Bear' decorated with an image of the Brandenburg Gate and an original Berlin gas lantern can be seen in the South Korean capital Seoul on 'Berlin Square'. The installation by Rolf Biser was given to the twin City in Korea by the Berlin Senate as a symbol of the friendship and connection between the two cities. Klaus Wowereit, Mayor of Berlin also left a message on a small column to give hope to the reunification of North and South Korea. "Berlin Square" was made possible by reconstruction works in the inner city. Blocked, and from then on used as a motorway due to the rapid expansion of the city at the end of the 1960s, the river Cheonggyecheon now flows once more and has since turned its surroundings into a leafy green area. Thousands of passers-by see the segments of the Wall every day. If you look closely, you can see the remains of the graffiti that had once been sprayed on the former West Berlin side of the Wall.

Location:
Peace Park –
Uijeongbu Station
Neighborhood Park

Thierry Noir in front of his
painted section with the Mayor
Of Teltow, Thomas Schmidt
© Stadt Teltow

Five original pieces of the Berlin Wall made their way to South Korea after the Mayor of Uijeongbu (a border city in South Korea) discovered them in Teltow during a visit to Germany.

They were put up in Uijeongbu Station Neighborhood Park, which is currently being remodelled to become a Peace Park. Uijeongbu is situated north of the capital city, Seoul, and lies 30 kilometres from the North Korean border. The segments of Wall stand as symbols of German reunification at their new location and, above all, as a symbol of the hope that the two Korean states will be peacefully unified.

The pieces of Wall had previously been in storage on the grounds of *Klösters* – a building materials company in Teltow, Berlin. The publicly owned concrete plant had bought sections of the Wall from the National People's Army at the start of the 1990s and intended to use them as steles to store mounds of stone. The remaining 160 sections of Wall stored in Teltow were taken over by *Klösters* two years ago. In 2001, the company's manger, Elmar Prost announced a project to "Paint the Wall". It was aimed at both professional and non-professional artists. One of the five sections now in Uijeongbu was painted by Wall artist, Thierry Noir.

The official unveiling took place on 19th March 2014 after the sections had been symbolically handed over to South Korean consul general, Eon-wook Heo, on 30th September 2013. Others present when the sections were handed over included Thierry Noir, Elmar Prost and the Mayor of Teltow, Thomas Schmidt.

The unveiling ceremony was opened by the Mayor of Uijeongbu, and numerous honoured guests were in attendance alongside German actor, Bruno Eyron (on behalf of Thierry Noir) and Tobias Dollase, legal advisor to the Federal Foundation for the Reappraisal of the SED Dictatorship. 500 further guests also attended.

A replica of the Brandenburg Gate can be found between the five segments of Wall. The ensemble is surrounded by illustrated information boards which explain the history of the inner-German division in German and English. A film commemorates the Peaceful Revolution.

Official unveiling of the five Wall segments in Peace Park, Uijeongbu

© Tobias Dollase

Location:
Taiwan Foundation for
Democracy, Alley 17,
Lane 147, Section 3,
Sinyi Road

The Wall in Taipei
© German Institute Taipei

An original section of the Wall was presented to the *Memorial Foundation of 2-28* by the German district of Oberhavel in time for the 20th anniversary of the Fall of the Wall. The idea behind the act arose during a meeting between the chairpeople from the *Memorial Foundation of 2-28* and Chiayi County with Karl-Heinz Schröter, district administrator of the Oberhavel district.

The foundation commemorates the massacre that took place from 28th February 1847 in Taiwan. An uprising by the people of Taiwan was brutally defeated by Chinese government troops. The chain of events was preceded by tensions between the native population and the new Chinese rulers who had occupied the island after the Japanese surrender in World War II. From 1985-1945, Taiwan had been under Japanese control and had seen a massive economical boost. The economical situation and the living conditions for the people of Taiwan deteriorated dramatically with the new Chinese military administration. The anger ended in a people's uprising in which, it is estimated, between 10,000 and 30,000 civilians lost their lives.

The martial law, called by the Chinese government over Taiwan, was in place until 1987. It was not until 1995 that an official government apology for the massacre came from Chinese president, Li Denghui. Under marital law which lasted for decades, commemorating the people's uprising was tabued, today, 28th February is an official public holiday in Taiwan. Wang Jin-pyng, former President of Taiwan, unveiled the 2.5 tonne section of Wall on 9th November 2009 in the gardens at the *Taiwan Foundation for Democracy* in Taipei.

Unveiling the Wall section

© German Institute Taipei

GDR civil rights campaigner, prominent member of the GDR opposition and contemporary witness of the Peaceful Revolution, Jörn Mothes, was present at the unveiling and held a speech.

In addition, a poster exhibition by the Federal Foundation for the Reappraisal of the SED Dictatorship entitled "20 Years of Peaceful Revolution and German Unity" illustrated the events that took place in Germany between 1989 and 1990. The section of Wall is to be moved into the yard of the reopened *Taipei 2-28 Memorial Museum*, which is primarily dedicated to the events that took place on 28th February 1947. As of yet, this has not taken place.

At least two segments of the Wall have found their way to Tonga. King Taufa'ahau Tupou IV bought a brightly coloured piece for several thousand Francs at the first auctions in early summer 1990 in Monaco. In 1999, a second piece of the Wall was to be shipped from Germany to the South Sea as a present from Tongan honorary consul, Alexander Müller. Whether or not these two segments ever arrived, and where they might be located within Nuku'alofa could not be found out. Neither German representatives nor the tourist office had any information relating to the segments of the Wall.

Founded in the beginning of the 1980s in the former Uzbek Sovjet Republic, the *Club of Friendship Esperanto* was one of the first unions of Esperantists. Dedicated to the historical heritage of Samarkands as a trading city on Silk Road, the people around Anatoly Ionesov built up a worldwide network. In 1986, the "International Museum for Peace and Solidarity" was opened – it was established during the International Year of Peace and tolerated by the national government. Even after the Fall of the Soviet Union in 1991, this initiative remained unique. The museum became a member of the *International Peace Bureau* in Geneva and the Association of Peace Museums worldwide, founded in 1992. Similar exhibitions on peace and pacifism have since been established in Europe, Asia and Latin America. In Uzbekistan, the museum was awarded the honorary title of a National Museum.

The exhibition is currently being renovated and is set to be housed in a new space. It is made up of over 20,000 exhibits from over one hundred different nations. Amongst them is a pieces of the Berlin Wall which was given by the "Friedensbibliothek / Anti-Kriegsmuseum" (peace library / anti-war museum) in Berlin. The pieces of Wall still bear graffiti and can be found today under glass in an open suitcase. There is also a picture of the donator standing in front of the Berlin Wall.

SAMARKAND
UZBEKISTAN

Location:
International Museum
for Peace and Solidarity

Pieces of Wall in Samarkand

© Museum of Peace and Solidarity
Uzbekistan

EUROPE

NORTH AMERICA

CENTRAL AMERICA

SOUTH AMERICA

AFRICA

ASIA

AUSTRALIA AND OCEANIA

MARS

Location:
Harmonie German
Club, 49 Jerrabomberra
Avenue, Narrabundah
ACT 2604

The Wall in Canberra

© German Embassy of the Federal
Republic of Germany Canberra

The German club 'Harmonie' was launched two months before the construction of the Wall in 1961 in Australia's capital city, Canberra. The club is dedicated to choir singing, football, dancing and maintaining German culture and has a clubhouse in South West Canberra. A segment of the Berlin Wall was put up on the drive on 3rd October 1993 to mark 'German Unity Day'. Dr. Otto Roever, permanent representative of the German embassy was at the unveiling. A small plaque commemorates the division of Germany:

"Harmonie Deutscher Verein Canberra / The section of the Berlin Wall reminds us that no man-made barrier can repress the spirit of freedom. / May we all unite to live in harmony, ensuring peace for further generations / Eingeweiht am 3. Oktober 1992 durch: Dr. Otto Roever, Ständiger Vertreter des deutschen Botschafters Canberra."

Günther Körner, long serving chairman of the club, tells the story behind this segment of the Wall:

"The Harmonie German Club committee decided, upon my suggestion, to open a Wall memorial on the site of the clubhouse to commemorate the reunification of Germany. A section of the Berlin Wall was to be imported from the German capital on the Spree. We were eventually able to get hold of a section of the Wall for 500 Deutsch Marks with help from friends in Berlin (Feely and Kilian Heerwig). The section of Wall arrived in Sydney a few months later on board a Russian container ship, packed in a container. In the

The Wall in Canberra

© German Embassy of the Federal Republic of Germany Canberra

meantime, a site had been created within the grounds of the clubhouse which was surrounded by a wall made from natural stone. The official unveiling took place on 3rd October 1992, the two year anniversary of German unification. The memorial was opened by Dr. Otto Roever from Canberra's German embassy, our mixed choir gave a musical accompaniment and hundreds of guests were in attendance. The section of Wall has become one of Canberra's most popular tourist attractions. Even Klaus Wowereit, Mayor of Berlin, has been to visit our memorial to German unification."

EUROPE

NORTH AMERICA

CENTRAL AMERICA

SOUTH AMERICA

AFRICA

ASIA

AUSTRALIA AND OCEANIA

MARS

MARS

Location:
Mars

The Wall on Mars:
"Broken Wall"
© NASA / JPL / DLR

The 'Pathfinder' mission to Mars in 1997 caused a great stir. The surface of the red planet was to be explored for the first time. Scientists from allover the world took part in the mission, including the German Aerospace Centre (DLR). The images beamed back to earth were recored by an international team and the most prominent rocks were given names. One set of rocks vaguely resembles the fallen Berlin Wall and German astrologer, Ralf Jaumann, suggested they should be named after the Fall of the Wall which took place on 9th November 1989. However, only one small piece of rock, approximately 85 cm long was given the name 'Broken Wall'. 'Frog' and 'Pumpkin' are in close proximity and were named by American scientists.

Naming this part of Mars after the Berlin Wall was of great significance to Jaumann as it commemorates "the Fall of the Wall and an event which was significant for everyone". The DLR also claims on its website that it is a sign that "the successful integration of scientists and engineers since 1992 from both East and West Germany at the DLR research centre in Berlin Adlershof" has been a success.

However, the official naming is yet to be confirmed. The decision to name the piece of rock, situated in a dried up valley, ultimately lies in the hands of the International Astronomical Union. Further trips to Mars have also left traces of German history behind. A team of researchers from Mainz university were allowed to name new rock formations as a token of thanks for their work developing a new measuring device 'Göstar Klingelhöfer'. 'Broken Wall' can now be found alongside 'Nikolaikirche' (St. Nicholas's Church), 'Montagsdemo' (Monday demonstrations) and 'Wiedervereinigung' (reunification).

THE MOST FREQUENTLY ASKED QUESTION: "SO WHERE EXACTLY WAS THE BERLIN WALL?" – THE NEED FOR A GENERAL CONCEPT TO DEAL WITH THE BERLIN WALL

I n the mid-1990s, the question being increasingly asked, not only by guests, but by Berliners themselves was, "So, where was the Wall actually?" Survivors and victims associations demanded that the Wall regime and its victims be commemorated. International surveys revealed that Berlin, and above all the Wall and its fall, were considered political icons around the world and, furthermore, that Berlin was considered to be the "the Rome of the 20th century" due its political state.

However, finding what remained of the Wall in Berlin was not easy. It was difficult to imagine what living with the Wall had been like. Creating an impression of what the division of the city had meant for its people was only possible with a lot of imagination. The media was beginning to ask why so much of the Wall had been torn down and destroyed and what could be done to make the Wall visible in the city again.

The few sites of memorial and remembrance and the few remaining sections of Wall lacked any kind of concept and were by no means connected to each other, many regarded this as insufficient. Above all, people's perception of the Wall had been connected since 1961 with commemorating and remembering its victims. When Günther Litfin was shot dead during an escape attempt at the Wall on 24th August 1961, just a few days after it was built, the image of the Wall that went around the world was that of a deadly construction that reflected the inhumane character of the GDR regime. Memorials and memorial crosses for the victims were continually put up by the people. Around 50 such memorials had been put up at the deadly Berlin Wall by 1989. Plaques and information Boards were later added by the senate and the victims were remembered on the anniversary of their deaths in special local services.

The first Wall memorial was put up in November 1961 by the 'Kuratorium Unteilbares Deutschland' (translated: committee for indivisible Germany) on Straße des 17. Juni, opposite the Brandenburg Gate. It has since been delegated to a site just in front of the Siegessäule (victory tower).

Whilst these existing memorials continued to be maintained and some even completed, there was a general consensus from the people of the GDR, the media and politicians that the Wall itself should be quickly torn down. Former GDR border soldiers, who had once guarded the Wall so fiercely, were now using their skills to tear down what was, until 1989, the most secure wall in the world.

Every street connection between East and West Berlin that was reopened was celebrated by politicians and the media. "Since 3rd October 1990, GDR border troops (under the command of the Federal army) have been dismantling the Wall with the same thoroughness they guarded it with for 28 years. They had already completed the task on 30th November 1990."[1]

There was a small group of monument conservationists, as well as experts from museums and some concerned citizens, who wanted to preserve at least a small part of the border-fortification as a memorial. However, they were unable to prevail against the euphoria most people were experiencing at the thought of Berlin's concrete and barbed wire nightmare being eradicated from the city landscape. The 1991 grand coalition was to create a 'New Berlin', and this meant getting rid of the concrete that ran through the heart of the city. The enormous pressure that had built up during the 28 years the Wall stood seemed like it was about to cause an explosion. The irrepressible joy seen allover the world when the Wall fell highlighted and made it clear to what extent the GDR had caused hopelessness and oppression amongst its people.

BETWEEN DISAPPEARANCE AND REMEMBRANCE
REMEMBERING THE BERLIN WALL TODAY

Rainer E. Klemke

---

1   Prof. Konrad Jarausch, quoted in "Gesamtkonzept Berliner Mauer", senate resolution from 20th June 2006, Imprint act Abgeordnetenhaus 15/5308 from 21.06.2006

DEN OPFERN DER MAUER
13. AUGUST 1961

The first Wall memorial stone in Berlin 1961

© Archiv Bundesstiftung Aufarbeitung

WHERE DO MEMORIALS COME FROM?

In democratic states, public memorials and places of remembrance are not built on orders from above as a demonstration of political or historical recognition, they are, in fact, the results of social engagement. Mostly, they are instigated by a group of citizens who all see the significance of a particular historical event and find a site (normally relating to the particular event) on which they want to commemorate it. Examples of this are the *Topography of Terror* and the *Memorial to the Murdered Jews of Europe*, neither of which would probably exist without the engagement of the people.

Further examples include the annual meeting between the people of Pankow and Wedding, who meet on 9th November on the Bösebrücke (Böse bridge) at the former border crossing point on Bornholmer Straße, or the Rosenzeremonie (rose ceremony) held by Berlin Mitte district officials to commemorate the victims of the people's uprising on 17th June 1953, as well as an initiative for a freedom and unity memorial in Berlin.

The broadening of this social engagement creates the basis for political and state institutions to recognise these topics and bring them to the forefront of public discussion, helping to find a solution which reflects social understanding. In this sense, these places of remembrance are adopted by the people. How this process developed in the case of the Wall will be discussed in this text.

and both of Berlin's Lord Mayors (Tina Schwiertzina and Walter Momper) worked on plans to build such a memorial on this site. On 13th August 1991, Berlin's first joint senate agreed to build a Wall memorial site.

The foundation stone was finally put down on 9th November 1997 and after more than eight years of talks and struggle, the memorial site was finally opened.

Pieces of Wall saved from destruction by the German Historical Museum, including an original watch tower from Acker/Bernauer Straße, were not permitted to be put up for reasons relating to monument protection and objections from the church. They can now be found at the *Allied Museum*.

The Documentation Centre was opened one year later, in what used to be a parish house for the Protestant Reconciliation Parish on 9th November 1999.

The Berlin Wall Memorial was enhanced with the opening of the Chapel of Reconciliation in 2000 and an observation deck in the Documentation Centre in 2003. These extensions were made to ensure that there was something on offer for everyone and helped to keep up with growing public interest.

Marking the former path of the Wall

At the same time the Wall was being torn down, thoughts were already being made as to how the path of the Wall could be made visible for future generations. Notable suggestions included marking the border with a yellow band of lupins (Manfred Butzmann, 1990), marking the path with a double row of cobble stones (Tiefbauamt Kreuzberg, 1990), a copper plate (Gernot Zohlen, 1992) and a red and blue strip – red for the border Wall and blue for the hinterland Wall – (Angela Bohnen, 1992). Models of the last two ideas were made and can still be seen on Niederkirchnerstraße, but a double row of cobbles marked with bronze plaques was the most popular idea and was laid along a few kilometres of the former path of the Wall.

The Berlin Wall History Mile

The Kreuzberg Museum came up with the idea to create a 'Berlin Wall History Mile' which is also part of the communication concept and has been been extended. It focuses on 30 significant sites of Wall history along the former course of the Wall and describes the events that took place at the site in question. The permanent exhibition is in four languages.

Marking the former border crossing points

In 1996, an artistic competition was also held to gather ideas for marking the abandoned border crossing points in the following locations: Bornholmer Straße, Chausseestraße, Invalidenstraße, Friedrichstraße, Heinrich-Heine-Straße (and four further subway stations), the Oberbaum Bridge and Sonnenallee. More artistic methods have been used in these locations, some of them ironic, like the life-size rabbits inlaid in the street on Chausseestraße, and some more eye-catching like the mast at Checkpoint Charlie where two enormous pictures of a Russian and US soldier can be found – each looking into the other's former border area. A reconstruction of the original Allied checkpoint was built alongside the *Berlin Wall Museum* and opened on 13th August 2000. The original was put in storage in the Allied Museum and was the subject of substantial public attention.

Schlesischer Busch/ Kieler Straße Watchtowers

The only watch towers still to mark the city landscape can be found at Schlesischer Busch in Treptow and on Kieler Straße there is also a tower from the hinterland on Erna-Berger-Straße at Potsdamer Platz. The watch

towers (former so-called command posts) are now listed constructions and were consigned to users who submitted plans to create Wall memorials. Fine arts platform, 'Kunstfabrik am Flutgraben' was consigned the watch tower at Schlesischer Busch and use the space for an artistic examination of the Wall. The watch tower on Kieler Straße was consigned to the brother of Wall victim Günter Liftin, who created a memorial site.

Crosses at Checkpoint Charlie

On 31st October 2004, Alexandra Hildebrandt, director at the Berlin Wall Museum, opened a Wall memorial to commemorate all the victims of the East German border regime. Part of it consisted of a reconstruction of the Wall and a further part of 1065 wooden crosses. The installation had been planned as a temporary exhibition and was taken down in July 2005 when the temporary lease contract came to an end. Whilst many people appeared to be moved by the exhibition and the discussion of commemorating the Wall victims was brought back to life, it was also criticised by historians since the Wall had cost nobody their life at this location. Furthermore, it transpired that many of the people commemorated by the crosses had died in altogether different circumstances, or were actually still alive.

The path of the Berlin Wall marked by cobble stones
© Archiv Bundesstiftung Aufarbeitung

THE OVERALL MEMORIAL CONCEPT FOR THE BERLIN WALL

Philosophy and communication concept

The following text concentrates on the concept, created by the Berlin Senate in 2004, which aims to memorialise and commemorate not only the division of Berlin, but the world. On the basis of this, selected sites of memorial are then described.

Twelve years after it fell, the Berlin Wall and its history became the focal points of plans by the Berlin Senate Department of Culture to integrate them into a memorial concept. The concept, by the first Socialist and Social Democratic coalition, aimed to achieve the following:

"The concept, focusing on the management of what remains of the Wall and the former border installations, should be further developed and implemented. The work carried out at the Berlin Wall Documentation Centre at Bernauer Straße should be permanently secured."[2]

The Senate Department for Urban Development developed a concept for a Berlin Wall trail, based on an initiative by delegates from Die Grünen (the Green party), Michael Cramer and Wolfgang Wieland. The trail should follow the former path of the Wall (wherever possible) and make what was left of the Wall accessible to pedestrians and cyclists. The Senate then went about making a list of sites where parts of the Wall still stood, or where Wall memorials already existed. Many sections of the Wall were then listed for the first time and, thus, saved from demolition. The senate drew upon a list compiled by the Brandenburg University of Technology (Klausmeier/Schmidt 2001- 2003). In this list, the locations of remaining pieces of Wall had been meticulously recorded. The Senate also called upon the 'Berliner Forum für Geschichte und Gegenwart' (Berlin forum for history and modern day) to draw up a list of all the existing Wall memorials and commemorative sites around former West Berlin.

A concept was needed that combined the leftovers of the Wall with an explanation behind the history and effect of the Wall – this explanation should be told with the aid of authentic remains. Also to be highlighted (appropriately) were those responsible for the Wall as well as those who died as a result of the Wall regime.

Alexandra Hildebrandt's Wall crosses on Checkpoint Charlie had a considerable part to play in spurring on this discussion, a desire to lay out suitable frameworks for such memorials.

The crosses also exemplified the fact that the location did not meet legal or scientifically sound standards – this also applied to the form of display and historical correctness. For this reason, there was no cause or possibility for the Senate to intervene when the crosses had to be taken down on the grounds that the private-land owner wanted his land back.

In 2004, the senate set up an inter-agency team under the coordination of the regional funding body for culture (Kulturverwaltung). On this team were delegates from the Berlin state departments (whose districts were affected), the Federal Government Commissioner for Culture and the Media (BKM), delegates from numerous memorial sites, the Federal Foundation for the Examination and Reappraisal of the SED and as numerous other specialist academics. It was their task to work on an extensive concept which focused on the Wall as a whole, and not on areas or events relating to it. The question at the heart of the discussions was whether or not it was suitable to reconstruct parts of the Wall. (This question always referred back to Hildebrandt's installation on Checkpoint Charlie.)

The question as to whether or not a section of the Wall should be constructed was always the focal point of discussions about how best to commemorate the Wall - this was in light of the exhibition on Checkpoint Charlie by Alexandra Hildebrandt. In particular, those who had been imprisoned in the GDR and those who had escaped adopted this assignment as their own. They were concerned that if the segments were not reconstructed, the cruelty of the Wall and the GDR regime would fade into obscurity and future generations would not be aware of what had taken place. This claim had also been discussed during plans for National Socialist memorial sites – in this case, the general consensus had been not to create reconstructions. Increasing numbers of visitors to these sites and the comments they made about them are testament to the fact that this decision not to reconstruct did not detract from the memorials.

---

2   Coalition agreement between The Social Democratic Party of Germany (SPD), Landesverband Berlin and the Party of Democratic Socialism (PDS), Landesverband Berlin, for the legislative period 2001-2006, II, 23, 3, historical culture

The fact that the Wall itself had changed many times during its 28 year existence made the task even more difficult. It had to be decided which version / stage of the Wall should be reconstructed. Furthermore, the final version of the Wall appeared optically to be the most harmless and it was sometimes asked why this final version of the Wall could not have been overcome.

Father Fischer, from the church of reconciliation, uses the following example to make the difference between the pre-1989-Wall and its appearance today clear: "Back then, the Wall was like a living, breathing dangerous polar bear. What is left today is, in part, just the fur. We prefer the latter today. Today we can cross the border between East and West without being shot – that is what makes the difference between the Wall as it was in the GDR and any kind of reconstruction."

Some of the reconstructions at sites of Nazi crimes had led to right wing extremists questioning and denying their authenticity. More ridiculously they had also been used as evidence to support the Holocaust denial. This had to be seen as a warning and lessons had to be learned from it, even more so in light of publications by former GDR officials which spoke out against the persecution of those responsible for crimes under Socialism.

On the basis of these records, several hearings and official statements, a decentralised concept for commemorating the history of the Wall was developed; it assigned specific themes to specific locations according to their history, which were to be represented with cross-references to the other memorials.

Checkpoint Charlie had served as the GDR's former checkpoint for foreign visitors and was therefore identified as the international site for Wall history.

It was here that the only direct confrontation took place during the Cold War. It was here that the Americans demanded their right to total access for western allies into the GDR. It was here that the checkpoint for foreign visitors to East Berlin once was and here that heads of state from allover the world travelled between West Berlin and the 'Capital of the GDR'.

In direct correspondence to this, the Brandenburg Gate became the national site for Wall history. Richard von Weizsäcker had once said: "As long as the Brandenburg Gate is closed, the German question is open!" this made it all the more clear that it should be the national symbol of German division – and later the national symbol of reunification.

Bernauer Straße was typical of the situation faced by the city due to the presence of the Wall. At the same time it was also one of the only places where a large section of the Wall could still be seen. It was also a place that had seen many significant events during the period in which the Wall stood: it saw the first stages of construction, it was one of the first places to be opened in 1989, one of the first areas where the Wall was dismantled, it saw escapes, church-demolition, building work on top of cemeteries, station closures (Stettiner Station, Bernauer Straße Station), relocation and the demolition of entire rows of houses etc.

It was the most documented Wall location, the media was stationed here around the clock in the sixties, photos of people fleeing that went around the world were taken here and it was home to the "Studio am Stacheldraht" (Studio at the barbed wire fence).

No other place in Berlin represents the historical events of the 20th century like Niederkirchnerstraße /Wilhelmstraße. The German Empire, the Weimar Republic and the National Socialists have all left their mark alongside the GDR regime with its Haus der Ministerien (house of Ministries), 17th June uprisings and escape attempts at the Wall.

The Fall of the Wall and the joy seen around the world also had to be documented, as well as telling how this period was documented artistically at places like the East Side Gallery and Parlament der Bäume.

All of these places are linked by public transport, in particular by Berlin's underground network and 'S-Bahn'. Bernauer Straße, the central location for Wall history, is just three stations from the Brandenburg Gate and 1300m from the new Central Station (Hauptbahnhof), itself a prominent part of 'New Berlin'. An ideal location for visitors to Berlin.

This is supported by a communication concept which creates necessary spatial and content-related connections. At the heart of this concept is the Berlin Wall Trail which runs through the city centre. It is made up of information markers and a collection of 29 different sites of interest along the former border line – each marked with an information board. There is also a multimedia tour available at www.berlin.de/mauer which includes films, witness interviews, photographs and GPS marked locations. This is available in six languages and is a good place to look for all Wall related questions and everything to do with the history of the Wall.

Information is also on display at the most significant Berlin tourist destinations: the Brandenburg Gate, Potsdamer Platz and Checkpoint Charlie. The information is aimed at tourists who have no prior knowledge of the memorial concept and intends to inform them of memorial sites and historical museums in Berlin.

THE ARRANGEMENTS

Checkpoint Charlie

A 360 metre long information wall has been in place at Checkpoint Charlie since summer 2006. It informs guests about the history of the site, the Berlin Wall and its victims and complements the private exhibition in 'Haus am Checkpoint Charlie'. In 'Haus am Checkpoint Charlie', visitors can find out about refugees and escape attempts from the GDR, there is also an exhibition about peaceful resistance.

The exhibition also points its many visitors in the direction of further places of interest around the city in relation to the Wall as well as highlighting the areas where authentic pieces of the Wall can still be found. Today, it is one of the most visited historical museums.

The so called "Black Box" has been home to an exhibition about the Cold War since September 2012. The site at the former checkpoint is currently being developed and considerations are being made to creat a "Cold War Centre".

Berlin Wall open-air exhibition at Checkpoint Charlie
© Archiv Bundesstiftung Aufarbeitung

Wall remains at
Potsdamer Platz
© Archiv Bundesstiftung Aufarbeitung

Brandenburger Tor

The Brandenburg Gate, alongside the government district, is Berlin's main tourist attraction. Almost all traces of the Berlin Wall disappeared when the new parliament was built, apart from the "Parlament der Bäume" (Parliament of Trees)

For this reason is a "contemporary history platform" in the new underground station at the Brandenburg Gate. It tells the story of Germany's national symbol throughout history and focuses on the events that surrounded the Fall of the Wall. This exhibition can be found directly under Pariser Platz and on the walls of the underground station. It also informs visitors where they can find remains of the Wall and at which memorial sites they can gather more information.

Potsdamer Platz

At Potsdamer Platz, an exhibition has been installed as part of the overall concept in Wall commemoration. The exhibition is in English and German and documents existing and planned places of remembrance. It was updated and redesigned to mark the 20th anniversary of the Fall of the Wall. Further sections of the Wall and a path of cobbled stones mark the Wall's former path and an information board in eight languages points out where visitors can find more significant Wall sites. A watch tower, which offered a 360 degree view over the eastern border, has also been preserved in a nearby street (Erna-Berger-Straße) and has been under monu-

ment protection since 2001. Further preserved sections of the exterior Wall are being relocated within the site of the new Department of Environment.

Bernauer Straße

The Federal Republic's central Berlin Wall Memorial came into being on 13th August 2011 – 50 years since the Wall was built. It attracted almost two million visitors in its first two years.

The project started with a competition in 2008 and the three existing components of the former Berlin Wall Memorial were merged together to form a comprehensive memorial landscape between Nordbahnhof and Mauerpark. The three existing parts were the memorial for the commemoration of the victims of Communist tyranny, Berlin Wall Documentation Centre and the Chapel of Reconciliation on the site of the old Church of Reconciliation, which was blown up by the GDR government.

A visitor centre at Nordbahnhof/ Gartenstraße welcomes guests, and the Documentation Centre is being remodelled to house a new permanent exhibition (as well as temporary exhibitions) about the Wall. The largest preserved section of Wall in the inner-city area along Bernauer Straße (1.2 km) makes the preserved traces visible and has paved the way for a dignified, individual memorial to the victims.

Here, those responsible for the Wall regime, the displaced people and the victims are all represented and explained alongside the history of the Wall.

Amongst others things, the following was carried out on the death strip to commemorate the events that took place there: a watchtower was put up on the memorial at Ackerstraße as a sign to the perpetrators, several plaques commemorating the events at the Wall and its victims were put in place, cellars (which had once belonged to over 2000 residents) were excavated, the former path of the Wall was marked out with the aid of steal rods alongside the remaining sections of the Wall. There is now also a guided tour along the sentry path, the course of which has not been made visible by steal plates.

In September 2008, the Berlin Wall Memorial was given a legal independent status and was to be run by government sponsored foundations (until then it had been run by a supporting association), this meant that the long term future of the memorial had been secured. The sponsors provide significant financial support for the memorial's acquisition of land and development.

Niederkirchner Straße

A 200 metre stretch of the *fourth generation* Wall has been preserved on Niederkirchner Straße and is an integral part of the *Topography of Terror*. It was made accessible to the public after reconstruction work on the open-air area was carried out, this work also took place on the western side of the Wall and on the former pavement in front of buildings used by the SS and Gestapo. The site's history is explained on an information board on the corner of Niederkirchner/Stresemannstraße in eight languages.

East-Side-Gallery

The East Side gallery was reconstructed in 2009 and repainted with original images by artists from allover the world (at least by those who were willing to take part in the project) in time for the 20th anniversary of the Fall of the Wall in 2009. A people's park has since been developed between the so called hinterlandmaucr (which makes up the East Side Gallery) and the Spree. Political and legal disagreements make it unclear whether or not the private land between the Wall and Spree will be used for urban development – such plans were made legal directly after the Fall of the Wall.

Parlament der Bäume (Parliament of Trees)

Plans to keep the Parlament der Bäume (Parliament of Trees) as the last authentic Wall site in the government quarter are being worked on at both a federal and a national level (at the moment, the area of land is reserved for an extension of the Bundestag). The plans also aim to keep the area accessible to the public, to ensure long-term maintenance and to ensure the history of the area is kept alive for visitors in the from of information boards and not forgotten.

Marienfelde Refugee Centre Museum

Alongside the various sites where failed escape attempts took place and those where dramatic escape attempts succeeded, the Marienfelde Refugee Centre Museum has become a significant and invaluable memorial site as far as the history of GDR migrants is concerned. For this reason, it was consolidated with the Berlin Wall Memorial association and its long term future secured.

Platz des 9. November 1989 (Nov. 9ᵗʰ 1989 Square)

The 'Platz des 9. November 1989' was officially unveiled and opened on the Bösebrücke bridge and documents the dramatic events that took place on that day in words and images. S-Bahnhof Bornholmer Straße serves as the starting point for tours along the path of the Wall and through Mauerpark and leads to the Berlin Wall Memorial on Bernauer Straße.

Further Wall sections

Four preserved watch towers make up part of the memorial concept.

One of these is the watch tower (leading post) on Kieler Straße. Alongside the artistic markings on Sandkrugbrücke (Invalidenstraße) and a preserved piece of the hinterlanadmauer in Invalid's cemetery, this watch tower forms the link between Hauptbahnhof (Central Station) and the memorial landscape between the strips of Wall at St. Hedwigs' cemetery (Elisenstraße) across the area around Nordbahnhof, Bernauer Straße and across Mauerpark up to Bösebrücke/Bornholmer Straße. The tower has been turned into a memorial to Günter Litfin, who died at the Wall. It is run by an organisation founded by Luftin's brother. There are plans to incorporate it into the Berlin Wall Foundation.

Another tower of identical structure to the one on Kieler Straße is the watch tower at Schlesischer Busch on Puschkinallee. It is run as an art gallery today by Flutgraben e.V. and focuses on projects to do with the Wall and former border. This segment of the Wall, further from the city centre, also offers guided tours.

A watchtower outside of Berlin corresponds to these two towers. It once served as the headquarters of Border Regiment 44 "Walter Junker" at the former GDR checkpoint Drewitz and is today operated by Checkpoint Charlie e.V. The former tank memorial on the motorway between Dreilinden and Drewitz makes up part of this memory space, the former Berlin checkpoint of the allied forces in Dreilinden with the bronze sculpture of the Berlin bear as well as the 17ᵗʰ June 1953 memorial on the centre strip on Potsdammer Chaussee.

The tower on Erna-Berger-Straße at Potsdamer Platz Teil also makes up part of the commemoration alongside the Wall exhibition, an information pillar, the many pieces of Wall (including those in the Federal Environment Ministry) and the road markings on Potsdamer Platz.

Visitor centre for the
20th anniversary of the Fall of
the Wall at Potsdamer Platz
© Archiv Bundesstiftung Aufarbeitung

NO PEACEFUL REVOLUTION, NO FALL OF THE WALL

Whilst the Berlin Wall and its history are at the focal point of public interest, and the Fall of the Wall has become an icon in international politics, the Peaceful Revolutions, the people behind them and the actual string of events have taken a back seat.

For this reason and to mark the 20th anniversary since the Fall of the Wall, the Berlin Senate ordered the first large exhibition about the Peaceful Revolution and the permanent marking of the sites where the events took place.

The senate then decided that creating this exhibition should not be undertaken by a state institution and, instead, offered the job to the Robert Havemann Institution - in a way as testamentary executer of the civil movement in the GDR.

The Peaceful Revolution took place on the streets and immediately became a threat to the GDR regime. For this reason it was decided that the exhibition should be open-air and at location where the events actually unfolded.

Therefore, it was decided that the exhibition to mark the 20th anniversary of the Fall of the Wall should take place between the dates of the GDR municipal elections and the Fall of the Wall. The exhibition enjoyed so much success, that it was extended by a year. At the same time, around 20 stationary audio guides were put up at significant locations and explained where and how the first successful revolution took place and came into force.

OUTLOOK – WHAT WILL REMAIN?

The last years have shown that interest in the Wall is growing with the distance of time. It is not only visitors to Berlin who want to find out what and where the Wall was and what kind of an impact it had on life in the divided city. Interest in the history of the GDR, and especially the Wall is growing quickly, and faster than it did in the case of National Socialist history. In this case, as in the case of the National Socialists, there will be no reconstructions, but an accurate presentation of selected traces as well as the historical backgrounds and responsibilities. Part of this involves an appropriate memorial to the victims of the Communist reign of violence and the Wall.

As witnesses to the system become no loner available to retell their personal memories and experiences, museums and media techniques are being used in their place, and present history alongside materials left by witnesses, documents and electronic records.

The task remains to explain the most significant events in Berlin's and Germany's history after the collapse of the National Socialist government (and the SED dictatorship as a result of the War, instigated by Germany) and to root them in an international context – especially in the context of Middle and Eastern European states, but also to think of the Fall of the Wall as the beginning of a new and widespread European integration, which had previously ended on the western side of the Iron Curtain until then.

Sources:
Overall Berlin Wall memorial concept – senate resolution and materials, 20th June 2006
2001 coalition agreement between the SPD and the PDS
Competition documents for the founding of a memorial to for the victims of the Berlin Wall and the Communist dictatorship
Competition documents for marking the former border
Competition documents for the extension of the Berlin Wall Memorial
Klausmeier/Schmidt, Mauerreste-Mauerspuren, Berlin 2004
www.berlin.de/Mauer
www.chronik-der-mauer.de

On 9th November 1989, the Wall fell unexpectedly and without the use of violence. A new chapter in the Wall's history was about to begin – a chapter that very few people could have expected at the time. The fortress around East Berlin, from which 10,000 armed border soldiers had prevented people leaving the GDR for the West, was now redundant. It had no function, the plug had been pulled. But it suddenly became something new – it became a memorial to itself.

Leo Schmidt

There is no better or clearer testament to this transformation and new status than the enthusiastic way in which the dismantling of the Wall began. Marion Detjen pointed out that it was now possible to 'cut off an ear' from the giant monster, and many people did just that. They quickly became known as 'Wall Peckers'. Who would have wanted a piece of the Wall before this moment? True, the Wall was on GDR territory, but it could be accessed from the West. However, there were other considerations to take into account. It was not only the danger of being shot by GDR border troops that had prevented people from hammering at the Wall and taking a piece of Wall to put on display in their homes. One also has to remember that such a piece of Wall would have only been suitable for display in a house of horrors. The Fall of the Wall changed that: it gave the depressing grey concrete a new meaning, it made it glow.[1]

This glow was called 'freedom'. Two hundred years previously, it had been called *Liberté*, when the Bastille, another construction of oppression, was stormed. This act ultimately brought about the fall of another ancient regime (spontaneous as well, then, but certainly not without the use of violence).

Much in the same way as the Berlin Wall had been intended to 'protect', the Bastille in East Paris dating back to the 14th century, intended to protect from the threat of the English, and also was pulled down and symbolically wiped from the city landscape. However, building contractor P. F. Palloy did not just consider the fortress as pieces of stone which could be recycled for new building. He saw the symbolism inside the stone. This is how his famous idea to build miniature models of the Bastille from the lime stone ashlars was born. He then sent the miniatures to the Départements of the New Republic as cult objects and symbols of freedom (ill. 1).

Segments of the Berlin Wall, comparable to Palloy's miniature Bastilles, were shipped in their hundreds to locations allover the globe. More often than not, they were then put on prominent display. They showed the changed world of the late 20th century, but above all the segments underlined the huge extent to which the Berlin Wall had become part of, and continued to have its place in contemporary consciousness.

What do these Wall memorials look like, how are they presented and what message do they convey? Time and again, it is one image that is being presented: 'Border Wall 75', made from prefabricated concrete elements called UL 12.41. These prefabricated elements had originally been developed for agricultural purposes. However, in 1975 and after extensive testing, they were used to build the 'forth generation' of Wall. These reinforced concrete elements had an L-shaped cross section and were 3.6m high and 1.2m long – they could be put up side-by-side almost seamlessly.

Once they had been sealed together, they formed what seemed like an endless concrete wall. Crowned with waste water pipes – making any attempt to climb over the top without aid almost impossible – this version of the Wall became the most notorious image of the entire construction. The fact that the Berlin Wall had been made from many other components disappeared from view, due to the overwhelming dominance of this one element.

---

1   The underlying mechanism of this observation has long been familiar: the Catholic cult of relics is based upon it. Polly Feversham, Leo Schmidt. Die Berliner Mauer Heute. Denkmalwert und Umgang. Berlin 1999. pp.12

III. 1:

Bastille model, made from an

original block

© BTU Cottbus,
Cottbus Department of
Preservation of Monuments

What is also equally noteworthy about this version of the Wall is that its smooth, seamless surface was an open invitation for people on the western side to use it as a canvas for graffiti. This had not been a problem with previous versions of the Wall, which had not had such a surface. To put it in other words: in the western perception of the Wall was reduced to the combination of concrete element, the round pipe along the top and graffiti.

Most of the memorials worldwide consist of just one single segment of the Wall. Sometimes, though, they appear in pairs or even groups. What they all have in common is their sober sense of memorial. Often they are found on pedestals bearing an inscription, almost as though they were sculptures of a famous historic character – which in a way is the case.

Although it is essentially the same object on display at each location – the Berlin Wall, represented by an authentic segment – each piece has been imbued with its own specific meaning. This meaning is conveyed principally by the context in which the Wall is on display, sometimes also by means of attributes.

The majority of the memorials are simple, the piece of Wall is presented naked, as though it were in a vacuum. Presenting them like this assumes that the object on show can be recognised easily and can speak for itself. The memorial presumes a silent understanding of the way it is presented – something along the lines of 'everybody obviously knows what the Berlin Wall looked like and what it stood for'. It many such cases, the memorials are the product of a private individual and their personal contemplation, like in the case of Hans-Olaf Henkel in Deauville, Normandy.

Presentation in such a way can only work within a homogeneous group and within a certain period of time. If this method was applied in a public, urban space, there is a risk that the understanding would be lost. An example of this can be found in Madrid, where sections of the Wall stand in the middle of a fountain with no hints as to what they are, rendering them ultimately 'invisible': Robert Musil claims there is "nothing more invisible in the world than memorials. They are put up to be seen…but at the same time they are shaped by something which deflects attention".[2]

There is a wide range of memorials where the context invites one to reflect, and from which interpretations can be made. Pieces of the Wall in the entrance to a publishing house, Editoria Perfil in Buenos Aires, put the Wall in the context of freedom of expression and information. Pieces at a train station in Chicago serve as a reminder of – what is now taken for granted – freedom of movement. A segment put on display by a language travel study company in Boston (Massachusetts) also has a certain charm: it highlights and compares being cut off from the world, as the Berlin Wall did to the East, with the vast extent of that which lies beyond the Wall. Segments in a supermarket, like in Seattle, seem to want to highlight the less sublime matter of consumer access to a choice of goods.

Another interesting and meaningful group of memorials offer varied interpretations on the basis of their locations, or by other means – implicit or sometimes very explicit – which take their meaning from the Wall itself, or more precisely, the Fall of the Wall. Pieces of the Wall in front of the NATO headquarters in Belgian Mons, or in front of the Imperial War Museum in London, draw a more obvious connection between foreign policy and military aspects of the border and the Iron Curtain. A three-dimensional collage on board the USS Intrepid in New York incorporates the air craft carrier's flight deck, a high-tech ship propellor, tank gun and segment of the Berlin Wall. The composition imposes an overly simplistic interpretation on the observer, that the Wall supposedly fell due to western superiority in the arms race, and that the Cold War was won by the West thanks to politics of strength.

The National Museum of the United States Airforce in Dayton (Ohio) commemorates the Fall of the Wall with a tableau consisting of a number of shop window dummies (wearing clothes which were untypical for a GDR citizen in 1989). They climb on the Wall from the roof of a Trabant, waving the GDR flag. The round pipe from the top of the Wall had obviously not been delivered and was replaced by one twice the size of the original. The installation in the Royal Air Force Museum in Cosford is even stranger: two figures stand on a ladder in the West and wave over the top of the Wall into the East. It commemorates the sudden and brutal division of family and friends in 1961. However, historians will spot the anachronism. The figures are waving over the top of 'Grenzmauer 75', which was not built until the late 1970s.

A bust of Ronald Reagan placed directly opposite a piece of Wall in the Ronald Reagan Presidential Library commemorates Reagan's famous speech in front of the Brandenburg Gate in May 1987 and his plea "Mister Gorbachev, tear down this wall". The arrangement of this wall memorial virtually 'proves' that this plea was answered.

This context belongs to a family of similar memorials. It is almost a must for a piece of the Wall to be on display in every late 20th century presidential library. As well as in Reagan's library, they can be found in the libraries of John F. Kennedy, Richard Nixon, Gerald Ford and George H. W. Bush, and they underline just how significant the Berlin Wall was during their time in office. Even memorial libraries of presidents who were in office before the Berlin Wall was constructed include a piece of it, Herbert Hoover and Franklin D. Roosevelt, for example.

---

2   Quoting Polly Feversham, Leo Schmidt: Die Berliner Mauer Heute. Dankmal und Umgang. Berlin 1999 p.165

Whilst references to the power politics of the Cold War are repeatedly made in presidential libraries and military museums, we find a different point of view towards the events on the 9th November 1989 in Fatima (Portugal). The presentation here aims to leave no doubt in anybody's mind that the Fall of the Wall was caused by divine intervention – or rather the Virgin's. By contrast, the section of the Wall in the centre of Catholicism, the Vatican itself, renounces this simplistic interpretation. Yet this is not just any old piece of Wall, but a section with a religious context: it carries a picture of Berlin's St. Michael's Church. The lower section of the Church can be seen (painted) on the Wall in Kreuzberg, creating the illusion that the whole church (on the other side of the Wall and facing the death strip) is in full view of those looking from the West – the Wall becomes transparent (ill. 2).

The topic of the Wall as art, or at least a canvas for art, is less important in the Vatican, but in countless other installations it is given a much greater role. The Yorkshire Sculpture Park is home to a piece of the Wall which was originally covered in bright graffiti and was most likely bought for just this reason. However, being on open-air display has led to the graffiti being almost completely weathered away. The issue of graffiti being regarded as something desirable, but not something which will last forever, has risen in many other places. For this reason, the solution most often put into practice has been to repaint the pieces of Wall. The way in which the Wall is painted says a lot about the reflection of those doing the painting. If one were to paint or graffiti the 'wrong' side, that is to say the side of the Wall originally facing the death strip, or if one were to paint over an area picked at by Wall Peckers, one removes oneself considerably from the situation in which the 'real' graffiti was originally created. In the quest to attain the original flair when restoring or creating new paintings on the Wall, many graffiti artists from Berlin have been hired to paint pieces at their

This self-centredness in West Berlin and the entire western world is still seen today in many Wall memorials, but it is not commented upon. Even in cases where sections from the 'hinterland Wall' have been put on display (sections which faced the East), such memorials do not critically reflect upon the meaning nor purpose of the section in question. Such pieces are mostly on display by coincidence or for practical reasons. When looking into the origins of such segments, it normally transpires that they were chosen because they were cheaper, as in Odense. Or in other cases, it is plain to see from the way in which they have been put on display, that little is known about their origins. For example, when such segments are put up vertically or have absolutely no graffiti on them, like in West Branch (Iowa) and in Portland (Maine).

If one asks which perception of the Berlin Wall these Wall segments represent around the world when they are put on display, the answer is obvious: the perception that was created during the years before the Fall of the Wall – and that is the perception from the western side.

The expectations of those who bought segments of the Wall at the famous auctions in 1990, went hand in hand with the compliance of the GDR sellers, that the Berlin Wall embodied the essence of the "Anti Fascist Protection Rampart".

The only Wall memorials that appear to show any interest in the functional aspects of the Wall as a border can be found in South Korea – this makes sense when one thinks that this country is still divided in two by a military border.

The Wall memorials around the world are based on an almost abstract western perception of the Wall that has little or nothing to do with the complex historic situation in Berlin itself. Those who put up Wall memorials focus on their own situations and their own experience of the threat of War symbolised by the Wall.

What the segments of Wall throughout the world do not address is the reality of the Wall in Berlin. They do not carry any information into the world what it was like to live in a divided city and what it meant to be a prisoner in one's own country.

But even if the memorials around the world have little to do with the Wall itself nor how it was seen by those in both East and West Berlin – a 155 km military guarded border that shaped their lives – it would be narrow-minded of the Germans to consider them irrelevant. On the contrary: has there ever been anything comparable? Is there any other monument distributed around the world in so many pieces and on so many continents? Has there ever been another monument that has had the same diverse and even contradictory history of reception and interpretation?

266

What the segments prove, which have found their way to all corners of the globe to make up memorials put up by all sorts of people and institutions, is the unique cultural significance of the Wall in every sense of the definition according to the Burra Charter, which claims that cultural significance means "aesthetic, historic, scientific, social or spiritual value for past, present or future generations."[6]

Seen individually, the segments of Wall seem out of place, uprooted. However, if all the segments of the Wall scattered throughout the world were put side-by-side, they would likely be longer than all of the remains left in Berlin – at least what is left of the border Wall. The Wall monuments around the world are, so to speak, ambassadors for the Berlin Wall – they represent the actual concrete construction and raise awareness around the world.

People are confronted with the Wall segments on their own ground. The memorials motivate people to go in search of their counterparts in and around Berlin. They inspire people to go and look for the real Berlin. The success behind this statement can be seen in the ever increasing numbers of visitors to Berlin, who come to see the Berlin Wall each year.

---

6   The definition continues: "The carrier of cultural significance is the object itself, its substance, its surroundings, its use, its associations, meanings, sources and the interrelating objects around it. Objects may have different meanings for different people and groups." Cf. Leo Schmidt: Einführung in die Denkmalpflege. Stuttgart 2008, 157.

FROM CONCRETE TO CASH
TURNING THE BERLIN WALL INTO A BUSINESS

Ronny Heidenreich

Anyone wishing to see the Berlin Wall today does not necessarily have to travel to the German capital. The symbolic remains of the border Wall can be found on every continent. There are perhaps more remains scattered around the globe than in Berlin, where the Wall has almost disappeared from the city landscape.[1]

Interest in the Berlin Wall had probably never been greater than when it fell on 9th November 1989. For decades, the death strip and the concrete Wall had embodied a divided world. When the Wall fell, its significance as a symbol of oppression crumbled with it overnight, and the Fall of the Wall became a success story in the struggle for freedom.

Those visiting Berlin in the following days were able to attack the Wall with a hammer and chisel and take a piece of world history home with them. There was equal interest in complete segments of the Wall – 2.6 tonnes in weight and 3.2 metres high – that had once divided the East from the West. More than 500 such segments have been scattered around the world in the last 20 years. They have become pieces of art, prize trophies and exhibition pieces. Very few of them were donated for free to their new owners. On the whole, the pieces were sold to buyers as commodities or as speculative investments for high prices.

Many took part in selling the Berlin Wall. From the GDR government, headed by the SED and responsible for the Wall's very existence, to marketing companies aimed at making large profits through the sales of the 'Antifascist Protective Rampart'. It actually came down to the GDR border guards, who had guarded the wall so intensely for decades, to carry out the task of selling the Wall.

On the evening of 9th November 1989, the world watched as the Berlin Wall fell. After a misunderstanding and a mistaken answer to a question at a press conference, SED official Günter Schabowski caused thousands of East Berliners to storm the border crossings a few hours after the conference. They demanded that the Berlin Wall, heavily guarded and impenetrable for decades, be opened. The first joyous GDR citizens crossed the border and entered West Berlin shortly before midnight.[2]

This historic event led to euphoria and meant the end of the GDR and the downfall of its stricken party. Internationally, opening the borders meant the effective end to the Cold War. Whilst diplomatic talks were still being held in Berlin to make sense of the situation, companies were already voicing their interest in the Wall. Now that the Iron Curtain had fallen and the Berlin Wall was history, companies and individuals wanted to secure a piece of the symbolic Berlin Wall.

The first to get in touch with the GDR's Minister of Foreign Trade, Gerhard Beil, was a Bavarian businessman. On 10th November, one day after the opening of the border, he offered Beil money in exchange for one of the 'unwanted sections of your border fortifications'.[3] Enquires were also being made to GDR embassies in the US and Great Britain a few days later, asking if and how the unwanted sections of the Wall could be bought.

This demand caused confusion in embassies around the world. The GDR had spent years defending their 'Antifascist Protective Rampart' internationally, and now they were to sell pieces of it to their class enemies. On 15th November 1989, clearly confused, the GDR embassy in New York called up the ministry for foreign trade in East Berlin to ask whether 'such a sale was possible'.[4]

1 See the entry in this book by Rainer Klemke as well as Gerhard Sälter: Das Verschwinden der Berliner Mauer. In: Klaus-Dietmar Henke (ed.): Revolution und Vereinigung. Deutschland 1989/90, published 2009 by dtv Verlag.

2 Hans-Herman Hertle: Chronik des Mauerfalls, Berlin 1990, Hans-Hermann Hertle / Konrad H. Jarausch / Christoph Kleßmann (ed.): Mauerbau und Mauerfall. Ursachen, Verlauf, Wirkung, Berlin 2002.

3 Letter from J. R. to the Minister for Foreign Trade, 10.11.1989. Bundesarchiv Berlin-Lichterfelde (BArchB) DE 10/21.

4 Telegram from Information Technology Department (IDP) New York to the Ministry for Foreign Trade, 15.11.1989. BarchB DE 10/21.

Perforated by Wall Peckers:

The Wall at the

Brandenburg Gate

© Archiv Bundesstiftung Aufarbeitung /
Coll. Rosemarie Gentges No. 238

In Berlin, the trading of pieces of Wall began immediately after the border had been opened. Wall Peckers in the West began to take small and large chunks unsing hammers and chisels. The armed GDR border guards could do nothing more than look on as people banged and hammered relentlessly on the once heavily guarded Wall. The Fall of the Wall came as as much of a shock to the border guards as it did to the citizens of the GDR and the divided city. It was also unexpected by state leaders and rulers around the world. The downfall of the SED regime was clear and nobody was prepared to put old methods back in place at the borders. The notorious order to shoot people at the border was officially reversed on 21st December 1989.[5]

Those who did not have tools of their own were able to exchange western cash with pop-up street vendors in exchange for pieces of the Berlin Wall.[6]

In November/December 1989, the price for such freedom souvenirs reached considerable amounts. People were paying between five and 30 DM for smaller and larger pieces. The consequences of the interest in Wall trade did not go unnoticed. By the end of 1989, large sections of the Wall between the Reichstag and the Brandenburg Gate had already been chipped away. The pieces chipped from the Wall were highly sought after and selling well but this 'wild' trade was also controversial. The fact that pieces of Wall were being sold as bright souvenirs was met with condemnation by many. New crossing

5   Thomas Flemming / Hagen Koch: Die Berliner Mauer. Geschichte eines politischen Bauwerks, Berlin 1999, P. 125.
6   "Sonntagsspaziergang mit Kamera, Hammer und Meißel". In: Der Tagesspiegel, 14.11.1989.

Pop-up Souvenir stand
at the Brandenburger Gate

points had to be created to keep up with the demand, and they too were reduced to rubble by Wall Peckers. One of the first new crossing points was created in the evening from 11th-12th November 1989 on Potsdamer Platz. Thousands of people were present alongside flashing cameras from around the world as eight sections of the Wall were lifted out. Dozens more followed in the weeks to come.[7]

If demand for the small pieces of Wall was already so high, how much profit could be made by selling complete segments?

The estimated value of such segments brought an entrepreneurial-spirit with it. A West Berlin building contractor arrived at Potsdamer Platz with a lorry on the morning of 13th November 1989. He and his companions, identified by the border troops as Austrian citizens, offered the border commando in Mitte 500,000 DM for the sections that had been removed. They were referred to the Ministry of Foreign Trade to obtain a transport permit. After all, the segments were on GDR territory. However, the deal was never closed as the ministry did not grant permission.[8] Others attempted to simply steal the valuable segments of Wall. Sixteen sections of the Wall which had already been loaded onto transporters were seized with the help of the West Berlin police.[9]

New lucrative offers were continually made to GDR officials. A lawyer from East Berlin passed on an offer from a Californian business which was willing to pay 500,000 US Dollars for the sections of Wall that

---

7   Hertle: Chronik des Mauerfalls, P. 263.
8   Note for Minister Beil, Head Department for the Minister, 14.11.1989. BArchB DE 10/21.
9   Based on the reports by West German TV channel Sat1, which had uncovered the theft of the Wall. Note made during a telephone conversation, 5.12.1989.

had already been taken down.[10] A citizen from the German city of Aachen offered 200,000 DM for the same segments.[11]

Other companies and intermediaries offered exclusive contracts to the Ministry of Foreign Trade which guaranteed that 'significant amounts of money would be made for the GDR'.[12]

A letter written to representatives of the GDR in Bonn on 14th 1989 summarises the situation as follows: The trade of the Berlin Wall cannot be prohibited any longer: "Despite some contradictions [...] you should still consider one aspect: trade is being made with the Wall, wherever these sections may come from. If anything, I consider it reasonable to make money from it."[13]

At the same time, there were mixed opinions and questions were raised about whether or not it was morally right to use the Wall to make money. If money was indeed to be made by selling the Wall, then the profits should at least go the "people of the GDR who suffered under the Wall for almost three decades".[14]

Hundreds of people had been killed at the inner-German border in the previous years – the concrete Wall was not just a symbol of oppression for those behind and locked in by it. Furthermore, the Wall, hated by so many, had cost the GDR government millions and was therefore the property of the people. On these grounds, calls for at least some of the money made by selling the Wall to flow back to the people of the GDR were warranted.[15] These factors may have been part of the reason that Hans Modrow's former GDR government did succumb to trading pieces of the Wall.

The threat of state bankruptcy since the 1980s had only been prevented by foreign loans. However, these reserves had almost been used up by autumn 1989. At a GDR parliamentary meeting in the People's Court four days after the Fall of the Wall, the declaration of state bankruptcy was made public.[16] An attempt by GDR leader Egon Krenz to convince Helmut Kohl to subsidise the opening of the Berlin Wall as a humanitarian act came to nothing.[17]

Not even border traffic between West and East created much money for the GDR government. An obligatory exchange rate at the border for visitors from the West failed to be enforced due to the chaotic scenes at the border and it was officially abolished around Christmas 1989.[18]

Even if the hope to top up the national budget with Wall trade was unrealistic, the chance to bring in extra money would have been welcome. In accordance with this, a letter to the GDR government from Gerhard Beil, Minister of Foreign Trade, was received with interest. Less then two weeks after the Fall of the Wall, he wrote a letter and pointed out that pieces of Wall and rubble could be sold for between 800 and 500,000 DM in 'capitalist countries' and the government should decide what action should be taken in light of such offers.[19] On Modrow's advice, the GDR government signalled their agreement and preparations began in December 1989 to coordinate the marketing of the Berlin Wall. The border commando in Mitte, who were responsible for the segments at the new crossing points, were ordered not to load the rubble onto transporters. Simultaneously, further damage to the Wall by 'Wall Peckers' was also prohibited.[20]

---

10 Telefax by lawyer P. to the Minister for Foreign Trade, 30.11.1989. BArchB DE 10/21.
11 Telefax about the Permanent Representation in Bonn to the Mayor of East Berlin, undated (Middle of November 1989). BArchB DE 10/21.
12 Letter of wholesale and foreign trade company C. R. to MHA, 23.11.1989. DE 10/21.
13 Telex of M. A. business consultancy to the Permanent Representation of the GDR in Bonn, 14.11.1989. BArchB DE 10/21.
14 Letter from the DSU to Prime Minister Modrow of 12.12.1989. BArch DE 10/21, o.P.
15 "Wenn der Specht das Volkseigentum zerhackt." In: Berliner Morgenpost, 11.02.1990.
16 Christoph Links / Hannes Bahrmann: Chronik der Wende, Berlin 1999, p. 77.
17 Hertle: Chronik des Mauerfalls, S.249f.
18 Hertle: Chronik des Mauerfalls, pp.249.
19 Note from comrade E's phone call, undated (End of November 1989), BArchB DE 10/21.
20 Note from comrade E's phone call, undated (End of November 1989), BArchB DE 10/21.

State leader Hans Modrow gave his consent for the sale of the Berlin Wall to commence on 7th December 1989. Theodor Hoffmann, Minister of National Defence (and also responsible for the dismantling of the Berlin Wall), and Transport Minister, Heinrich Scholz, also agreed to the plans.[21]

An official ruling by the GDR government also followed and outlined the "commercial use of complete segments of the Wall, officially granted during the Council of Ministers meeting on 4th January 1990".[22]

The execution of trade was to be carried out by the Foreign Ministry since potential buyers were in western countries abroad. Import and export company 'Limex' were tasked with marketing and selling the Wall. The publicly owned company had worked on numerous construction projects in western countries and Latin America since the 1960s. To the annoyance of trade unions in West Berlin, 'Limex' had sent temporary workers from East Germany in the 1980s.[23] Now, the government had ordered them responsible for the sale of the Berlin Wall.

An inspection of the dismantled segments of Wall at the border commando in Mitte followed in December 1989 and was led by Limex's general director, Dirk Pfannschmidt. Discussions about how best to store sections of the Wall which had already been torn down were held, and decisions made about tearing down further, interesting pieces of Wall.[24]

A 300 metre long area along West Berlin's Waldemarstraße and Leuschnerdamm was of particular interest. In the mid 1980s, wall artists including Thierry Noir, Kiddy Citny, Keith Haring and Jürgen Große alias 'Indiano', had begun brightening up the ugly grey concrete with bright graffiti. Both the Ministry of Foreign Trade and art experts were of the opinion that these areas of Wall were the most valuable.[25]

Border patrol soldiers were ironically ordered to protect the area from 'vandalism' by Wall Peckers. These 'smearings' on the West Berlin side of the Wall had, for the last few decades, been a thorn in the GDR's side. Now, the same soldiers were to do everything in their power to protect the graffiti, now officially deemed 'art', so that the same government could make money from it.

Work to dismantle this section of Wall began on the evening of 22nd January 1990 under the protection of darkness. Approximately 50 sections of Wall were carefully lifted by crane and transported over the next three days. This was the first large section of Berlin Wall to disappear from Berlin's city landscape. However, calling this act an act of good will by the GDR would be mistaken and the holes in the Wall were quickly blocked again with a two-metre high fence. The planned sale of the Wall was the only reason for dismanteling it. The process was done at night (as explained to the press by a border soldier), "so as not to cause a stir."[26]

These valuable segments of Wall were put in temporary storage on an industrial estate on the border between Kreuzberg and Treptow. All 360 dismantled segments of the Wall were eventually brought and stacked up here, where they then awaited sale.

---

21 Handwritten by the Minister for Foreign Trade, Beil, 7.12.1989. BArchB DE 10/21.
22 Resolution of the cabinet of the GDR 8/I.8./90 from 29. December 1989 about the commercial use of entire segments / single pieces of the border fortifications ("Wall") to West Berlin. BArchB DC 20/I/3 2891.
23 "Konkurrenz hinter der Mauer." In: Die Zeit, 11.08.1989, 33/89.
24 AHB Limex letter to the MHA, 14.12.1989. BArchB DE 10/21.
25 Note for Gen. Minister Beil, 15.12.1989. BArchB DE 10/21.
26 "Statt Mauer jetzt ein Metallgitterzaun." In: Berliner Morgenpost, 24. January 1990.

Worth millions: the Wall on

Waldemarstraße before removal

© Archiv Bundesstiftung Aufarbeitung /
Coll. Rosemarie Gentges No. 10

On 28th December 1989, reports in GDR newspapers were published outlining plans for the sale of the segments.[27]

It was emphasised that the GDR government intended to use the profits for humanitarian purposes. 'Limex' also made a press release via ADN[28]. Due to worldwide interest in the Wall, 'Limex' had taken over the responsibility of selling the Wall on behalf of the GDR government. Reports that the sale of the Wall had already begun moved many GDR citizens to get in touch with the government, demanding to know more about it. The Wall had brought so much misery to so many people and had even cost some their lives. For many, the idea that it was to be put up for sale, seemed suspect.[29]

However, the response to these statements was huge. A Japanese company offered 185,000 US Dollars for a segment of the Wall from the Brandenburg Gate and many thousands of DM were also paid for less symbolic sections.[30]

Existing 'Limex' business ties were to help in organising the logistics of shipping the sections. 'Herfurt', a construction company from Spandau, which exported grit and gravel from the GDR, also offered 'Limex' their services to help with distribution and transportation.[31] The company boomed in the coming months. 900,000 DM (then equivalent to 2,700,000 GDR Mark) were paid into a special account by mid-April 1990.[32]

27 "DDR verkauft Teile der Berliner Mauer." In: Neues Deutschland, 28.12.1989. As well as a draft for an ADN-message, signed by Pfannschmidt, AHB Limex, undated (December 1989). BArchB DE 10/21.

28 The Allgemeiner Deutscher Nachrichtendienst (ADN) (General German News Service) was the state news agency in the GDR.

29 Draft of a reply by AHB Limex undated End of December 1989. BArch DE 21/10, o.P.

30 "Wie die DDR mit der Mauer ein Geschäft machen wollte." In: Der Tagesspiegel, 9.11.1999.

31 "Mauerbrocken auf schwarzem Samt und weißer Seide." In: Berliner Morgenpost, 29.12.1989.

32 Reasons for the resolutions made by the cabinet of the GDR 4/13/90 from 2. May 1990. BArchB DC 20/I/3 2930.

However, 'Limex' alone can not be thanked for the massive sales. Another business was also born in the western side of the city. Owners of 'LeLé Berlin Wall Verkaufs- und Wirtschaftswerbung GmbH' Judith B. LaCroix and Christian Herms had already made business contacts in the East during the 1980s whilst exporting beer within Germany.[33]

An exclusive cooperation contract was drawn up between 'Limex' and 'LeLé Berlin'.[34] According to the contract, 'Limex' was in charge of dealing with enquiries from museums and institutions which had been in contact with the GDR government regarding remains of the Wall, whilst 'LeLé Berlin' were in charge of the unequally profitable trade with private customers, businesses and gallery owners.

This meant that the actual marketing of the Wall lay in the hands of West Berlin businesses. This set a new standard. The less representative East Berlin 'Limex' office – based in an industrialised apartment block – was replaced with a new upmarket apartment on Tempelhofer Ufer. The offices were completely refurbished: modern furniture, contemporary art and, obviously, pictures of the Wall graffiti. This new image was meant to impress people from allover the world. In order to show the concrete sections of the Wall in their best light, 'LeLé Berlin' commissioned East Berlin photographer Karl-Heinz Kraemer to photograph each individual section still standing in Treptow. The pictures were then published in a 'LeLé' and 'Limex' sales catalogue which was sent to potential buyers all around the world.

Some sections of the Wall, damaged by weather or Wall Peckers, were given a facelift. Fading graffiti was given a new lick of paint. Some sections were painted to look completely new in the hope that this would create a bigger profit margin.

In spring 1990, Judith B. LaCroix went about finding young Berlin artists who could continue the work of the West Berlin Wall artists on a commercial scale. Some of the images painted by these artists echoed the works of Thierry Noir and Kiddy Citny, which had been deemed the most valuable of the 1980s era.

 Several segments of the Wall were commissioned by 'LeLé' and later sold as 'original' pieces of Wall art. Such pieces can be found today in Singapore, or in front of the Ronald Regean Presidential Library in California. It seemed that it was no longer important for buyers whether or not the expensive images had been painted before or after the Fall of the Wall. Other companies and artists also used 'aids' to make unattractive sections of the Wall more appealing to buyers. Work by five Soviet Union artists who had travelled from Moscow to Berlin in summer 1990 to paint 100 small sections of Wall, was sold for hundreds of thousands of US Dollars.[35] In order to dispel any fears that segments of the Wall sold by 'Limex' and 'LeLé' were not authentic, both companies later produced certificates of authentication for all 360 sections of Wall painted for sale.

Individual certificates with an official bronze seal guaranteed the authenticity of the segments. In summer 1990 'LeLé Berlin' was demanding high prices for such segments. A piece of Wall, complete with Wall graffiti, cost 90,000 DM, a piece without graffiti could be bought for 40,000 Marks. Even small segments, 20cm x 20cm, cost up to 2,500 DMs.[36] Sale notices were published in art and collectors journals all over the world and in order to create as much publicity as possible, 'Limex' and 'LeLé Berlin' organised two auctions. The idea to auction sections of the Wall had already been brought to the table in December 1989 by GDR culture

33 The Wall. Le mur de berlin vente aux encheres exceptionelle, Auktionskatalog eds. by Limex and LeLé Berlin, Berlin 1990.
34 Letter by LeLé Berlin to Jens Galschiøt Christophersen, 26.02.1990. Archive Jens Galschiøt.
35 "Auch Moskau will ein Stück Mauer." In: Tagesspiegel, 08.08.1990. The pieces of art are up for sale again in the USA. Disclosed by Outdoor Arts Foundation, 22.01.2009.
36 Price list by lelé Berlin GmbH, undated (spring 1990). Archive Jens Galschiøt.

Genuine Wall for the whole world: Limex certificate in German and Japanese
© Maruho Co. Ltd.

minister Dietmar Keller. He made a suggestion to auction sections of the Wall to the Ministry for Foreign Trade.[37]

The auction took place on 28th April 1990 at the West Berlin Hotel 'Interkontinental', near Kurfürsten-damm. Three segments were selected for auction: two from Checkpoint Charlie and one from the Brandenburg Gate. However, there was not a great deal of interest. Only one segment found a buyer amongst the 80 present. A representative from a Swiss firm was able to take the 2.6 tonne section of Wall home for 1,500 DM.[38]

Despite the disappointing result, 'LeLé Berlin' and 'Limex' did not lose faith in their concept. It was announced at the end of the auction that further international auctions were to take place in the coming months. Art lovers from allover the world were to be offered the segments in Paris and Monaco. The plans for an auction in Paris never came to fruition, but as a consequence even greater efforts were made whilst preparing for the auction in Monaco.

'LeLé Berlin' managed to gain the support of Monegasque gallery owners Francoise and Louis Jeze-quelou, who, until then, had specialised in 17th and 18th century paintings.[39]

---

37 Note after conversation with Minister Keller, 28.12.198. BArchB DE 10/21.
38 "Versteigerung von Mauerteilen mangels Geboten schnell zu Ende." In: Der Tagesspiegel, 29.04.1990.
39 The Wall. Le mur de Berlin vente aux encheres exceptionelle, Auktionskatalog eds. by Limex and LeLé Berlin, Berlin 1990, a part of Waldemarstraße for the Hennessy-Kids. In: Die Tageszeitung, 25.06.1990.

The extravagant Hotel Metropole on the French Riviera was chosen as the location for the auction. A press conference took place on the 30th May 1990, where the sale of 81 original sections of Wall art was announced.[40]

Almost a month later, the auction was held. Around 100 art lovers and brokers from all over the world had made their way to Monaco on the evening of 23rd June 1990. 70 pieces were on sale, amongst them, many pieces by famous West Berlin Wall artists, Noir and Cinty. Further segments – labelled in the catalogue as being by 'anonymous artists' – had been commissioned and repainted by 'LeLé Berlin'.[41]

Eleven smaller pieces were also on auction for a bidding price of 40,000 Francs. The foreword in the sale catalogue noted that all proceeds were to be given to the GDR. To emphasise this noble action, the president of the East Berlin Charité hospital was invited to Monaco. Sections of the Wall not permitted to go on sale were those originally situated where people had lost their lives or sections that bore bullet holes. This was supposed to detract from the horror of the 'Antifascist Protection Rampart' and prevent buyers from feeling guilty. The auction was a success. For example, Italian publisher Jaguba Rizzoli and French businesswoman Ljilijana Hennessy bid 170,000 DM for their pieces of Wall. A Swiss entrepreneur even paid 1,300,000 Francs. It is still not clear today how much money was actually made at the auction, but it is reported to have been between 1.8 and 2.2 million DM. In a newspaper report, 'LeLé Berlin' refused to disclose any information.[42]

GDR company 'Limex' and the hospitals to which the proceeds were donated investigated this. According to press reports, the West Berlin company still owed between 700,000 and 1,000,000 DM.[43] Wall artists Noir and Citny, whose work had been sold at the auction without permission, tried to gain reparations for the works sold at the auction. However, it was not only the GDR in dispute with the West Berlin company. In autumn 1990 they took their case against 'LeLé' to the regional courts in Berlin. They were unsuccessful. According to a statement by 'Limex', their paintings on the Wall had ultimately been "damage to GDR property" and Noir and Citny should be thankful that they themselves had not been prosecuted.[44] The case went to the German Federal Supreme Courts. Senior judges granted in favour of the artists whose copyrights had been damaged. Noir and Citny, therefore, were to be paid almost 500,000 DM in damages, which was to be used for charitable purposes decided upon by an advisory board established in 1990.[45]

By this time both 'Limex' and 'LeLé Berlin' had been dissolved. The official end of the GDR also saw the end of the duties for 'Limex', who had been working under the name VGH Bau GmBH since the economical and currency reforms in June 1990. Since then, they had been less and less involved with selling the Wall.

After disagreements between 'LeLé Berlin' and 'Limex' concerning the money made at the Monaco auctions, the West Berlin company were forced to find other sources from which they could buy sections of the Wall. Newspaper reports claim that 'LeLé Berlin' continued to be supplied by one of the largest demolition firms.[46] 'LeLé Berlin' dissolved in 1992/1993 when reports about dishonest practice and hidden money escalated.

---

40 Mandy Schielke: Das Mauerpuzzle. Eine kleine Geschichte der Berliner Mauer. Radiofeature by Deutschlandradio Kultur.http://www.dradio.de/dkultur/sendungen/laenderreport/527213/, last accessed 22.03.2009.

41 Patrice Lux, who liaised the Wall artists with LeLé Berlin, confirmed, that most "anonymous" pieces of Wall art were specially designed for the Monaco auction. Interview with the author with Patrice Lux, 04.02.2009.

42 Statement by Limex as quoted by: "Gericht: 492301,65 Mark für Mauerkünstler."In: Berliner Morgenpost, 13.07.1999.

43 On the controversy surrounding the proceeds of Monaco: "Wem gehört die verkaufte Mauerkunst?" In: Die Tageszeitung, 8.12.1990, p. 34 as well as "Ein Teilsieg für Mauerkünstler." In: Die Tageszeitung, 13.02.1991.

44 "Citney-Mauer-Graffiti an Museum verkauft." In: Der Spiegel 22/1990.

45 "Gericht: 492301,65 Mark für Mauerkünstler." In: Berliner Morgenpost, 13.07.1999.

46 "Klammheimliche Millionengeschäfte mit der Mauer?" In: Berliner Morgenpost, 16.12.1990.

Dismantling the border
installations Pankow, Berlin
© Archiv Bundesstiftung Aufarbeitung /
Coll. Leonore Schwarzer No. 134

In March 1990, the first freely elected GDR government came to power and also had their suspicions that proceeds made from sales of the Wall were being channeled elsewhere. On 2nd May 1990, culture minister Herbert Schirmer submitted a proposal to government leaders to have all money in the 'Limex' account controlled by a specially formed advisory board. Indeed, it had been decided in December 1990 that the proceeds from the sale of the Wall should go towards the health system and preservation of historical monuments, but this money had not been monitored and controlled. Furthermore, 'Limex' and the GDR government were still receiving calls and queries from concerned citizens who, despite assurance, did not believe that the proceeds were being used for altruistic purposes by all parties involved. Reports focussed solely on the large scale corruption in the former GDR and mistrust amongst citizens was great.[47]

The newly elected government under de Maizière adopted a resolution on 2nd May 1990 to form a board of trustees (consisting of representatives from the Ministries of Culture and Health, as well as ten other public personalities) who would administrate and distribute the money.[48] The board was headed by High Consistory Martin Ziegler, who had moderated the round table between December 1989 and March 1990. However, the constitution of the board took a long time and only really existed on paper when reunification took place on 3rd October 1990. More than 2,000,000 DM made from the sales by 'Limex' were frozen by

47 Due to several enquiries by the public to 'Limex' its management found itself in the position of having to prepare a statement in December 1989 and January 1990. The recorded draft states that all proceedings from the sale of the Wall flow into national budget and are then used for charity purposes. Draft of a reply, signed by Pfannschmidt, undated (January 1990). BArchB DE 10/21.
48 Resolution of the cabinet of the GDR 4/13/90 from 2nd May 1990 about the formation of an advisory board on the use of the proceeds from the sale of the segments from the "Berlin Wall". BArchB DC 20/I/3 2930.

the treasury in late 1990 until further notice. Next on the agenda was the issue of the artists: had the sale of their work actually been legal? Furthermore, with the signing of the Unification Treaty the Wall had become property of the Federal Republic, along with any profit made from the Wall. All the same, the treasury granted use of the money for charitable purposes, which the board should decide upon.[49] After this agreement was reached, more than 70,000 applications for funding were made. The applications had a sum total of over 50,000,000 DM.[50] 25 projects ranging from equipping hospitals to the redevelopment of churches and castles, were granted funds. However, it was not until 1997, when the issues surrounding the artists were settled, that the treasury transferred the first payment of 250,000 DM.

A further sum of half a million DM was transferred three years later. Estimates by the committee of the board leave a total of approximately 650,000 DM which remained tied up in the federal budget. The board dissolved in 2002. Nonetheless, a number of hospitals in Berlin and Plauen, a disabled sports group and a few churches in need of redevelopment continue to benefit from the money made from selling the Wall.[51]

The Monaco auction in 1990 was probably the biggest success story in the history of Wall trade. Until then 'Limex' and 'LeLé Berlin' were the only companies able to offer complete segments of the Berlin Wall for sale. The circle of those able to get their hands on a section of the Wall became larger with the complete destruction and, above all, the disposal of the Wall that began on 13th June 1990.

When work (which largely went unnoticed) to dismantle the border fortifications began between Potsdam and West Berlin in March 1990, interest in the concrete sections was great. The task of demolishing the Wall was given to border troops. They offered pieces of the Wall at low prices to private customers and businesses who wanted to use the remains to build garages or fill silos.[52] According to one border officer, "a few hundred thousand Marks" were taken in the first few weeks of March.[53]

Private companies were also called in to help with the complete demolition of the 155 kilometre long border-fortification around West Berlin. As well as GDR companies, the job was given predominantly to companies in West Berlin and neighbouring firms from the Federal Republic. They helped the border troops with the dismantling and, in return, were given the remains of the Wall at low prices as building material. It was an open secret that the odd section of Wall never made it to the grinder, but instead into the hands of collectors on the art market. Newspapers reported that the pieces that had disappeared from storage areas were those that had been painted with graffiti.[54]

The story of Volker Pawlowski, whose company was one of the lucky few to be granted subsidies from the government, shows how appealing the remains of the Wall were to some. Volker Pawlowski had the idea of setting small pieces of the Wall in plastic cases and sticking others to postcards. These products are still popular with tourists today.[55] The value of the Wall was not recognised right away by everybody. A farm in Mecklenburg bought several segments from border troops in summer 1990 for use in constructing silos.

49 "Die Mauer ist weg, das Geld auch" In: Hamburger Abendblatt, 08.08.1991.
50 "Erlös aus Mauerverkauf fließt ins Gesundheitswesen." In: Der Tagesspiegel, 6.11.1990.
51 "Die Wende, fünf Aktenordner und viel Frust." In: Berliner Zeitung, 14.03.2002.
52 "Mauer-Silos." In: Tagesspiegel 04.05.1990.
53 "Millionengeschäft mit der Mauer." In: Tagesspiegel, 18.03.1990.
54 "Klammheimliche Millionengeschäfte mit der Mauer?" In: Berliner Morgenpost 16.12.1990.
55 "Geschichte, bröckchenweise." In: Berliner Zeitung, 11. August 2001.

It was not until a few years later that the owner recognised the true value of the bits of Wall. Cut into small pieces and covered in new graffiti, the pieces would go for thousands at auction today.[56]

In order to better regulate the demolition of the Wall and know the whereabouts of the remains, the government announced that the remains of the Wall were allowed to be sold. The proceeds should go back into the national budget.[57] This was only applicable to rubble and not entire segments. Demolition commandos should now be able to ensure that sections of the Wall, which were to be donated as gifts by the GDR, would be readily available.

Furthermore, potential buyers who contacted the army had to prove their 'charitable intentions'. This way, the black market would not profit. The government were still aware of the fact that segments could reach between "1,000 and 10,000 Mark" on the market.[58] However, the Wall was not only sold in complete segments: grey concrete sections of the Wall were rented out to companies as advertising spaces. Smaller bits of Wall memorabilia, including signs and fences, could also be found in shops and on flea markets.

Interest in the Wall did not subside after reunification. The border troops who had been given the task of demolishing the Wall were put under the control of the Federal Armed Forces. The Federal Armed forces were under the direction of General Rolf Ocken and completed the demolition by mid-1991.

Requests for sections of the Wall were still made to the armed forces. When reports about dishonest handling of such segments continued to be made by the press, General Ocken prohibited the sale of the Wall in October 1990.

The incoming requests and offers for sections of the Wall were collected and passed on to the Ministry of Defence in Bonn. It was from here that official instructions were given to proceed with the sale of the Wall. Between December 1990 and mid-1991, more then six million DM is said to have been paid into the Ministry of Defence's budget – more than three times the amount raised by the GDR when selling the Wall. Compared with this, the demolition of the Wall had cost the treasury an estimated 170,000,000 DM.[59]

However, it was not only the GDR border troops and private companies who had to get to grips with the Wall. Units were put together from British troops stationed in Berlin in order to help with the swift dismantling of the Wall. To thank them for their work they were (officially) allowed to take a number of section back home with them. These sections can be found today in a number of military museums in Great Britain.[60]

The biggest quota was secured by US troops. American General Raymond Haddock had numerous complete segments and smaller sections sent to army museums in the US.[61] American interest in the Wall was second only to Germany. It is estimated that there are more pieces of the Wall in America than there are in Berlin. Remains of the Wall were highly sought after in the states as victory trophies and as concrete proof of the rightfulness of the American dream for a better world. Such pieces were making their way to the States after the Wall had been opened, but before the topic of demolition had been discussed. 60 tonnes of Wall rubble were shipped to the US two weeks after 9th November 1989 in order to keep up with demand during the Christmas shopping period. Not even hundreds of Wall Peckers would have been

56 Catalogue of the 26th Brecht Immobilien GmbH Auction, 14. March 2009 in Berlin, p. 28/29.
57 Order Nr. 10/90 of the Minister for Disarmament and Defense, as quoted by Rathje: Mauer-Marketing,Vol. 1, p. 913-14.
58 File memo for the State Secretary for Disarmament, 23.08.1990, as quoted by: Rathje: Mauer-Marketing, Vol. 1, p. 919.
59 "Mauerabriss verlief 'wie's Brezelbacken'". In: Berliner Morgenpost, 21.08.1999 as well as "Ein Mann räumt auf". In: Süddeutsche Zeitung, 11.06.2009
60 As in Royal Engineers Museum, Gillingham, Royal Air Force Museum, Cosford or in National Army Museum, London.
61 As in US Air Force Museum in Ohio, in military prison Fort Leavenworth or at the CIA in Langley/Washington D.C.

able to come away with so much of the Wall in such a short amount of time. The Bloomington department store chain put an estimated two million tiny pieces of the Wall on the market complete with certificates of authentication at the beginning of December 1989.[62] The questionable origin of these pieces did not seem to bother anybody.

Some resourceful Americans hammered away at the Wall themselves, and had paid significant amounts of money to have their heavy freight flown back to the States. Professional coin dealer Barry Stuppler offered to buy the entire Wall for 50 million US Dollars. Private Wall Peckers from New York to Washington and California earned themselves a mint at the end of 1989.

What was missing from the American market were complete segments. They were considerably more difficult to get hold of than the small pieces hammered from the Wall. Nevertheless, in spring 1990 some Americans tried to have segments stolen and sent to the US. The West German customs authorities, however, were suspicious of the extremely heavy freight and had the sections sent back to East Berlin.[63]

'Limex' sales director Helge Möbius flew to New York in January 1990 to build up an American sales network. More than 300 American companies had been in touch by then to offer their broker services. In the end, only three companies would be given the exclusive contract to market sections of the Wall, amongst them were the "Berlin Wall Commemorative Group" and "JAK Productions"[64] The latter was specialised in professional fundraising for American police, whilst the "Berlin Wall Commemorative Group" was coined by New Jersey building contractor Joseph Sciamarelli. His concept to create a Wall memorial in all 32 American places named Berlin and generate millions quite clearly convinced 'Limex'.[65]

On 2nd February 1990, sales began onboard the US warship Intrepid in a New York harbour shortly after the contracts were signed. The 'Berlin Wall Commemorative Group' got Berlin born pop-artist Peter Max involved in a 'Berlin Wall Happening'. He painted two segments, which had been brought to the US with the representative from 'Limex', with a small Statue of Liberty and signed them. Smaller limited edition versions of this piece were supposed to have been made and sold for 7,000 US Dollars.[66] Demand for these segments was within reasonable limits. Potential buyers waited for the complete segments of Wall and smaller fragments of the Wall which were still on board a ship somewhere on the Atlantic. Joseph Sciamarelli delivered segments of the Wall to almost all American presidential libraries, as well as to private buyers and art collectors. Those interested in segments of the Wall could also order them from Europe, or they could fly over to Berlin themselves and pick out a piece from the storage areas. American entrepreneur Fred Meijers did just that and returned home with three segments of the Wall.[67] There is no information available that discloses how much money was made by the 'Berlin Wall Commemorative Group'. The total amount of the sales discovered just from research for this book run into many hundreds of thousands of US Dollars. However, not all entrepreneurs were so successful. Irvin Deyer paid 165,000 US Dollars in the summer of 1990 for segments of the Wall with the intention of reselling them in the US – but he was simply unable to sell them. A similar story can be told of a lawyer from Chicago who was also unable to sell the sections of wall he purchased.[68]

---

62 "Großes Mauerspektakel im New Yorker Hafen." In: Berliner Morgenpost, 04.02.1990.
63 "Eine Unze Freiheit." In: Der Spiegel 5/1990, 29.01.1990.
64 "Heute in New York...". In: Die Tageszeitung, 01.02.1990.
65 Self-portrait by the Berlin Wall Commemorative Group. www.berlin-wall.com
66 "Eine Mauer für die ganze Welt". In: Der Stern 56/1990, p. 81.
67 Today they are in the Public Museum, Grand Rapids, at Grand Valley State University, Allendale and in the Gerald Ford Presidential Library in Grand Rapids.
68 "Eine Mauer für die ganze Welt." In: Der Stern, 56/1990.

Two Berliners came unstuck in 1990 when their idea to open a Wall amusement park failed. Watch towers, spring guns and 90 sections of the Wall had already been shipped to the States, where tourists were supposed to have been given the creeps by a reconstruction of the death strip. No sponsor was found in America for the macabre amusement park.[69]

Such stories are, however, exceptions. The Wall continues to sell very well in the US today. The 'Outdoor Arts Foundation' in Florida had more than 350 sections of the Wall brought to the States in time for the 20th anniversary of the Fall of the Wall. Any American corporation that can raise the asking price of between 60,000 and 100,000 US Dollars can buy one of these sections.[70] Further sections, for example those from Steinstücken (one of West Berlin's exclaves), are still waiting to be bought.[71]

Waiting for buyers:
350 Segments of the hinterlandmauer in Florida
© Outdoor Arts Foundation

Interest in the Berlin Wall is still great today. Its complex and worldwide symbolic power will continue to promote its trade. However, not many have become rich by selling the Wall. Least of all, the GDR government, Modrow or de Maizière, who had hoped for at least a small contribution towards the cost of demolishing the Wall and also to put some money back into society. For them, the Wall remained what it had always been: a losing game.

69 "Freizeitspaß auf dem Todesstreifen". In: Süddeutsche Zeitung, 20.05.1995.
70 www.outdoorartsfoundation.com.
71 www.berlin-wall-monuments.com

Ruth Gleinig: employed at The Federal Foundation for the Reappraisal of the SED Dictatorship since 1999 as contact person for victims of political persecution in the GDR and Soviet occupation zone, also project coordinator for "memorial sites for the communist dictatorship".

Ronny Heidenreich: research associate at Unabhängige Historikerkommission (Independent Commission of Historians) for research into the history of the Bundesnachrichtendienst (Federal Intelligence Service) since 2011, 2009-2011 research associate at the Berlin Wall Memorial, 2007-2009 employee at the Federal Foundation for the Reappraisal of the SED Dictatorship. Studied early modern and modern history, Eastern European studies and political science in Leipzig and Berlin. Research and publications on German and Eastern European contemporary history and commemorative culture.

Anna Kaminsky: doctorate and title Dr. phil. 1993-1998 collaboration in various research and exhibition projects including the Berlin Institute for Comparative Social Research, The University of Münster, Memorial and Museum Sachsenhausen and the German Historical Museum, research fellow since 1998, Director of the Federal Foundation for the Reappraisal of the SED Dictatorship since 2001.

Rainer E. Klemke: graduate of political science, Communication Consultant and Project Developer, former Director of the Berlin Senates inter-agency team 'Gesamtkonzept Berliner Mauer' (overall Berlin Wall memorial site concept) and 1995-2012 director of inter-agency team 'Museum' with government support, memorial sites and contemporary history in the State Chancellery.

Maria Nooke: studied religious education and has been active in youth ministry work, studied sociology, psychology and pedagogy at the TU in Berlin from 1989, has worked on contemporary historical projects relating to National Socialism and GDR history, PhD at the Otto Suhr Institute for Political Science at the FU in Berlin in 2007.

Research associate and senior position at the Berlin Wall Memorial from 1999, Deputy Director of the Berlin Wall Foundation since 2009. Released historical publications about dealing with the National Socialist past, GDR opposition and the history of division.

Member of the board of directors at Verein Gegen Vergessen – Für Demokratie (Against Oblivion – For Democracy)

Tina Schaller: M.Phil. freelance historian. Collaboration on various historical and art history exhibitions. Recent publications (currently only available in German): "Grenz- und Geisterbahnhöfe im geteilten Berlin", 2nd edition, Berlin 2014, "Weltende – Die Ostseite der Berliner Mauer. Mit heimlichen Fotos von Detlef Matthes", Berlin 2011 (ed. Gerhard Sälter and Anna Kaminsky), "Verschwunden und Vergessen. Flüchtlingslager in West-Berlin bis 1961", Berlin 2012 (ed. Bettina Effner und Enrico Heitzer).

Leo Schmidt: studied history of art, classical archaeology and history at the universities of Freiburg and Munich, 1980 Ph.D. in Freiburg, 1980-1995 employed at Landesdenkmalamt Baden-Württemberg (the Baden-Württemberg Monument Authority), most recently as Director at Denkmalinventarisation (Record of Monuments) in Baden, Director of historic preservation at BTU Cottbus.

Specialist research areas in: monument science (practice, theory and the history of the notion of monuments), history of the city and urban archeology, history of architecture and the preservation of 18th century stately homes in England, architecture in the Wilhelmine Empire (1871-1918), commemorative significance of the Berlin Wall.

ACKNOWLEDG-MENT

The remains of the Berlin Wall have sometimes taken long and meandering paths to arrive at their new locations. Enquiries have often proved difficult, and retrieving answers would have been impossible without the obliging and active support from our on-site contacts. For this support, the Federal Foundation for the Reappraisal of the SED Dictatorship is indebted to numerous authorities, institutions, memorials and museums. It is equally indebted to many private persons, who call a piece of the Wall their own and have readily provided information and photographs and supported the work in various ways.

American Overseas Schools Historical Association (USA), Andrej Sacharow Zentrum (Russia), Associación Civil "Club Berlín" (Argentina), Ministry of Foreign Affairs Costa Rica (Costa Rica), Bausch & Lomb Dr. Mann Pharma (Germany), BerlinBrats Association (USA), Bezirksamt Treptow-Köpenick von Berlin (Germany), Costa Rican Embassy Berlin (Germany), German Armed Forces Command, United States and Canada (USA), Carlo Accorsi (Italy), Chapman University (USA), City of Leavenworth (USA), Colgate University (USA), Dankmar und Christel Hottenbacher (Germany), Defense Language Institute (USA), Embassy of Germany in Vatican, the Holy Sea (Vatican City), Embassy of Germany in Buenos Aires (Argentina), German Embassy Canberra (Australia), German Embassy Guatemala-City (Guatemala), German Embassy Cape town (South Africa), German Embassy Kingston (Jamaica), German Embassy Copenhagen (Denmark), German Embassy Kiev (Ukraine), German Embassy La Pas (Bolivia), German Embassy Madrid (Spain), German Embassy Montevideo (Uruguay), German Embassy Moscow (Russia), German Embassy Ottawa (Canada), German Embassy Riga (Latvia), German Embassy San José (Costa Rica), German Embassy Santiago de Chile (Chile), German Embassy Seoul (South Korea), German Embassy Singapore (Singapore), German Embassy Sofia (Bulgaria), German Embassy Stockholm (Sweden), German Embassy Tel Aviv (Israel), German Embassy Warsaw (Poland), German Embassy Washington (USA), German Embassy Zagreb (Croatia), Deutsche Luft- und Raumfahrtgesellschaft (Germany), German honorary consul in Nassau (Bahamas), German honorary consul in Tonga (Tonga), German consulate general Chicago (USA), German consulate general New York (USA), German consulate general Sevilla (Spain), Dirk Verheyen (Germany), Division for Trade and Tourism Miyakojima (Japan), Dustin Holmes (USA), Editoria Perfil (Argentina), Edwina Sandys (USA), Ein Hod Visitors Centre (Israel), Elena Codecà (Monaco), Fanny Heidenreich (Germany), Federación de Asociaciones Argentino-Germanas (Argentina), Franklin D. Roosevelt Presidential Library (USA), Genting Highlands Resort (Malaysia), George H. W. Bush Presidential Library and Museum (USA), Capital University (USA), George Patton Museum (USA), Winston Churchill Memorial and Museum (USA), Gerald R. Ford Presidential Library and Museum (USA), Gerd Mielke (Bolivia), German Institute Taipei (Taiwan), Grand Valley State University Library (USA), Great Passion Play Park (USA), Halifax Regional Municipality (Canada), Hans-Olaf Henkel (Germany), Hartmut Jahn (Berlin), Herbert Hoover Presidential Library (USA), Hochschule für Musik Hanns Eisler Berlin (Germany), Holcim Italia S.p.A. (Italy), Hoover Institution (USA), Imperial War Museum London (Great Britain), Institute for Peace Studies Jeju (South Korea), J. James Kinley (Canada), James A. Baker III. Institute for Public Policy (USA), Jean Browaeys (Germany), Jens Galschiøt (Denmark), Jens Schöne (Germany), Jerusalem Foundation (Israel), John F. Kennedy Presidential Library and Museum (USA), John Hopkins University / SAIS (USA), Kelly Cutchin (USA), Kentuck Knob (USA), Kevin W. Smith (USA), Klaus Groenke (Germany), Konkuk University Seoul (South Korea), Kurt Goerger (Germany), Landratsamt Oberhavel (Germany), Lode Anseel (Belgium), Loyola Marymount University (USA), Ludwig Johannsen (Mexico), Ludwik Wasecki (Berlin), Lunenburg Foundry (Canada), Manuel Steinbrecher (Germany), Marbles Kids Museum (USA), Margareta Hulthén

(Sweden), Martin S. Young (Canada), Maruho Co. Ltd. (Japan), Microsoft Art Collection (USA), Museum House of Terror (Budapest), Museum of Peace and Solidarity (Uzbekistan), Museum of World Treasures (USA), National Army Museum London (Great Britain), Nemacolin Woodlands Resort (USA), Odsherreds Turistbureau (Denmark), Olaf Stölt (Spain), Olympisches Museum Lausanne (Switzerland), Outdoor Arts Foundation (USA), Patrice Lux (Germany), Public Affairs Office Fort Gordon (USA), Public Museum Grand Rapids (USA), Reagan Ranch Centre (USA), Richard Nixon Library and Birthplace (USA), Robert Brendel (Germany), Robert Golzen (USA), Robert Gulyás (Hungary), Ronald Reagan Building and International Trade Center (USA), Ronald Reagan Presidential Library (USA), Royal Air Force Museum (Great Britain), Santuário de Fátima (Portugal), Berlin Senate (Germany), Stefan Pannen (Fernsehbüro Berlin), South Dakota Memorial Park (USA), Stacey Warnke (USA), City administration Gent (Belgium), Steve DiMillo (USA), European Solidarity Centre Gdansk (Poland), Supreme Headquarters Allied Powers Europe (Belgium), Takahisa Matsuura (Japan), Teguh Ostenrik (Indonesia), The Freedom Forum (USA), Thierry Noir (Germany), Tom Hood (USA), Town of Truro (Canada), TÜV Rheinland Japan Ltd. (Japan), U.S. Airforce Museum (USA), U.S. Department of State (USA), U.S. Naval Academy (USA), Ulrike und Jochen Guckes (Germany), Wally Gobetz (USA), Wende Museum (USA), Wikimedia Commons public domain (world map), World Trade Centre Montréal (Canada), Yorkshire Sculpture Park (Great Britain).

Out thanks go especially to Mr. Frank Rainer Mützel (Berlin), who painstakingly edited the manuscript and supported our work with valuable tips and suggestions.

Despite intensive research, it has not been possible to contact all right holders. We will of course pay any legitimate fees in accordance with Mittelstandsgemeinschaft Foto-Marketing (MFM) regulations.

Geographic Register

Albania 36	Flagstaff 121	Lunenburg 116	Saumur 64
Albinea 82	Fort Gordon 138	Luxemburg 87	Schengen 87
Argentina 206-208	Fort Knox 149	Madrid 105	Seattle 187-188
Australia 242-243	Fort Leavenworth . . 146	Mars 245	Seoul 233-235
Bahamas 198	France 55-68	Merone 83	Seville 106
Baltimore 152	Fulton 161	Mexico 202-204	Simi Valley 132
Belgium 37-44	Gdansk 89	Mexico City 202	Sofia 45
Bible Hill 114	Ghent 42-43	Miedzyrec Podlaski . 93	Sosnóvka 95
Bolivia 209	Germany 69-74	Monaco 88	South Africa 214
Boston 154-156	Gillingham 76	Montréal 118	Spain 104-107
Bretton Hall 79	Grand Rapids . .157-159	Moscow 103	Spartanburg 177
Bringolo 55	Great Britain 75-79	Mountain View 125	Spilamberto 84
Brussels 37-39	Guatemala 200-201	Nagoya 223	Stanford 133
Budapest 80-81	Guatemala City 200	Nassau 198	Strasbourg 65
Buenos Aires . .206-207	Halifax 115	Nemacolin 176	Sucre 209
Bulgaria 45	Hamilton 165	Newport News 183	Sweden 108
Caen 56	Hikone 221	New York City . .167-171	Switzerland 109
Cala Vadella 104	Honolulu 139	Nuevo Berlín 212	Taipei 238
Canada 114-119	Hope 141	Nuku'alofa 240	Taiwan 238-239
Canberra 242	Houston 182	Nykøbing 51	Tampere 54
Cape Town 214	Hungary 80-81	Odense 52	Timişoara 101
Casteau near Mons . 40	Hyde Park 166	Orange 127	Terespol 93
Chalk Hill 175	Ibiza 104	Orlando 136	Tirana 36
Chicago 142	Indonesia 217-218	Osaka 224	Togitsu 225
Chile 210-211	Israel 219-220	Ottawa 119	Tonga 240
China 216	Italy 82-84	Paris 60-63	Trelleborg 108
College Station 179	Jakarta 217	Poland 89-98	Ueno 227
Columbus 173	Jamaica 120	Portland 150	Uijeongbu 236
Copenhagen 48	Japan 221-229	Portugal 99-100	Ukraine 110-111
Cosford 75	Jeju-si 230	Powiat Bialski 93	Uruguay 212
Costa Rica 199	Jersey City 164	Presidio of Monterey 128	USA 121-196
Croatia 46-47	Kentuck Knob 175	Rapid City 178	Usbekistan 240
Culver City 123	Kiev 108	Redmond 185	Utrera 107
Dalian 216	Kingston 120	Reston 184	Vatican City 112
Dallas 181	Kobylany 93	Riga 85	Versailles 67
Dayton 174	Korea 230-237	Rochester 172	Washington D.C.
Denmark 48-53	Krzyżowa 91	Romania 101-102	189-194
Deauville 58	Langeland 49	Russia 103	West Branch 144
Ein Hod 219	Langley 195	Saint Petersburg . . 137	Wichita 147
Eureka 143	Lausanne 109	Samarkand 240	Yokohama 229
Eureka Springs 122	Latvia 85-86	San José 199	Yorba Linda 134
Fátima 99	London 77-78	Santa Barbara 130	Zagreb 46
Finland 54	Los Angeles 124	Santiago de Chile . . 210	Zwevezele Wingene . 44

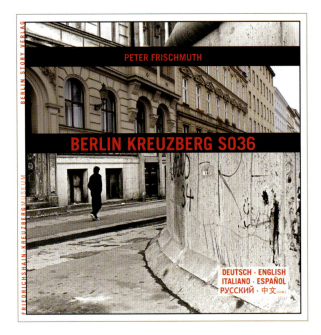

Peter Frischmuth
BERLIN KREUZBERG SO 36
128 pages, b/w and colour photos, hardback **19,80 Euro**
ISBN 978-3-95723-004-1

From the most significant West Berlin district and back to the heart of the city. When the Wall was built, Kreuzberg found itself at the edge of the border and life between East and West Berlin was cut off. In 1982, Peter Frischmuth documented the situation. In 2006 – quarter of a century later and after the Wall had fallen – he retraced his footsteps and tried to spot the differences.

His side-by-side photographs – before and after the Fall of the Wall – are particularly impressive. The observer is magically taken back to the Wall years, only to be then set free on the other side. The wound has been healed, the Wall had to go – and it really has gone.

Frischmuth has even tracked down the same people he photographed in 1982, as well as the locations. He shows how Kreuzberg SO 36 has found its place again in the heart of the city.

Tobias Seeliger
ZEITENWENDE
128 pages, 150 b/w photos **19,95 Euro**
ISBN 978-3-95723-021-8

"Let the little one go first", called Willy Brandt. He was talking about Tobias Seeliger, just turned 16 and pushed back by the hordes of press photographers. Today, Seeliger is a professional photographer. As a student and member of the Gethsemane Church congregation, he was always at the heart of the action capturing images – always in the right place at the right time. His unique pictures were taken at his school during protests against ballot rigging, large demonstrations and finally, the Fall of the Wall in November 1989. Seeliger already follows the route to the Fall of the Wall from a press photographer's perspective and sells his pictures. Nobody else photographed the Peaceful Revolution, the Fall of the Wall and reunification from so close-up and so uninhibitedly.

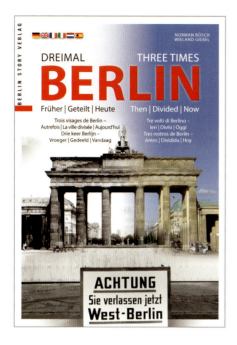

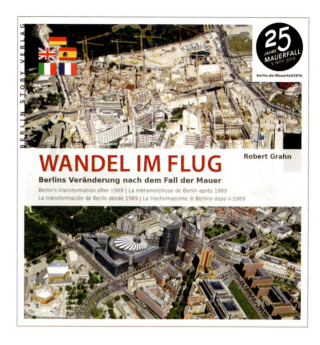

Norman Bösch/Wieland Giebel
DREIMAL BERLIN
80 pages, 170 illustrations, paperback **9,95 Euro**
ISBN 978-3-95723-030-0

Pictures of Berlin from the last 100 years: from the City Palace, once the most popular postcard image, to the Palace of the Republic and areal photos of the Berlin Palace building site – 13 images over 6 pages.

The Brandenburg Gate in the midst of imperial celebrations, Nazis marching, the four defenders of the fatherland during the time of the GDR and modern day party – ten photos over six pages.

Potsdamer Platz, Checkpoint Charlie, Mauerpark and the Oberbaum Bridge – the changes of important places, buildings, bridges and railway stations.

Robert Grahn
WANDEL IM FLUG
144 pages, aerial photos, hardback, **19,95 €**
ISBN 978-3-95723-009-6

No European city changes itself as quickly as Berlin. The city has undergone unique changes incomparable to any in modern world history. New buildings and projects including Central Station, Potsdamer Platz, the Holocaust Memorial, the government district and the new American embassy have sprung up – and those are just a few in the area around the former deathstrip.

Robert Grahn has photographed the changes. His impressive aerial photos show Berlin in a way you have never seen before. A unique then & now comparison of the metropolitan on the Spree. Available now in its third edition with new photographs.

BUNDESSTIFTUNG AUFARBEITUNG

REMEMBRANCE AS DUTY

The Federal Foundation for the Reappraisal of the SED Dictatorship, established by the German Bundestag in 1998, is called upon by law to promote a comprehensive reappraisal of the causes, history and impact of dictatorship in the Soviet zone of occupation in Germany and the GDR. Furthermore, its tasks are to assist and to strengthen the process of German Unity, and to foster the reappraisal of dictatorships on an international scale. In cooperation with other institutions and numerous partners both in Germany and abroad, the Foundation supports the critical reappraisal of the communist dictatorship in the Soviet zone of occupation in Germany / GDR and in Central and Eastern Europe, in order to promote public awareness of communist totalitarianism and injustice.

The Stiftungsrat (Board of Trustees), elected for a five-year term, is the head of the Foundation. It consists of MPs of the German Bundestag, members of the Federal and Berlin government, as well as individuals especially committed to questions of reappraisal. The Stiftungsvorstand (Board of Directors), commissioned by the Stiftungsrat, works on an honorary basis and guides the operations of the Foundation. The Foundation is supported by highly reputable Advisory Teams.

To initiate and to facilitate, to inform and to build networks: these are the guiding themes of the Foundation's work. The Foundation pursues these themes as a partner for memorial sites, museums, historical associations, independent archives, victims' organizations, German federal states and local governments, academic research, civic education, as well as school and extracurricular education. It supports the projects of its partners by providing know-how and, if possible, funding. The Foundation develops a broad range of information offers and publications, and provides a forum for cooperation and networking. Arranging panel discussions, workshops and symposia, discussions with witnesses, colloquia and trainings, it fosters debates and provides impulses in order to promote processes of "coming to terms" through knowledge transfer, communication and consultation.

www.Bundesstiftung-Aufarbeitung.de